Changing Your Management Style

Changing Your Management Style

How to Evaluate and Improve Your Own Performance

Robert C. Benfari

LEXINGTON BOOKS
An Imprint of The Free Press
NEW YORK   LONDON   TORONTO   SYDNEY   TOKYO   SINGAPORE

RAP 339 6662 ✓

Library of Congress Cataloging-in-Publication Data

Benfari, Robert.
    Changing your management style : how to evaluate and improve your
own performance / Robert Benfari.
        p.   cm.
    Includes index.
    ISBN 0-02-902635-0
    1. Executive ability.   2. Management.   I. Title
HD38.2.B457   1995
658.4'09—dc20   95-13619
                                                                                      CIP

Lexington Books

An Imprint of The Free Press

A Division of Simon & Schuster Inc.

866 Third Avenue, New York, N. Y. 10022

Printed in the United States of America

printing number

1 2 3 4 5 6 7 8 9 10

Contents

Preface

"Media discussion of prominent executive officers and the continued speculation in the business press about the possible departure of others attribute those respective companies' inability to master their difficulties significantly to the management style of their chief executives." This statement was made by Harry Levinson, a noted business psychologist, in an Award Address at the 101st Annual Convention of the American Psychological Association, in August 1993.

Some of the factors in the "fall of the behemoths" include:

- Difficulties with rigid corporate structures.
- Inability to grasp the importance of foreign competition.
- Subtle *psychological assumptions* of which many business leaders are unaware.

Levinson cautions us to be wary of mere description without explanation. If one lacks an appropriate diagnosis, one will have trouble finding appropriate solutions. Part of the diagnosis is understanding our management style and the key assumptions underlying our behavior.

In my book *Understanding Your Management Style* I addressed the four main building blocks of management style: psychological type, needs, power, and conflict styles. The main purpose of that book was to explain management styles. In my numerous corporate workshops and graduate seminars on this topic the inevitable question arose: "Now that I know about my style, how do I change it?" I offered some personal interventions in my earlier book, but not to the extent needed to ensure positive results.

Over the past four years I have searched the psychological literature to find the most viable techniques for this important change task. Psychology underwent a vital transformation during the 1970s and 1980s. New cognitive theories and methods gained scientific and clinical acceptance. These new methods provide stepping-stones for changing one's behavior without undergoing the long and expensive process of psychoanalysis or subjecting oneself to behavioral modification. Cognitive theory respects both the depth aspect of psychoanalysis and the here and now action orientation of behaviorism. In this respect it is an integrative approach that captures the best of the two worldviews.

This book builds on the previous one, but adds the dimension of corporate culture and the role of occupational stress to my analysis of management style. Each factor affecting management style is diagnosed with the explicit intention of maximizing individual and group potential.

During the past four years I have devised a number of cognitive-behavioral techniques and used them in my management development workshops. In these field trials I have invited feedback on the effectiveness and utility of my methods. I am indebted to the hundreds of managers who played a vital role in the construction and testing of the model for changing management style.

The theorists and practitioners in the field of cognitive-behavioral psychology have provided the critical links to the chain of understanding and changing management style. In this regard I have attempted to give attribution to all who helped me in this process.

I offer my special thanks to Beth Anderson (Senior Editor of Lexington Books) who made the project possible with her enthusiastic support, backed with careful, insightful comments and suggestions. Judith Hildebrandt provided day-to-day scrutiny of both my writing and my ENFP tendencies to avoid details at all costs. Her help tempered my overly enthusiastic intuitive approach and helped in bringing forth the final product. My students at Harvard University and Tufts Medical School and numerous corporate clients provided the critical input that fine-tuned the process.

David Lajoie and Tom Zommer, training and development managers at Raytheon, gave immeasurable contributions in the formulation of the book.

Introduction

Managers today face volatile and often unpredictable changes within their own organizations and outside them—changes ranging from the sudden obsolescence of skills to hostile takeovers to downturns in the economy, both local and global—and they must respond effectively to them. Certainly, they have no control over the external factors; they do, however, have control over their own management style. Accordingly, the first step to being an effective manager is self-understanding. My previous book, *Understanding Your Management Style*, is a guide toward attaining this knowledge of self and others and the complex situations that arise from inherent human differences. The second step in the process is learning how to change your management style. This book is intended to help you achieve that goal of change for the better.

The organization of the future will see more interdependencies at all levels of management. Richard Hogan, a psychologist, asserts that effective leaders rely on persuasion, not domination. Authority can no longer be used as the sole source of power to influence others because the team concept has gained prominence; it is a more positive approach that includes participation from everyone, both managers and workers, who have no direct reporting obligations among each other. Team building is an essential element of total quality management and can be accomplished when attention is paid to developing good people skills.

Managers largely agree that good interactive managers have the following characteristics:

- An understanding of their own management style, both its strengths and its weaknesses.

- Skills for resolving conflict at the lowest level. Conflict is natural; timely effective solutions can prevent problems down the line.
- Effective communication skills for influencing people; for negotiating roles with subordinates, peers, and superiors; for dealing with difficult people; and for building morale.
- An understanding and acknowledgment of interdependent roles and the team concept.
- Techniques for dealing with stress and daily pressures to prevent burnout.
- An understanding of the organization's unique culture.

This last point—understanding organizational culture—is an important consideration. In truth, individual managers have little control over an organization's culture because so many factors determine its character. No individual manager can turn around a culture that has evolved over years or even decades, but every manager can learn to be more effective in that predetermined environment, and every manager can effect subtle changes in that culture through spheres of influence. The key to this process is a simple truth: each manager can control his or her own behavior and can change his or her own interaction within the organizational environment. For example, a manager may introduce process changes that improve group and individual problem-solving techniques: delegating, coaching, managing conflict, and dealing more effectively with difficult people.

So how do you change your management style? Follow these four steps:

1. Understand your style—both its strengths and its weaknesses.
2. Identify situations in which you have been effective and those in which you have been ineffective.
3. Determine what aspects of your management style played a role in both positive and negative outcomes.
4. Work on modifying your behavior to achieve more positive outcomes all of the time.

The exact procedures are presented in the following chapters.

My approach is to integrate various views on behavior modification, beginning with an examination of behaviors, both innate and learned, and an exploration of current views on behavior modification, from a variety of psychological and behavioral schools.

In *Understanding Your Management Style*, I presented four critical building blocks that can be used in understanding managerial style: psychological types, needs, conflict management styles, and the effective use of power. These building blocks fit together to form an individualistic mosaic, one that varies from manager to manager. This book reexamines those building blocks, adds one more to it—managing stress—and explains how to use them within the context of the organizational environment.

Changing Your
Management Style

1

The Origins of Your
Management Style

In a sense, all styles of management stem from personality and be-havior. How we react to problematic situations and individuals in an organization is largely based on the sort of people we are—whether we are extroverts or introverts, for example, or whether we meet conflict head-on or shrink away from it. Some of us almost instinctively make the right moves, but most of us do not. Never-theless, we all have within us the capacity to modify our manage-ment style and to become more effective in dealing with our bosses, peers, and subordinates.

Personality and Behavior

Are personality and behavior predetermined by biological and ge-netic factors, or are they more malleable? The debate about the roles of nature and nurture has been a lively one throughout this century, with proponents of one or the other striving to prove that they alone are right—and in the process failing to appreciate the es-sential interdependence of both the genetic and the environmental influences in shaping behavioral and psychological traits. The reali-ty thus lies in the reconciliation of these two positions to create a third position that proposes an interaction between nature and nur-ture. In other words, behavior is shaped by both nature *and* nur-ture: some facets of behavior are totally the result of nature, some are totally the result of nurture, but most facets of an individual's behavior are determined by some mix of the two.

Nature

When Freud intoned "Biology is determinism," he was coming down solidly on the side of nature. Nature supporters have since used animal research to uncover ingrained behavior patterns and have amassed impressive data to support their position. Studies on monozygotic twins (identical twins derived from a single egg) too have produced powerful evidence for the inheritability of many human traits, including extroversion or introversion and some psychiatric conditions.

Most of these inherited traits follow the Mendelian model, whereby the traits are largely predictable. Some inherited traits, however, follow a different path referred to as *emergence*. Richard Lykken, a geneticist, has proposed that certain traits "emerge" when unique combinations of genes come into play. He uses the case of the great thoroughbred Secretariat to explain this concept. As a result of careful breeding, race horses had seemingly reached a plateau of excellence. Then Secretariat, the wonder horse, came along. Paradoxically, his numerous offspring were mere plodders. In explanation, Lykken suggested that genius—rare strength and speed in the case of Secretariat—comes from the emergence of unique genes and that this unique combination will not be passed on to the next generation. True geniuses fall into the emergent category. Rarely do their offspring demonstrate the same genius. Cases in point include Shakespeare, Benjamin Franklin, and Gauss (one of the princes of mathematics), none of whose progeny were distinguished.

Nurture

B. F. Skinner was an extreme experience advocate. He dismissed the significance of any mental phenomena that could not be observed, and he insisted that all behavior is determined by learning. This extreme behaviorist position was modified in the 1960s by social learning theorists. Although they still emphasized the role of conditioning and reinforcement, they also recognized the importance of cognitive processes, self-reinforcement, and imitation in the development of behavior. Yet in neither its radical nor its modified form did behaviorism leave room for genetic determinism, that is, for nature.

The Interactive Position

Between the nature and nurture extremes is a position that reconciles the differences. This interactive position has been well defined by Jerome Kagan, a developmental psychologist at Harvard University:

> One of the happy consequences of the marriage of the modern synthesis in evolutionary theory with increasingly sophisticated research in neuroscience and genetics is an acceptance of the view that the young infant's behavioral profile interacts with the social environment to produce, over time, a particular constellation of moods and behavioral propensities. The psychological characteristics are neither fixed permanently by biology nor shaped entirely by social interaction. Rather, each child's changing profile is a historical product of genetically influenced reactions accommodating to particular sequences of experience.

Lykken has identified what he calls *impact traits*, traits seen only when the right circumstance arises to promote use of a natural talent. Charismatic leadership is an example of an impact trait. For example, George Patton was a genius on the battlefield, and Eisenhower was a master of coalition building. If either had changed roles, his effectiveness most likely would have been diminished.

When these three positions are united, we see a continuum regarding the sources of behavior, extending from pure nature, to a mix of nature and nurture, to pure experience-based behaviors. My view is that we can assign selected managerial behaviors to places along this continuum and thereby achieve a realistic approach to changing managerial style. We can pinpoint behaviors that are inbred and impossible to change, and we can also identify behaviors that are amenable to change.

Management Style

The key to changing one's management style is the development of a wholeness based on strengthening weaknesses and maximizing strengths (or what Carl Jung called "striving toward individuation"). Each opposite strives to be dominant, thereby creating one-sidedness; wholeness is achieved when thesis and antithesis are integrated. William Whyte in the 1950s described the one-dimensional organizational man, a conformist shut off from his individuality. Since that time a plethora of self-help books have advised people about how to avoid this fate, but few have taken into account the integrating concept of wholeness. Becoming a three-minute manager does not make you a whole or complete person. Therefore I am not offering one quick fix to improving management style.

In *Understanding Your Management Style*, I pinpointed four critical factors: how we perceive and judge the world around us, how we gain a sense of personal satisfaction and competence, how we handle conflict, and how we use power. Combinations of these four factors constitute the building blocks of management style. This book adds one more factor, the management of stress, and looks at all four in terms of their interaction with another factor: organizational culture.

The Psychological Types

The psychological types I posit are based on Jungian theory and the Myers-Briggs Type Indicators (MBTI), a significant personality test designed after World War II by Katherine Briggs and Isabel Briggs Myers, a mother–daughter team. The following four polarities of human nature form the psychological types:

1. *Extroversion versus introversion.* This polarity defines how we use our psychic energy. Extroverted persons find their orientation in the objective, outer environment, through people and institutions. Introverted persons derive their orientation from within.
2. *Sensing versus intuition.* This polarity defines the perceptive function. Sensing people focus on details, facts, and data derived from the five senses. Intuitive people focus on possibilities, go beyond the facts, and use their sixth sense.
3. *Thinking versus feeling.* This polarity defines the judgment function. Thinking types use impersonal, logical, and analytical approaches to judging situations. Feeling types base their judg-

ments on individual value systems and focus on the personal impact of their judgments.
4. *Perception versus judgment.* The last polarity determines which function, sensing versus intuition (the perceptive function) or thinking versus feeling (the judgment function), is used in dealing with the outside world.

Significantly, these types arise more from nature than from nurture. For example, recent research indicates that patterns of shyness and assertiveness—or the extroversion–introversion polarity—emerge at an early age. Kagan has asserted that "[t]he temperamental category we call uninhibited to the unfamiliar refers to a select group of children . . . who are likely to become sociable, effectively spontaneous, fearless 10-year-olds, and very unlikely to become quiet, shy, and timid, although a small proportion of these children who are outgoing at age 2 acquire a timid demeanor later on because of intervening stressful experiences."

Research on the sensing versus intuition polarity has revealed chemical and neurological differences between these two groups. For example, brain scans of the intuitive types show more interaction between the hemispheres, with many crisscrossing firings in the brain, while those of the sensing types demonstrate more linear firings, with fewer crossovers between the hemispheres.

Regarding the thinking versus feeling polarity, Lawrence Kohlberg has amassed a large body of solid evidence indicating that children develop definite logical (thinking) versus moral (feeling) judgment throughout puberty.

Psychological types do seem to be determined early in life, and they appear to have a genetic source, a conclusion with far-reaching implications for behavioral modification of psychological types. One is that an intervention intended to change a person's psychological orientation (his or her mix of the four sets of polarities) will introduce stress factors, which are potentially damaging to the person. For this reason, attempts at long-term alterations are not recommended. However, adjustments designed to respond to particular situations can be made. (Jungians call this "rotating your axes.") For example, an introvert can engage in assertiveness training and project his energy outward for particular roles. An intuitive type can learn to deal with details and time management and to be more precise to meet the requirements of a specific job. Then once the situation is dealt with, the person's natural orientation comes to the fore again. The preferences can be likened to the concept of plastic memory, in physics, whereby an object returns to its original shape after bending for short periods of time. The preferences of the psychological type operate under the same principle.

If a person is pressured to change her natural orientation, tension, internal conflict, and even mental disorder can result. For example, parents who demand that their children be clones of themselves cause their offspring psychological stress. A parent who tries to change a shy, introverted child into an extrovert may be thwarting a natural pattern of behavior; the consequence can be mental disorder. This situation has a parallel in organizational life: bosses who demand conformity to their preferences stress their subordinates.

The concept of psychological types not only explains why people behave in different ways, it explains why it is so difficult to change basic behaviors. But when people of differing psychological orientations clash, their conflict can be turned into a positive force that leads to greater synergy in the workforce. All efforts at team building must start with examination of the temperaments of the participants. Otherwise the result will be unresolved conflict at both a conscious and a subconscious level. The participants will be trapped in a dance of death that none of them understands. Irrational and cruel behavior can result.

Although a person cannot permanently change his or her basic profile in terms of the psychological types, he or she can train himself or herself to change temporarily when circumstance dictates flexibility. The polarities of extroversion versus introversion, sensing versus intuition, thinking versus feeling, and judgment versus perception can be viewed as on–off switches that can be activated by the individual as circumstances change. For example, extreme extroverts have their E switch on most of the time. However, there are times when the I (introversion) switch can and should be switched on. The same principle applies to the other preferences. The trouble begins when an extrovert or an introvert tries to keep the opposite switch open all the time.

The Needs

Human needs are determined by nature (e.g., the needs for air, water, food, and safety) and shaped by experience. Richard Gregory, in his book *The Mind*, identifies other needs: "the needs that one may call social: the need for companionship, the need to be part of a group with a hierarchical structure, the territorial needs of a group of which one forms a part."

Needs are forces that organize our perceptions, judgments, and actions to attain competence. A need presupposes that a condition is unfilled. All of us have complexes of needs that demand satisfaction and that express our personalities—for example, the need for achievement or autonomy. Interpreting these individual patterns is one of the challenges of understanding management styles. Understanding and accepting people's different needs can bring us another step on the way toward appreciating them as unique individuals, putting their skills to the best use, and resolving management difficulties.

I will use some of the new techniques from the field of cognitive psychology to demonstrate how needs can be modified. The rationale behind changing them is that sometimes we can be too needy. Conversely, our strengths can become our weaknesses if they are overplayed. For example, if a person with a high need for achievement and dominance tries to control the task in a small problem-solving group, the result may be negative for all.

The Bases of Power

Acquiring power and using it effectively is vital to achieving success in organizations, to managing relationships, and to individual fulfillment. The manager's sense of self-esteem, desire for self-fulfillment, and competence are enhanced by his or her ability to use power effectively.

A simple definition of power is that its goal is to influence the beliefs, emotions, and behaviors of other people. In this sense, power is neutral until it is translated into action. In a one-sided relationship, there will be only one recipient and one wielder of power. The behavior of the wielder of power will be perceived as negative when the wielder is trying to exploit, manipulate, or control the actions of others. But power can be a positive force when other people feel that they are sharing in the interaction.

Some people have an uncanny ability to use power effectively (and positively). Why these individuals can skillfully influence others is not entirely known. Other people use power to manipulate, disinform, and subvert (this is negative power). People are used like fuel in the furnace of power or cleared away like worn-out gears for more efficient replacements. Both types of power—positive and negative—operate out of an instinctive base.

The effective use of positive power is an acquired skill. Its opposite, negative power, can be shaped as well by our environment. In either case, it is a learned response. In the first case, it is an active, conscious attempt to be effective. In the second instance, it is probably negative conditioning from the environment.

Our use of power depends on our assumptions, perceptions, and feelings (APFs) about it, which themselves are shaped by our value system, our culture, and our experiences. For example, the glare of power bothers some people. Some believe that power poisons, and they shun its use. They may use power on a subconscious level, but probably in an ineffective way. Other people recognize the reality of power—both its uses and abuses—and try to build effective power skills. Another part of the learning process is to know when to use the various bases of power given the requirements of the task. This is situational management.

Each of us can do something about our power orientation since it can be developed by skill building.

Conflict Styles

The biological basis of how we handle conflict is the "fight-or-flight" response, a primitive pattern based on our perceptions of any danger posed by a situation. On some rare occasions the fight-or-flight response is appropriate. Most of the time, however, we need to develop other means of communicating in order to resolve conflicts. These skills can be learned.

In various ways, overtly and covertly, we are always being conditioned to avoid or dominate conflict; therefore, our strategies for conflict resolution are culturally overdetermined. And, in most cases, we are not wholly effective in resolving conflicts. We take a reactive (learned but not effective) rather than a proactive (learned but differentiated and conscious) stance toward conflict. The model for changing our conflict style is based on training in the steps that lead to win–win strategies. In addition, a perceptual shifting from either fight or flight needs to take place.

Stress

How we respond to stress is akin to how we handle conflict. Our response to stress is rooted in fight or flight, but modified by our own life experiences. Therefore, an understanding of stress encompasses the role of individual differences in responding to both internal and external stressors. Some individuals are particularly likely to become stressed, some apparently live stress-free lives; most experience stress only under certain conditions.

Fight or flight is not an adequate response to stress. Herbert Benson of Harvard University has done extensive research on the physiological and psychological consequences of stress, and he has proposed some remedies. The field of cognitive behavior therapy has also contributed techniques for reducing the negative effects of stress. It is possible to manage stress through behavioral modification methods, a topic I will address in Chapter 6.

Organizational Culture

Organizational culture has a strong relationship with all the variables of management style. It can be instrumental, positively or negatively, in the shaping of any of the building blocks of management style, and it can be a source of stress to everyone in the organization. Unlike the other management style factors, it is not easy to change (and a complete treatment of the matter is outside of the scope of this book). Understanding organizational culture is like reading a chart to navigate unfamiliar waters. Managers have some control over their microenvironments, including the network of interdependent relationships, subordinates, peers, and bosses. In this context, some change can take effect.

The behavior modification tools involve forms of skill building tailored to each building block. A basic model of change is cognitive restructuring—the exploration of assumptions, perceptions, and feelings that influence our management style. Clarification of this style can lead to a restructuring of our mind-set and eventually to behavior change.

This book takes an integrative approach to modifying management style because the management style building blocks are interactive and should be treated as a whole. Understanding one's style is the linchpin in the sequence of change. From this point, we can proceed to modifying our behavior.

2

A Model for Change

Cognitive Restructuring

Cognitive restructuring, one of the newest approaches to changing behavior, is based on a framework developed by Albert Ellis, a psychologist. The basic goal is to identify internal monologues that are related to stressful events, to evaluate this self-talk for its rationality and influence on behavior, and then to produce new self-talk to modify the original cognition and the undesired behavioral pattern.

Dubbed the ABC chain, it begins with the trigger event (A). How the event is perceived, which is the function of the person's core beliefs and assumptions, forms the (B) of the chain. The (C) part is the response: behavioral, physiological, and psychological. The technique stems from findings that over time we all build up cognitive scripts that are always present in our brain. Through the process of perception, we label events in a positive or negative way, and this labeling in turn gives rise to emotional or behavioral reactions. Our perceptual labeling may be accurate, or it may be inaccurate, inappropriate, or irrational. When this happens we put ourselves into a state of *stress*, as Joe did when his boss, John, called him into the office.

John immediately set out the problem: "The damn circuit failed for the tenth time. Joe, we have to fix the problem, or we'll have a severe overrun." As Joe paced around the room, constantly looking at the test documents and slamming them on his desk, Joe could only think, "This is awful. John is accusing *me* of fouling up. I only did what the design people told me to do. He is really mad at *me*. There go my stomach cramps again. What am I going to say?" He stood immobilized with anxiety and fear, until John demanded of him, "Joe, what are we going to do? We need answers. We need action—and promptly!" Finally Joe stammered, "I'll do my best. I'll go back to the lab and see what I can do."

Joe misperceived the situation, and subjected it to negative distortion. He evaluated John's emotional reaction as directed at him rather than at the situation. Further, he allowed his negative emotional reaction to overwhelm him and prevent engaging in dialogue with John to examine and solve the problem. Finally, he left to avoid further emotional damage.

Cognitive restructuring would take this scenario and:

- Demonstrate that Joe's reaction did not fit the reality. He had an irrational or distorted view of the interchange.
- Demonstrate that if he continues to allow false perceptions and beliefs to shape his present and future behavior in a negative way, he will set himself up for failure.
- Help Joe to change his thinking (his cognition) and abandon his irrational beliefs.
- Help Joe to develop a more rational appraisal of such situations and generate alternative interpretations.

Three elements are key to understanding and using cognitive restructuring: assumptions, perceptions, and feelings (APFs).

As we pass through life, we build up an assumptive system of what is, what should be, and what ought to be. These assumptions, highly charged by emotional events and our upbringing, come from encounters that we take for granted. We all have assumptions based on our beliefs, values, and attitudes, though the range and depth of them vary from person to person. Because these assumptions and beliefs in part determine our needs structure, becoming conscious of them can help us modify these underlying elements and lead to change.

Perception is what we process through the five senses or how we interpret these sensations through intuition. A sensing type of person relies on what she perceives as facts and details in the situation. An intuitive type of person can arrive at a perception without being aware of the concrete basis for it. Intuitive types can make imaginative leaps from the past or present to future possibilities. Given that there are different ways of processing a situation, there is tremendous latitude in what we perceive. There are general laws of perception, but individuals create their own spin in a given situation. Cognitive restructuring makes us acutely aware of the role of our perceptions in determining our behavior in a situation. By modifying our perceptions, we alter our emotional state and our reactive behavior.

The following components are important to an understanding of perception:

- We structure our perceptions to fit our wishes, biases, needs, and expectations.
- Emotions may influence the perceptual process, either intensifying it or interfering with it.
- We are unaware that we are distorting reality; our defenses are at work.
- Inner determinants—memory, emotion, wishes, cultural factors, our psychological type—carry more weight than outer determinants—immediate perceptions, and logical input from others.
- Previous experience with positive or negative reinforcement in similar situations generates strong biases that influence the current perception.
- Life experiences and traditions in our culture can influence how we process information, particularly when we interact with a different culture.

Feelings—pain, pleasure, hate, love, disdain, grief, hope, joy, disgust, and so on—are our evaluative reactions to a situation. Our emotional state is critically linked to our immediate perceptions. For example, love can change our perception of another's thoughtless action into acceptance, or hate can intensify our perception of the same act into a deliberate affront or worse.

Assumptions, perceptions, and feelings interact, each influencing the other. Deeply rooted assumptions can distort our perceptions such that they reinforce the old assumptions. By opening up our perceptual field by "floodlight" vision versus "spotlight" vision, we have the opportunity to alter these assumptions. The emotional tone can reinforce or alter either assumptions or perceptions. Assumptions can set the stage for a positive or a negative emotional state. A current perception that triggers a previous negative or positive image can affect our emotional state.

Behavior modification was a common approach in the past for changing management style, but it ignored the role of cognition and perception. Cognitive psychologists put perceptions at center stage. For example, criticism from a tyrannical boss can be perceived differently by different people. Joe has been taught that perfection is the sole goal in life. He perceives his boss's criticism as an unconditional putdown of him personally, not his behavior. As a result, he suffers anxiety and fear of failure whenever he has to interact with his boss. Eventually he may avoid his boss—a perceived solution that only compounds the problematic situation. A vicious cycle of the boss's anger and Joe's terror flights develops. Cognitive restructuring would help Joe deal with his difficulties.

Practitioners in the field of cognitive restructuring have identified three core activities that are necessary to bring about behavioral change:

1. Identification of the thoughts, beliefs, and values that cause negative affect and behavior. This is a systematic attempt to bring to the surface automatic, and sometimes dangerous, thoughts so that we can recognize them.
2. Evaluation of these thoughts, beliefs, and values in an attempt to judge their validity.
3. Shifting of any irrational or untenable beliefs to a more rational basis. The anxiety level is reduced by repeated attempts at mastering the irrational belief.

Cognitive restructuring takes into account self-talk, all our internal scripts, of a positive or a negative nature, that promote or deter our purpose. We all talk to ourselves. In this ongoing process, we may build up scripts that are so negative that they interfere with our well-being and performance.

In order to diagnose your self-talk, take into consideration the following particulars:

- *Self-concept:* The degree of your self-worth and any corresponding negative thoughts about the outcome.
- *Self-instructions:* Corrective scripts that promote new behavior.
- *Self-reinforcement:* Changes of approach, even in moderate degrees, that you reinforce with positive self-talk.

Mary, a staff coordinator, once held these beliefs about her role and her boss, Harry: "Harry is the boss. I must be doing something wrong if he needles me. My role is to obey authority—without questioning it. We are all helpless when faced with a superior force. The boss does the problem solving, not me."

Mary now uses a different, more positive kind of self-talk when she is in difficult situations. She has accepted the truth that life can be unfair and that people can be difficult, so she has developed a strategy based on challenge and mastery. When Harry starts needling her, she says to herself, "Well, here he goes again, same old Harry. I don't know whether he realizes what he is doing. But regardless, I can't control him, and I don't want to. I will be in charge of myself and try to work out a solution to the problem. I am not helpless and powerless. I am in control." Mary has applied cognitive restructuring techniques to change her perceptions and reactions to a chronic situation.

Now let's look at Joan, a perfectionist who suffers all the self-imposed defeats of the extreme perfectionist. When things go wrong—and they frequently do—Joan takes it out on herself and her employees. As the manager of a graphics design studio, she works with a diverse group of people, including secretaries, graphic designers, and her boss. The business is very cyclical: a four-month crunch period when everyone is taxed to their limits, followed by a breather. Joan's secretary does not have the same high level of drive to achieve perfection that Joan does. She doesn't finish work on time, misses follow-up calls, and slights customers. When these events occur, a sequence of tension, emotional reaction, and nonproductive self-talk develops, as in this scenario:

JOAN: Betty, did the customer receive the package?

BETTY: No. [blank stare]

JOAN: Did you follow up on where it might be?

BETTY: Oh, was I supposed to?

JOAN: [clenching teeth] Obviously, Betty, if the client didn't get it, you should have tried to locate the package.

Joan goes into her office, shaking her head in disgust. She feels frustrated and thinks: "I have only myself to blame. I hired her. She fooled me. I thought she was smart. Do I have to do everything myself to make sure it gets done correctly? Damn her and me." This negative self-talk in no way helps to work through the problem with Betty. In fact, by practicing self-flagellation Joan has escalated the problem to a new level. Promotive self-talk might go like this: "This occurs all the time. I have to figure out why this happens. It could be that I don't communicate my expectations very well; if that is the case, I should outline them for Betty. Betty may have a different perspective of the job than I do, but I have to find a solution to prevent this from happening again and to encourage Betty to follow through when these things occur."

Joan takes some time to cool off and to distance herself from the problem, and then she outlines her next steps. At that point she says to herself: "Good first step." Her primary emotion shifts from defeat and frustration to a sense of self-efficacy, and with this newly acquired ability, she is able to deal effectively with Betty. Once she practices these skills, they become natural and automatic. Self-reinforcement is an integral part of promotive thinking. Joan must avoid putting Betty down in her thoughts, because such thoughts will turn into self-fulfilling negative prophecies.

Cognitive restructuring can be used to modify most elements of management style. It can be directed at these elements:

- Modifying psychological type for a given situation.
- Strengthening and changing motive patterns.
- Developing positive power and influencing skills.
- Overcoming barriers to effective conflict resolution.
- Managing stress.
- Coping with organizational culture.

Techniques for Cognitive Restructuring

Counters

Counters are thoughts that go against a firmly held belief or assumption. They can be well-articulated sentences, short imperatives, or phrases. The theory behind countering is that when you repeatedly counter a thought, belief, or assumption, you weaken it. In the A → B → C series it is the B that is modified by countering. By repeatedly countering an assumption, you build up an effective charge that reduces the potency of the original assumption. For example, the irrational belief that I must be loved by everyone can be countered by: "Baloney! Fat chance in hell! Really, there are many people who are incapable of showing respect, affection, or compassion for others. When I encounter them, I must take this truth into consideration." The more counters you muster against the assumption or belief, the more likely you will succeed in reducing the power of the thought.

In the usual practice of cognitive restructuring, countering is used to erase noxious, irrational thoughts. (However, as we will see, it can be applied as well to restructuring our needs, power bases, and conflict styles, and to managing stress.)

There are at least three types of counters: alternative interpretations, coping statements, and countering protective beliefs.

ALTERNATIVE INTERPRETATIONS

Our assumptions, beliefs, and perceptions are based on a set of automatic thoughts that can be changed by using alternative interpretation. Murray, a stockbroker, believes that he must succeed in everything that he undertakes. His high need for achievement has been inculcated in him by his family, the schools he attended, and the competitive environment in which he now works. He is regularly anxious, tense, and depressed. An alternative interpretation of success could be: "I have only so much energy to expend. If I squander it on many endeavors, I will be mediocre in all of them. Therefore, I must focus on what I really want to do." Or, "My family was a stress-ridden bunch of workaholics who never enjoyed life and were miserable for it. I should not follow their imperative." Or, "Those high-priced schools had a set of values that inbreed competitiveness and lack of compassion. After all, look at the products of the British public schools!" These alternative interpretations refocus Murray's achievement need to a manageable level, away from his frenetic drive for an impossible-to-obtain level of success.

Henry, a middle manager, believes that if he is not in total control, all will be lost. This belief strengthens his need to dominate his subordinates, his wife, his friends, and his children. Henry needs to reappraise that assumption. He might have this dialogue with himself: "Now, Henry, what would happen if you delegated the authority to Jim on the next project? Well, he could fail, and my boss would come down on me. Do you really believe that Jim will fail and your boss would blame you? After all, Jim has followed your orders faithfully in the past. Don't you owe him the respect to prove his competence to you and himself? Well, I could try a small project out with him and see what happens." Henry can repeat this dialogue with all the catastrophes that he imagines would happen with his wife, his children, and his friends and work out a worst-case scenario. If he repeatedly does this, his catastrophic mode will diminish.

COPING STATEMENTS

The use of coping statements is based on the reality that some people believe that they will fail miserably. Albert Bandura, a prominent cognitive psychologist, calls this expectation "low self-efficacy." Coping statements can prevent this pattern and improve self-efficacy. When you use coping statements, you anticipate problems and devise ways of dealing with them.

Coping statements are effective in countering self-fulfilling negative prophecies. Sally thinks to herself: "I can't face telling Mary [her boss] about the overruns on the Apex project. She will blame me, and I will suffer." So Sally does *not* tell Mary, and the overruns are discovered at the end of the quarter by the accountants. Mary angrily confronts Sally on why she withheld the information. Now Sally feels guilty and depressed—another case of a self-fulfilling negative prophecy.

Instead, Sally can construct a script so that she can cope with the situation and reach a wise solution. For example, she can reject thinking like this: "I can't face Mary. She is a lethal weapon and will explode when she hears the bad news. It will be 'kill the messenger time.' I feel depressed. Maybe it will go away." Instead, she can try to create a positive coping message, such as this one: "There are three reasons why the project is overrun: (1) the client added scope to the work, (2) some estimates for parts were off, and (3) Nick, our programmer, had a heart attack. These seem to be plausible reasons why we are overrun. I know this may be difficult for me to convey to Mary, but I will rehearse this five times and go in and discuss the problem with her."

Sally goes through her coping routine and enters Mary's office: "Mary, I want to update you on the Apex project. We have encountered three significant problems, and I want your advice on how we should handle the projected overrun." Mary then replies, "I'm glad you came to me before the quarter was up. Maybe we can do something about it."

After the problem-solving session, Sally should give herself some positive reinforcement: "Boy, that was easy. I'm going to try this every time I have these negative thoughts."

COUNTERING PROTECTIVE BELIEFS

Protective beliefs are cherished assumptions that serve as security blankets. They act as magical thoughts that maintain a strong defensive armor against change. "If I don't ride herd on my subordinates," says a manager, "they will goof off." The assumption behind this belief is the old shibboleth, "Spare the rod and spoil the child." It is also tied to a need to dominate and be aggressive. The belief is so strong that the manager feels that if he gives it up, something will go wrong.

Protective beliefs arise because we want to maintain personal power. Putting down another person with a negative belief about them elevates us. Protective beliefs can arise from one's social support system. If the group believes strongly in a protective belief, group members will find it hard to criticize or deny that belief, for they will fear being ostracized. The protective belief bonds us to the group.

Some people like to be contrary and negative. They believe that their autonomy is threatened if they agree with someone else's position. But, in the long run, they only alienate themselves with their chronic negativity.

Finally, a person may feel that it is dangerous to change beliefs because something disastrous will happen. The protective belief wards off unwanted anxiety. For example, a person might think: "I've been very successful in using the old purchasing system. If I try to learn the new one, I will fail. I will stick to what I know." This protective belief reduces anxiety in the short run but is self-defeating for long-run competence. The use of countering takes time and commitment. The easy way out is to stick with the old protective belief.

Agnes, the head of the publications department in a large financial firm, uncovered her protective beliefs when her company upgraded its hardware and software and this action disturbed her. First, she uncovered her beliefs:

1. The old word processor worked quite well. Why fix what is not broken?
2. I am an expert with twenty years' experience. What do those young, wet-behind-the-ears kids know about my job?
3. My boss has praised me in the past, and he will stand by me.
4. If we change to the new system, my subordinates will think I am giving in.
5. Giving up power in any area is always dangerous.

Agnes relied on these five protective beliefs to guard her against these anticipated disasters:

1. I may show my incompetence if I try the new system.
2. I am getting old, and I may be slipping.
3. Maybe I am uncertain about my relationship with my boss.
4. I cannot lose control over my subordinates.
5. This a political environment. Anyone who shows weakness will be swallowed up.

But protective beliefs can be used to gain access to underlying concerns. Then counters can be employed to break down these concerns. Agnes used the following counters to her protective beliefs:

1. I can attend training sessions. They offer a risk-free environment because mistakes are part of the learning process.
2. Age equals wisdom. I can use my experience with the previous system to help integrate the new one. I can act as a consultant when problems arise.
3. I will set up progress meetings with my boss to discuss the new system. He will be grateful for my positive attitude.
4. I will discuss the new system with my subordinates to get their perceptions about the new system. This will maintain my stature as a caring, receptive boss.
5. Everyone else is in the same boat—naive and anxious. My positive attitude can lend support to others. This can lead to positive bonds and break down destructive competition.

Perceptual Shifting

The focus of this technique is the manager's perceptions and the impact of those perceptions on his or her performance. The first step is to identify any perceptions that have a negative effect on interpersonal relationships, defining objectives, and attaining goals. An example of a perception that has a negative effect is a belief that the person with whom you are interacting is like someone else you know who once caused you psychological harm. The immediate perception is influenced by a past event. The former negative event now colors the present perception, leading to negative feelings and judgments.

Usually the unfavorable pattern is not corrected until the faulty perception is changed and a more realistic, less damaging pattern replaces it. In other words, the manager requires a basic perceptual shift in how he or she perceives certain experiences. Only then will the negative emotion be removed. Five techniques prove useful to managers in effecting a perceptual shift.

BASIC PERCEPTUAL SHIFTS

We are constantly bombarded with input from the outside world. The brain has the capacity to select and transform this informational deluge into patterns, and these patterns shape our beliefs, attitudes, and values. For example, a flashing yellow light means caution or slow down; a red light means danger or stop. The meanings attached to the perceptual inputs are determined by constant reinforcement and become embedded assumptions, or beliefs. More complex assumptions/beliefs are formed in the same way. We select what is salient for that circumstance. We employ the same kind of selective attention to most of the stimuli that we receive in our day-to-day existence.

Most of our beliefs, attitudes, and values are positive, constructive, and reality-based. However, some are based on distorted perceptions. Sometime in our life we were taught to respond to cues in a distorted manner. Usually these distorted beliefs were based on negative reinforcement and result in negative emotion. Because of early traumatic learning or poor role models, we incorporated these events into harmful life themes. Our subsequent day-to-day perceptions are then guided by these former happenings. We use the old schemata to organize what we perceive today in the light of the past. For example, you may think:

• I am helpless. My strategy to resolve this discomforting feeling is to attach myself to people who can help me. If this is a persistent pattern, I become a dependent person.

- Errors are bad; I must not err. I become constantly alert to cues that may disrupt my drive for perfection.
- People are potential adversaries. I organize my perceptions to be on guard against signs of competition from others. I become a wary person.
- I could be stepped on. I develop resistance strategies to cope with this perception of the world. I am uncooperative even when it is in my best interest to be a team player.
- I may get hurt. I organize my perceptions to avoid any potential threat to my self-esteem. My behavior becomes avoidant.
- I am special. I seize on any opportunity to promote myself.
- People are there to be taken advantage of, or they will take advantage of me. I scan the environment for hostile signs and mobilize my attack mode.
- I need to impress. My perceptions are ordered to allow me to dramatize most interactions with others.
- I need plenty of space. I perceive that every interaction closes in on me. I seek isolation.

These patterns of behavior based on previously embedded assumptions are maladaptive if they become habitual ways of organizing our current perceptions. Aaron Beck, an expert in cognitive restructuring, states:

> Egocentricity, competitiveness, exhibitionism, and avoidance of unpleasantness may all be adaptive in certain situations but grossly maladaptive in others. Since we can observe only the overt behavior of other people, the question arises as to how our conscious internal states (thoughts, feelings, and wishes) are related to strategies. If we examine the cognitive and affective patterns, we see a specific relationship between certain beliefs and attitudes on the one hand and behavior on the other.

These habituated themes can be changed by undertaking a basic perceptual shift in how we perceive a given experience. Perceptual shifts can be guided by using a worksheet for gathering data. It consists of four columns:

Column 1: List every thought or belief that causes negative effects in a particular situation.

Column 2: Identify whether the belief is true or false. Look for evidence both for and against it. Decide which is stronger. It is fundamental that you make a judgment based on objective data in order to counter your subjective feelings about the belief.

Column 3: Record the best argument against the theme. Ideally, this argument will be emotionally persuasive as well as rationally sound.

Column 4: List evidence in support of this argument. This is the key to the perceptual shift technique.

To bring about the actual perceptual shift you must meditate for five to ten minutes a day on critical past incidents that disprove the irrational belief.

Bob successfully made a basic perceptual shift when he found his self-confidence plummeting. Bob is the manager of a seven-scientist project team charged with developing new enzymes for genetic splicing. He was promoted to head the team when he discovered, quite by accident, a new enzyme mutation that proved to be useful in developing a new project the research department was working on.

Bob's boss, Gregory, is a scientific entrepreneurial gadfly. He flits from project to project, reviewing progress in a cursory manner, rarely taking time to meet with project leaders. He gives his managers great latitude but little direction. Gregory, like many other entrepreneurial leaders, looks to the future and has little regard for the past or the present. His style disturbs Bob, who is highly conscientious and cautious about his work. He needs constant affirmation from the external environment and has achieved this by building a tight, cohesive group that works well as a team. Bob acts like a member of the team rather than the project head. He receives most of his internal esteem from the group, who are appreciative and supportive of him. But Gregory too has repeatedly expressed confidence in Bob's work throughout their relationship.

The latest project, involving an elusive enzyme derivative, has been bogged down for months. Bob is concerned but has not gone to Gregory to report on the status of the project. Now Gregory, with no warning, has thrust a new scientist on Bob's group. Alexis showed up one day unannounced but carrying a letter, signed by Gregory, saying that he would be working with the group.

This event threw Bob into a panic state, especially since Alexis turned out to be a brilliant individual contributor but brash and inattentive to the culture of Bob's group. In fact, right away he seized all the current data and started reworking the design. To the astonishment of Bob and the group, Alexis was right most of the time. Alexis had no patience with the group problem-solving techniques Bob had instituted for the project. He charged on in his own individualist way and openly criticized some of the group's previous methods.

Bob's anxiety grew. He avoided confronting Gregory, but he did go to the human resources department to see a company counselor, who asked him to fill out a perceptual shift worksheet. It was a painful operation, but Bob went forward with the request. Table 2–1 contains the filled-out worksheet.

Bob's fragile self-esteem has been challenged by the presence of a semigenius, Alexis. His self-doubts about his competence have led him to question his ability to lead and contribute. His negative assumptions were reinforced by his selective perception of isolated events: the unannounced arrival of Alexis, Alexis's success, and his own inability to confront Gregory about the role of Alexis. His perceptions of mistrust, spying, and Alexis's great intellectual powers prevented him from taking positive steps to unravel the web of uncertainty. He has not taken into account the laissez-faire management style of Gregory: he misinterprets Gregory's loose style as "keeping him in the dark." As a result of these faulty assumptions and misperceptions, his anxiety level climbs well above his ability to cope. But by using counters Bob can restructure his original assumptions and perceptions and take positive action. The first step should be to reassume true control of his group and relate to Alexis as a valuable resource person working for him. Second, he should set up a meeting with Gregory to discuss Alexis's role in the present and the future, and to talk about the problems and progress of the new project. This conversation would allow Gregory to give him input that could allay most of his anxieties.

PHILOSOPHICAL SHIFTS

Philosophical shifts are changes in overall viewpoint. A basic perceptual shift involves one set of assumptions, perceptions, and feelings.

Creating a personal goal inventory is one way to establish specific goals and philosophy in five areas: career satisfaction, status and

TABLE 2-1
Perceptual Shift Worksheet

Thought/Belief	True/False	Best Argument against Thought	Evidence from Own Experience Proving Best Argument
I am incompetent as a scientist. I discovered the enzyme by luck.	False	Since that time my group, through my direction and support, has made significant contributions.	The Beta project was a huge success. My boss praises me, and my project team appreciates me.
Gregory does not trust me. He sent Alexis to spy on me.	False	Gregory asked me about Alexis's progress. Why would he do this if Alexis was a spy?	Gregory has stated his support for my work. Up to this point Alexis has not met with Gregory.
Alexis is brilliant; I pale in his shadow.	False	Alexis is an individual contributor in a narrow technical field. I have knowledge in a broader spectrum. I am able to synthesize ideas, while Alexis is one-dimensional.	I have shown in the past that my management style works. The group has always worked best under these conditions. My successes affirm me.
Gregory is keeping me in the dark for some reason. Maybe he wants me to fail.	False	In my encounters with Gregory, he asks me about my work and the progress of others. However, I don't open up and discuss any problems. Maybe I am keeping myself in the dark.	On the occasions when I have discussed problems and progress, Gregory has been open and supportive.
My group has lost respect for me. Alexis has soured them on me.	False	The group still responds to my suggestions. They ask for my guidance and support. Alexis is just Alexis.	Some of the group have raised concerns over Alexis's abrasive style. Even Gregory has asked me how he was doing. I need to take charge.

self, personal relationships, leisure satisfactions, and learning and growth. The inventory is a seven-step process:

1. Identify the specific goals in each category.
2. Rate the importance of the goal.
3. Rank-order the specific goals.
4. Determine the level of current attainment (low, medium, or high.)
5. Assess whether the specific goals are in conflict.
6. Select the most important ten goals, and rank them in order of importance.
7. Determine what barriers lie in the way of their attainment and what steps need to be taken to achieve success.

The following case is an example of a person, Herbert, who looked at his life and made a major philosophical shift.

For three generations Herbert's family have owned and managed a midsize apparel manufacturing company. Herbert went to the prestigious Wharton School, another tradition in the family. Upon graduating with honors, he received numerous job offers. Much to the dismay of his father, Herbert decided not to enter the family business until he had proven his own success. He is now an accountant in a large consulting firm.

Herbert had felt the pressure to continue in the family's retail tradition, but he was not yet ready to make that commitment. Nevertheless, he viewed this tradition as a sacred responsibility that could not be violated, so with reluctance he had mastered the elements of finance and accounting. His boss was very pleased with his work. On the other hand, Herbert was besieged with doubts about his chosen profession.

His only pleasures and passions in life, other than his family, were scuba-diving trips and a newfound interest in marine biology.

Herbert's boss called him into the office one morning and told him that he was being considered for a promotion to manage the accounting department of a regional office. This job included a large salary increase and the opportunity to become a partner in the firm. Herbert's immediate reaction was mixed: he felt both gratification and anxiety. He graciously thanked his boss and told him he would give him an answer in the next two weeks. He told his boss he needed to settle some family matters. His boss understood and shook his hand.

That evening Herbert fell into a state of depression. His wife tried to get him to talk about his reactions about the job offer and his feelings about the promotion. His family still wanted him to work with them rather than in his current position and now he had to make some difficult decisions.

After three days of self-analysis and discussions with his wife, he came to realize that he was in an existential bind. Accepting the promotion would lock him into a career path that he was uncertain about and probably would bar him from ever working in the family business. Neither option was palatable to him. Herbert was a prime candidate for philosophical shifting.

After considerable soul-searching, Herbert came to the insight that he was haunted by repressed feelings of meaninglessness and unfulfilled desires. He carried out, competently but resentfully, his job obligations. This behavior was governed by an imposed philosophical view.

Herbert tried to uncover the tenets of this philosophical view. Early in his life, his family had structured a worldview and a set of roles based on their assumptions and beliefs. He was not allowed the luxury of defining himself and thus was ruled by these underlying philosophical tenets:

- I am defined by my adherence to traditional family values.
- Acceptable career paths are in retail and finance, the family business.
- My lifestyle is dominated by responsibility and conservative understatement.
- Self-fulfillment is secondary to group conformity.
- Life is a journey of duties on the road to salvation.
- Pleasure is a deterrent to salvation.

Here is Herbert's new philosophy after his philosophical shift:

- It is possible to be faithful to family and self at the same time.
- Career choices should be based on abilities and interests.
- Spontaneity can define one's life as well as understatement; this is a matter of choice, not dictate.
- Self-fulfillment requires more than group conformity. Inner convictions must be considered.
- My own personal philosophy will determine my salvation.
- There is no evidence that responsible pleasure causes harm.

Herbert came to the conclusion that he had to be the initiator in his life and not let himself be controlled by external pressures. He decided that he needed to reassess his career goals to determine what he really wanted to achieve in his professional and personal life.

Through this process, Herbert resolved to combine his valuable skills in accounting and finance with his intense interest in marine biology. With his personal savings, he invested in a scuba-diving company specializing in educational tours. He had made philosophical shifts that enriched his life.

CONCEPTUAL SHIFTS

We all have a basic view of the world and how we fit into it. The Germans call this our Weltanschauung, our personal worldview. It is based on sets of assumptions that form a pattern. Sometimes this pattern forms a coherent whole; then there is harmony in our thoughts and actions. But the pattern may also form a distorted view of ourselves that needs a conceptual shift—a realignment of underlying assumptions about ourselves.

Brooke had strong feelings of anxiety when she became a district manager in a retail clothing company. She had to deal with ten other district managers, all male, at the division meetings. She developed a shy and reclusive stance in these meetings, in spite of the fact that she was extremely extroverted and confident with her subordinates, mostly females. Brooke feared that her new shyness was hindering her performance, and making her look bad to her peers and her boss. Her anxiety became so overwhelming that she decided to do something about it.

The human resources counselor asked Brooke to list all the negative thoughts connected with her anxiety attacks. She came up with this list:

- I fear I will be looked on as aggressive if I speak my mind.
- The other district managers are more experienced than I am.
- I never feel comfortable in a group when I am the only woman.
- I fear reprisal if I speak up, even though I know I am right.
- My mother was brilliant but knew her place. I am the oddball.
- Power is unbecoming to women.
- Men see me as pushy; therefore I must adjust my behavior.

Brooke was next asked to describe her behavior in other areas of her life:

FAMILY: I let my husband make the decisions. He wears the pants.

FRIENDS: At social gatherings at home and elsewhere, I mingle mostly with women.

BOSSES: With men, I become submissive and compliant. With women, I feel like an equal and am comfortable.

SUBORDINATES: I like to manage women. I feel distant with males even though I am the boss.

ATHLETICS: I am an accomplished tennis player and rank number one in the women's division at the club. In mixed doubles, I usually let the males dictate the play.

Brooke and her counselor analyzed the list and realized that Brooke was operating under a strong set of assumptions that women should not be assertive. She was then able to realign these assumptions, thereby creating a more positive perception of each negative belief. Following, we see the shift from negative to positive assumptions.

Negative Assumption	New Assumption
• I fear I will be looked on as aggressive if I speak my mind.	• Good managers, male or female, need to be assertive when the situation requires it.
• The other district managers are more experienced than I am.	• I bring a new perspective to the group.
• I never feel comfortable in a group when I am the only woman.	• Mixed groups offer opportunities for growth.
• I fear reprisal if I speak up, even though I know I am right.	• If I focus on the problem, no one can attack me.
• My mother was brilliant but knew her place. I am the oddball.	• This is an outdated way to behave.
• Power is unbecoming to women.	• Positive power is a skill that all managers need to develop.
• Men see me as pushy; therefore I must adjust my behavior.	• All men do not hold this perception. A minority might, but that is their problem. In most business situations assertiveness is viewed as a strength.

The last step that Brooke took was to collapse her new beliefs into one core thought: *I am a female who can be part of a productive team by acting in a natural, assertive manner.* Brooke continued to reinterpret her anxiety attacks as they occurred. She practiced this exercise until her sense of the new fit was automatic.

Discovering Personal Values. Most people hold to a set of values that give meaning to their lives. Some individuals have developed a highly articulated set of core life values. Most people, though, have a less differentiated set.

There are two levels of values: the universal, which involve the limited number of common human problems for which all peoples at all times must find some solution, and variations of the universal core values, which emerge from subcultures or enclaves that evolve their own art forms, lifestyles, and status rituals, independent of the dominant core values. Organizational values, for example, are variations on the dominant core values of our society.

Florence Kluckhohn, an anthropologist, and Frederick Strodtbeck, a sociologist, have identified five areas that have universal significance:

1. The character of innate human nature (human nature orientation).
2. The relation of the person to nature (person–nature orientation).
3. The temporal focus of human life (time orientation).
4. The activity focus of human life (activity orientation).
5. The modality of a person's relationship to other people (relational orientation).

For each of these areas, Kluckhohn and Strodtbeck then set out three alternatives:

1. View of human nature: evil, mixed, or good.
2. View of person/nature orientation: subjugation to, harmony with, or mastery over.
3. View of time focus: past, present, or future.
4. View of activity focus: being (emotional expression), being-in-becoming (personality integration), or doing (action).
5. View of social relationships: lineal or hierarchical, collaterality or group-focused, or individualism.

Table 2–2 defines the orientations and alternatives to life.

All human societies must solve common problems. No matter how cohesive a society is, its members will exhibit variations based on the alternatives. Most people find it difficult to identify core values. Moreover, we may subscribe to one set of values but have inner conflict over its primacy in our lives. In American life, indi-

TABLE 2-2

Kluckhohn and Strodtbeck's Value-Orientations Model with Alternatives

Orientation	Alternative		
Human Nature	*Evil:* People are born with evil inclinations. Control of evil behavior is the only hope.	*Mixed:* People are both good and bad at birth.	*Good:* People are basically good.
Person/ Nature	*Subjugation-to-Nature:* People have little control over natural forces. Nature guides one's life.	*Harmony-with-Nature:* People are one with Nature. Nature is one's partner in life.	*Mastery-over-Nature:* One is expected to overcome natural forces and use them for one's own purpose.
Time Sense	*Past:* Traditional customs are of central importance.	*Present:* The past and future are of little importance. Here-and-now events are most important.	*Future:* The temporal focus is on planning change for events which are to occur.
Activity	*Being:* Emphasis is on activity which is spontaneous self-expression of emotions, desires and impulses.	*Being-in-becoming:* Emphasis is on the self-expression aimed at integration of the personality through control.	*Doing:* Emphasis is on action-oriented self-expresssion which is measurable by external criteria to the acting person (e.g., achievement).
Social Relations	*Lineal:* Lines of authority are clearly established and dominate subordinate relationships.	*Collateral:* Individual goals are subordinated to group goals (collective decision making).	*Individualism:* People are autonomous of the group. Individual goals are more important than group goals.

vidualism takes precedence over collaterality, but an organization is a web of interdependent relationships demanding a shift from radical individualism to collaboration. These two solutions, individualism and collaboration, come into direct conflict when they are not articulated and integrated. When the conflict is not directly addressed, the manager exists in a confused state of being.

Generating Promotive Thoughts. The techniques of cognitive restructuring we've already looked at—removing barriers in one's self and the environment and eliminating negative thoughts, beliefs, and assumptions—are not enough to ensure future optimal performance. You must develop a strategy for generating promotive thoughts, the cognitions that people use to achieve their core life values. With core life values, promotive thoughts move people toward optimal performance.

Cognitive Restructuring to Change Management Style: A Case Study

Beth, an assistant vice-president in a retail clothing company, began by identifying her core values:

- View of human nature: mixed—that is, good and bad but changeable.
- View of person/nature orientation: mastery over the environment.
- View of human activity: doing.
- View of time focus: future.
- View of social relationships: individual.

Beth's set of value orientations follows the dominant pattern characteristic of middle- and upper-middle-class Americans. Almost all the managers in her company seemed to have the same future. Sometimes she questioned whether this hard-driving pattern, which sacrificed the present for the future and focused on mastery and doing, was what she really wanted. As a student in the 1970s, she recalled, mastery over the environment was secondary to harmony with nature, as was being-in-becoming to doing, and collaboration to individualism. In those days the past and future were far less im-

portant than the present moment. She wondered if she had not sacrificed too much for "success." After much soul searching, Beth determined that she wanted to shift her core values: "I want to have
more balance in my life without sacrificing my career goals. I think
I have embraced the dominant orientation while discarding my
inner needs." Beth's restructuring sought to give different priorities
to the following core values:

- *View of person/nature orientation:* "I would like to return to a
  harmony with nature and place less priority on mastery over nature, which puts me at odds with the world." Here Beth used
  two promotive thoughts to help reinforce a shift in core values:
  "I can function equally well in my job while maintaining a sense
  of oneness with nature," and "I was able to do this in the past
  and can regain this ability by reading, sailing, and visiting and
  appreciating the shore. I have a special affinity for the water."
- *View of activity:* "I have devoted the last ten years to doing and
  producing while letting my inner self become walled off. Being-
  in-becoming allows me to be more spontaneous. By maintaining
  a doing orientation to the exclusion of all else, I have developed
  a one-sidedness." Beth again settled on two promotive thoughts:
  "I can explore my inner self through meditation, self-reflection,
  and reading *The Book of Life*, by the Italian Renaissance writer
  Marsilio Ficino" and "I can set limits and priorities for my
  doing/producing and the search for my inner self; they need not
  be opposed to each other."
- *View of time focus:* "I have lived too long looking to the future,
  looking to what I should do to make things bigger and better,
  without enjoying the here and now. I need to balance this with
  an appreciation of the past and enjoyment of the present." Beth's
  first promotive thought was: "I need to take my lunch hour, not
  work at my desk with sandwich in hand, and go home by six
  o'clock each day. I also need to stop anticipating what is going to
  happen next. I can concentrate on small pleasures, like looking
  at the sky and spending more time with friends, enjoying their
  sheer presence." Her second promotive thought was more ambi-
  tious: "I can visit South America or southern Spain and learn
  from the people there the value of a present orientation. Possibly
  I can develop and embrace the flow experience."

- *View of social relationships:* "I was taught to be self-reliant, and to be an individual contributor. But these values produce a sense of isolation and extreme competitiveness. I work in a strained atmosphere, where people are on guard most of the time, in spite of the company message that we have to work as a team. I want to develop more collaborative relationships with fellow workers and friends." Her first promotive thought was: "I can engage in team activities—maybe even attend an adult Outward Bound program—to develop a sense of interdependence." Her second promotive thought related to her organization: "I can encourage team-building exercises for my work group and develop a sense of collaboration. This may take some doing, but I can prevail!"

Beth has articulated her core values and the shifts that she wants to make. With the help of promotive thoughts, she will be able to reinforce any changes over time and reduce internal and external conflicts.

Relaxation Techniques: An Adjunct to Cognitive Restructuring

An impressive body of scientific evidence demonstrates that use of relaxation techniques can foster a state of readiness for changing one's assumptions, perceptions, and feelings. Relaxation can be used as a simple stress-reduction technique, and it can be combined with cognitive restructuring techniques.

Herbert Benson, a noted researcher on stress and the relaxation response, confirms that executives in a pressure-cooker environment cannot escape the realities of the situation but can counteract them with the relaxation response. Relaxation, when appropriately and regularly used, creates a mind-set of receptivity to undertaking other tasks related to stress problems.

Deep relaxation, practiced every day, will help you reach a state of calmness and serenity, where a state of suspended animation sets in. At this high level it has extremely beneficial effects. When relaxed, you are able to suspend negative critical thinking and open up to other techniques to deal with your problems. It is possible in a state of deep relaxation to reach your inner thoughts and to use them consciously. For example, you can mentally rehearse tasks and performances that will prove to be very effective when dealing with difficult employees or bosses. In a broader context, deep relaxation can help you in dealing with life's problems. When used in conjunction with perceptual and philosophical shifting, you will reach toward wholeness and completeness.

When you are ready to try deep relaxation, go to a private area and sit in a comfortable chair. Then close your eyes, take a deep breath, breathe slowly and deeply, and progressively relax your body by suggestions of further deepening. The following script encapsulates the key elements. Memorize this, or read it first and practice as you go along:

You are going to do three things. First, raise your eyes toward the ceiling without moving your head. Hold them like this. Now take a deep breath, exhale, and close your eyes. Take three deep breaths. Sink deeper and deeper into your chair. Let your arms go limp. Breathe deeper and more slowly. Now focus on the muscles in your head. These muscles need to be relaxed. Feel the tension flowing out of the muscles of your forehead. Now focus on your eyes. Let the lids totally relax. Now relax the muscles in your cheeks. Feel them go limp. Now relax the muscles around your lips and chin. Feel how your head is perfectly relaxed. Breathe more deeply and slowly. Now relax your shoulders, your arms, and your fingers. Focus on your upper back, and let all the tension drain from these muscles. Breathe more deeply and slowly. Relax the muscles in your lower back, buttocks, and thighs. Now relax your calves, feet, and toes. Feel how deeply you have sunk into your chair. You are floating on a cloud. Breathe deeply and slowly. Keep repeating the words "calm and serene." Stay as long as you like in this calm, ever calmer state. When you are ready to stop, take a deep breath, exhale, slowly open your eyes, and stretch your arms.

This is an easily learned procedure. You may prefer transcendental meditation or yoga. The end result is the same: lower tension, greater calm, and an open mind.

3

Modifying Psychological Type

Psychological types are based upon a theory of human behavior that is grounded in the interplay of opposites, or polarities. Carl Jung, the founder of this theory, identified four components to psychological types. He used the word *preference* to classify the four components. Each preference is composed of two distinct poles.

The first preference is an *energy orientation*. At one pole is an outward-going extroverted side (E), and at the other, the inward-looking, introverted side (I). Each of us is capable of shifting from one pole to the other, but we usually have a preferred pole.

The next two preferences are *functions* that describe how we perceive and judge the world. The first function, *perception*, is divided into the poles of sensing (S) and intuition (N). The sensing type uses the five senses to comprehend the environment; the intuitive type uses a sixth sense to seek out possibilities. A sensing type (S) is more comfortable with facts, details, and concrete reality. The intuitive type (N) feels at home with future possibilities and the integration of data. Perception is idiosyncratic: sensing and intuitive types who examine the same data may come up with very different pictures of the world around them, and conflict can result from their different ways of processing data.

Judgment, the second function, is divided into the poles of thinking (T) and feeling (F). The thinking function (T) is based on rational, principled logic and has an impersonal tone to it. To make a judgment, criteria are sufficiency of data, validity, and reasonable-

37

ness. The feeling function (F) (an unfortunate label because it incorrectly conjures up emotional tones) uses a personal set of values to judge perceptions. It is very subjective in nature, uses empathy, and calculates subjectively whether a judgment is important or unimportant, valuable or useless.

There is a *dominant function* that is the cardinal function of the four. The extroverts use their dominant function outwardly, while the introverts use their dominant function inwardly. A dominant function is easier to use than an auxiliary function.

The fourth component is the *preference,* used in dealing with the outside world. This can be a perceptive function (**P**), sensing or intuition, or a judging function (**J**), thinking or feeling.

These four preferences essentially define psychological type:

Extroversion (E) versus Introversion (I)—how we use our psychic energy.
Sensing (S) versus Intuition (N)—how we perceive the world.
Thinking (T) versus Feeling (F)—how we judge the world.
Perceptive (P) versus Judging (J)—how we deal with the world.

Each of us has a preference from each of these four categories that combine to define our type, represented by four letters. The first letter denotes how we use our psychic energy, whether as an extrovert (E) or as an introvert (I). The next two letters combine to show perception and judgment: sensation and thinking (ST), sensation and feeling (SF), intuition and thinking (NT), and intuition and feeling (NF). Finally, the fourth letter reveals whether we have a perceiving orientation (P), using sensing or intuition in interactions with others, or a judging orientation (J), using thinking or feeling in interactions with others. When all of these polar positions are combined, we arrive at sixteen psychological types.

The Tasks of Types

The goal is not to change anyone's psychological type. If we accept the prevailing belief that the types have a nature more than a nurture basis, an attempt to change type drastically can have serious psychological consequences. We must accept our own orientation and learn to cope intelligently with the differing orientations of others. But that does not mean we are stuck with our type. As individuals, we should learn to recognize our strengths and weaknesses, become conscious of the impact of our preferences on others, and develop the skills that can be used in a temporary fashion to achieve *individuation*, that is, the integration of all our capacities and capabilities so that our personality is balanced.

Paradoxically, individuation begins with the differentiation of the functions, moves on to the clear development of each, and finally ends with integration of the four functions. We each have a dominant, an auxiliary, a tertiary, and an inferior function. Rarely do we integrate all four functions in a harmonious style. The inferior function, the least preferred and possibly most submerged function, will never become the dominant function, but one can learn how to accept and strengthen it so that it is not locked out. Understanding the natural order that is unique to you is the first step. If you can identify your dominant function, then you will know that your inferior side is at the opposite pole.

Introverts use their *dominant function* internally. Others will rarely see this part of their personalities except under demanding or stressful situations. Extroverts use their dominant function externally, that is, when dealing with the outside world.

The *inferior function* is the opposite of the dominant function. If S is dominant, then N is inferior, and vice versa. If T is dominant, then F is inferior, and the reverse.

The fourth letter in the psychological type acronym tells which function we use in dealing with the outside world: J or P. This preference defines the use of *perception* or *judgment* in dealing with the outer world. The J types use a judging function (thinking or feeling). They live according to a planned, decisive, and regulated fashion. The P types depend on the perception function (sensing or intuition) for interacting with the outer world. They are more flexible, spontaneous, and adaptive in their approach to life.

Extroverts, by definition, use their favorite process (dominant function) in dealing with the outer world. The following extroverts are judging types: **ESTJ, ESFJ, ENTJ, ENFJ**, with T or F dominant. The following extroverts are perceptive types: **ESTP, ESFP, ENTP, ENFP**, with S or N dominant.

With introverts the favorite process is used in the inner world.

Their auxiliary process, **J** or **P**, is used in the outer world. The following introverts are judging types: **ISTJ, ISFJ, INTJ, INFJ**. The perceptive introverts are: **ISTP, ISFP, INTP, INFP**.

Dominant **intuition** has **sensing** as the inferior function, and vice versa; dominant **thinking** has **feeling** as the inferior function, and vice versa.

Once you know your dominant function, the next step is the connecting process, whereby the inferior function is awakened and used. Apart from entering formal analysis, there are some simple but effective ways to achieve connectedness. In addition to connecting the four functions, you can learn how to appreciate and use your psychic energy, either outward or inward.

The following section describes the sixteen types. Before you read about them, you might want to turn to Appendix A, which contains a short assessment instrument for determining your psychological type. If you complete this instrument now, you will have an unbiased assessment of your type.

The Sixteen Types

Extroverted Thinking Types: ESTJ and ENTJ

Both of these extroverted types judge their environments through thinking, their dominant function. They draw their conclusions from objective external information. The external world is their reality, and they demand that the rest of the world conform to their view of it. In describing this type, Jung warned, "The more rigid the formula, the more he develops into a martinet, a quibbler, and a prig, who would like to force himself and others into one mold."

Extroverted thinkers interpret their environment through logic and careful organization. Their analytical approach to problem solving sometimes seems impersonal and cold, but in emergencies their decisiveness is welcome. When a decision must be put on the table, they willingly supply one.

Since their dominant function is thinking, feeling is their inferior side. This often causes trouble for both themselves and others. When the inferior feeling side remains ignored and unconscious, it can break out in undifferentiated emotions and values. As the psychologist Marie-Louise von Franz pointed out, if the inferior function is not integrated, it can explode "like a banshee." Von Franz wrote, "The extroverted thinking type has . . . a kind of mystical feeling attachment for ideals and often for people. But this deep, strong, warm feeling hardly ever comes out."

ESTJs use introverted sensing as their auxiliary function. They observe the world through their five senses, but they must apply the orderliness of thinking to their sensory impressions before they have meaning. Since their sensing function is introverted, it primarily services their extroverted thinking. They take a matter-of-fact approach to problems. Strongly developed ESTJs generally distrust intuition and feeling. They need to play down their extreme realism and their penchant for logical positivism. There are no mystics among ESTJs.

ENTJs use introverted intuition to guide their inner lives. With them, vision and a sense of possibilities enter the picture. The ENTJ's dominant judgment function is based upon grasping the meaning of facts and things and their unique associations. An ENTJ would be at home with an ESTJ in offering opinions, but the two would violently disagree about whether their opinions were based on fact or fiction. ENTJs have been called natural "commandant" types who insist on ruling by their particular vision. In organizations, they are the ones who look to the future and conceive new ventures. If their tertiary sensing function is not brought into play, however, their formulations may be nothing but pure fantasy. Successful ENTJs are able to balance their visions with relevant facts.

Extroverted Feeling Types: ESFJ and ENFJ

Extroverted feeling types are in tune with their environment, especially with other people. They use their judging function—feeling—to evaluate each situation according to an individualized set of values. Instead of principled reasoning, the criterion behind their values is whether something has relative status or personal worth. Cold logic is not part of the picture. There are many do's and don'ts in their life scripts, and the moral imperative is their watchword. Extroverted feelers are excellent at sizing up or creating an atmosphere. They lend themselves beautifully to arranging and creating wedding parties, for example. Because thinking is the function most likely to disturb feeling, they suppress it. They make friends easily and vent their feelings often. But their feelings and statements are not always appropriate. Anyone who exclaims on a dreary, rainy Monday, "Oh, what a beautiful day!," is overdoing it.

Introverted thinking is the inferior function of extroverted feeling types. They have no patience with philosophical ramblings, and they back away from conversations that require careful analysis. If suppressed too much, the inferior thinking function can erupt in a volley of negative criticism, some of which is apt to be illogical or crude. When that happens, the individual is possessed by the inferior function. But when extroverted feeling types try to integrate their inferior thinking function, they sometimes overdo it and become dogmatic and conventional. Inexperienced in critical analysis, they embrace a new idea without reservation, swallowing it whole.

Good judges of people and situations, ESFJs keep in tune with their environment by using sensing as their auxiliary function. They are service-oriented and can be extremely self-sacrificing. Because their sensing function is introverted, their keen awareness comes from internally scanning details and images from the external world.

ENFJs, on the other hand, use introverted intuition as their auxiliary function. Instead of focusing on present realities, they look at future possibilities. They find great satisfaction in creating growth experiences for themselves and others. They also place high value on trust and cooperation. If this value is violated, ENFJs can become formidable enemies. They are very expressive individuals, but they often assume that others understand them, despite their unusual value-based judgments. Their quest for perfect work relationships can get them into frustrating situations, because they base their perceptions of individual potential on intuition, not facts. A well-developed ENFJ can be a positive group leader, however, creating a productive atmosphere and tuning into the needs of group members. There are not enough of these types in organizations.

Extroverted Intuitive Types: ENTP and ENFP

Extroverted intuitives use their dominant function to sort through the choices their external world presents. They have a great sense of anticipation. If they have fully developed intuition, they are successful in predicting the future. They focus their energy outward toward what will happen next, and they see many alternative possibilities for objects, people, and situations. In the 1950s, it was probably an extroverted intuitive who noticed some children playing with a thin metal tire hoop and created a similar hoop out of a new material—plastic—thereby inventing the Hula Hoop. This ability to sniff out possibilities makes extroverted intuitives entrepreneurial and innovative. Some extroverted intuitives get no further than the search, however. Their weak decision-making ability or poor organization prevents them from completing tasks or following through on their inspirations. They are little more than gadflies, dropping one idea for another, then another, and so on.

The inferior function of extroverted intuitives is introverted sensing. They give scant attention to details and tend to overlook essential facts. Since their inferior sensing function is introverted, they pay excessive attention to bodily sensations or to minor, misplaced facts. They notice insignificant details, imagining that those details have personal importance. A twinge in the lower back can portend a grave illness. An astrological forecast can paralyze their decision-making ability on the day when the company needs it most. This signals that the inferior function has taken over, crippling an otherwise spontaneous and creative individual. Extroverted intuitives need to develop their inferior function and bring it out of its unconscious lair so that it can do good rather than harm.

ENTPs use thinking as their auxiliary function, putting a critical spin on their intuition. They tend to be interested in projects involving things rather than people. They are good at the innovation and integration of various systems. Their judgment function, which is secondary, is logical and analytical. They are always on the lookout for new and better ways to do things. Entrepreneurship is one of their specialties. They are fun to work with because they can not only play with ideas but critically evaluate them. They make excellent "devil's advocates." The ENTP is a good member of a brainstorming group. But the ENTP's weak point is lack of thorough preparation. They are great at generating ideas but poor at following through. This may be why many entrepreneurs fail just when an innovation most needs good management. When careful follow-through is needed, a good ENTJ, ESTJ, INTJ, or ISTJ is a more welcome partner than an ENTP. For many ENTPs, ego and power needs get in the way of success.

ENFPs use feeling as their auxiliary function. They shift from objects and analysis to people and values. When presented with a task such as developing a more marketable product, they consider their real task to be developing their own potential and that of their colleagues. Enthusiastic crusaders, they are engaged in a lifelong quest for perfection, authenticity, and spontaneity. They are delighted when their quest inspires their fellow workers; when it does not, they may become depressed and even vindictive. As intuitives, they look for information to confirm their preconceived biases. When their cloudy judgment interacts with their inferior function, they may draw erroneous conclusions. When their judgments of people and situations are correct, they are brilliant; when they are wrong, they are disastrous. ENFPs like to work in freewheeling environments and have difficulty adjusting to institutional or organizational constraints. They are the bane of organizers and enforcers of policy. Placed in a suitable role, an ENFP can inspire the development of human potential in an organization.

Extroverted Sensing Types: ESTP and ESFP

Extroverted sensing types are masters at observing external details. They focus on people and things, and they remember exactly what someone wore on a particular occasion and what they said and did. Recognition of details and events is primary, while recognition of their significance is secondary. The extroverted sensing type is the most accurate eyewitness, whereas the introverted intuitive is the worst. Extroverted sensing types are practical, down-to-earth people. They reject intuitive fantasizing out of hand, preferring to focus on the present. They bring a splash of reality to any situation or discussion. When their pedestrian tendencies are extreme, they seem to be spoilsports and obstructionists. Materialism is their forte; they revel in a world of things. Every detail of a management-by-objectives program enthralls them. They are the realists of organizations who stockpile reams of information. But to be useful, their facts need sorting and categorizing.

Intuition is the inferior, dark side of extroverted sensing types. They regard with great skepticism anything that is only a hunch. Their undeveloped intuition may break through in suspicious thoughts about people or events—thoughts that are more often wrong than right. Because their intuitive function is not refined, when used at all it is egocentric. Marie-Louise von Franz pointed out that when extroverted sensing types let go of their egos through drink or weariness, they sometimes tell fantastical, imaginative tales. They are apt to deny having done so when their egos come back in charge again. Von Franz also cited examples of no-nonsense extroverted sensing types who became obsessed by their inferior function and rushed with complete abandon into esoteric Eastern religious sects or new wave movements. This illustrates the pull of *enantiodromia*, the philosophy of opposites.

Thinking is the auxiliary function of ESTPs. They are logical in gathering data and resourceful in using it, keeping information logically sorted and ready for action. Because their perception function is finely tuned, they are on the lookout for change, anticipating their neighbor's next move. They are excellent negotiators and "firefighters." Because of the dominance of their sensing function, ESTPs live fully in the present but can focus the energy of their auxiliary function on future plans. But their organizational abilities are not as refined as those of an ESTJ, and some of their actions and judgments are shot hastily from the hip.

ESFPs use introverted feeling as their auxiliary function. Empathetic and hypersensitive, ESFPs are naturally friendly people. They seek company and have an uncanny sense of tact, sympathy, and social ease. For them, life itself is a performance into which they throw their artistic and aesthetic talents. But ESFPs are not strong at analyzing events or at offering criticism. They shy away from any form of conditional negative feedback—a serious weakness for them as managers.

Introverted Thinking Types: ISTP and INTP

With introverted types, the dominant function is directed inward, and what is seen in their dealings with the outside world is the secondary or auxiliary function. Thus, introverted thinking types use thinking internally. They are the people of ideas and principles. Taking a logical, systematic approach to the world is their raison d'être. But this approach is internal and guarded from the world. Because their auxiliary function is a perception function, they come across as quiet and reserved. Their judgment function does not surface unless they are required to explain the logic behind a particular plan, whereupon they unveil a highly systematized procedure. In problem-solving groups, introverted thinkers are the silent minority who need to be prodded for their input. Their thinking emanates from a subjective source and does not apply to external matters. Jung described Darwin's classification of external factors as the prototype of extroverted thinking and Kant's inner critique of knowledge as the prototype of introverted thinking.

The inferior function for introverted thinkers is feeling. Their judgments are black and white, a characteristic of undifferentiated feeling. "You could compare the inferior feeling of an introverted thinking type," wrote von Franz, "to the flow of lava from a volcano; it only moves five meters an hour but it devastates everything in its way. But it also has the advantages of a primitive function, for it is tremendously genuine and warm. When an introverted thinker loves, there is no calculation in it." Unfortunately, the introverted thinker hates with an equal lack of calculation.

ISTPs use sensing as their auxiliary function to relate to their friends and their employment. They gather facts and details from the real world to make internal judgments. Since they deal with external matters through their perceptive function, they sometimes seem laid-back. They have a penchant for economy of effort. Most of their psychic energy is expended on subjective assessments about what facts mean to them. They view action as an end in itself, and they want the freedom to follow their own assessments. ISTPs are the most taciturn of types; verbalization is not their thing. They are also patient, accurate, good with their hands, and appreciative of the outdoors.

INTPs are quite different in demeanor from ISTPs. Both use thinking as their dominant function, but the INTP deals with the outside world through ideas and possibilities, gathering insights from the environment. Of all the psychological types, INTPs exhibit the highest precision in thought and language. They are good at detecting inconsistencies in thought and logic. INTPs are the natural architects of ideas, using logic, perceptiveness, and ingenuity. Because of this talent, they are sometimes viewed as intellectual snobs or even as dilettantes. Although they are good at developing ideas, they are weak at putting them into practice. Action is not their strong suit. They generously supply problems with new alternatives and clear reasoning.

Introverted Intuitive Types: INTJ and INFJ

Introverted intuitives deal with the external world with the logic and analysis of thinking. Their dominant function, however, is introverted intuition. Jung saw the introverted intuitive as a peculiar combination of mystical dreamer and eccentric artist. Introverted intuitives must sometimes be brought back to reality and asked what their ideas mean. Their perceptions tend to be single-minded, and their views unshakable. As introverts, they see their visions clearly, but they are not always aware of how others perceive them. The development of the introverted intuitive's judgment function—either thinking or feeling—is critical for balancing and systematizing their inner visions.

It is interesting to note that Jung himself was an introverted intuitive, as are many of today's Jungian analysts.

The inferior function of introverted intuitives is sensing. They are not in close touch either with their own physical senses or with those of others. Von Franz pointed out that the introverted intuitive is vague about facts, plucking from the environment whatever they need to verify their preconceived conclusions. Therefore, their facts must sometimes be questioned. When unchecked by their judgment function, they can deceive themselves. In extreme introverted intuitives, external facts present themselves as isolated islands of information, unrelated to any structure or larger meaning. Selectively and subjectively processing information, introverted intuitives often make wildly incorrect assumptions.

INTJs have thinking as their auxiliary function. Therefore, thinking keeps their visions in balance, making them logical, critical, and decisive, although they may not communicate the premises behind their judgments. Ironically, many CEOs in American industry are INTJs. A *Wall Street Journal* article stated that the occurrence of INTJs among CEOs is twenty times greater than among the general population. It seems as if most INTJs become either Jungian analysts or CEOs! As managers move up the corporate ladder, their communication skills become more crucial—except, apparently, for

INTJs. They seem to be promoted on the strength of their insights and determination, regardless of their inability to communicate well. A manager working with an INTJ can ward off potential conflicts and misunderstandings by frequently reviewing roles and objectives. Here a psychological contract is useful.

INFJs are more aware than INTJs of their impact and influence. They are less concerned with moving an organization or institution toward a future vision than with learning the meaning of events. They are something of an enigma, for although their differentiated feeling function is extroverted, they are reluctant to share their private intuitions. Interested in what others think and feel, they reveal little about themselves. Although they are concerned about the general welfare, they are not as communicative as ENFJs.

Introverted Feeling Types: ISFP and INFP

The dominant function for introverted feeling types is inward-directed feeling. They have highly differentiated sets of values but rarely express them. Because of this, the introverted feeling type is poorly understood. Their intuitive function communicates in a somewhat distant manner, while their feeling function remains buried deep within. Directed by their differentiated introverted feeling, they display an uncanny sense of ethics and moral propriety. Although they have strong preferences, they seldom verbalize them. Idealists, they put a tremendous amount of energy into philanthropic causes. Intensely loyal to their internalized values, they seem driven by internal forces. In fact, without a unifying value system, the introverted feeling type is like a floundering ship. But armed with a strong, personal set of values, he or she is the backbone of organizations.

The inferior function of the introverted feeling type is thinking, which tends to be undifferentiated. Pushed by the inferior function, introverted feeling types drive to amass data indiscriminately. Needless to say, the volume of disorganized data can quickly overwhelm them. While a well-differentiated extroverted thinker is an organizer and an astute evaluator of information, the introverted feeling type is not. Von Franz recommended that the introverted feeling type should always check thoughts against facts, frequently subjecting them to reevaluation.

ISFPs use extroverted sensing as their auxiliary function and are therefore in tune with their world, using relevant facts and details to meet the requirements of their jobs. They see the needs of the moment and respond accordingly. They like to express themselves and their values through actions instead of words and work devotedly at projects that satisfy this need.

Because extroverted intuition is their auxiliary function, INFPs have more insight into their actions. But their intuition is shy, almost reticent. They have a deep sense of traditional values, and they like to pledge themselves to a cause. Because of their feeling function, they seek continuity and coherence, but they are vague about what this entails. They are able to interpret symbols and view situations from a broad perspective.

INFPs make good novelists and character actors, having a good sense of mood or atmosphere and a strong interest in people and their potential. In organizations they are adaptable and sensitive. Impatient with conditional or hypothetical possibilities, they prefer their own real or imagined truths.

Introverted Sensing Types: ISTJ and ISFJ

Introverted sensing types take in their environment through their dominant sensing function. Placid but absorbed, they interpret the world through their five senses. To those who do not know them well, introverted sensing types may seem entirely unaffected by external events, as if little from the outside world had penetrated their consciousness. This appearance is deceptive, for their acute perception and memory make them tremendous organizational assets. When their auxiliary function—thinking or feeling—is in operation, they pour out details and impressions that others never thought existed. Their patient attention to detail and shades of meaning is without parallel. Introverted sensing types deal with external matters through their judgment function, presenting encapsulated evaluations of events and information. They like to have things, people, and facts under control. Their business and personal affairs are organized to a degree that is hard for extroverts to fathom. They make up for their lack of spontaneity by their dependability and carefulness. But if anything useful is to come from their deeply stored impressions, introverted sensing types must develop their auxiliary judging function.

The inferior function of the introverted sensing type is extroverted intuition. Sensing types are in danger of seeing no further than the present. When intuition occasionally does break through, it is apt to be undifferentiated and unreliable. Actions that are suggested by this kind of intuition should not be trusted. But this type may throw caution to the winds when intuition takes over. A prudent, dependable financial accountant will squander hard-earned money on a whim, for example. At the other extreme, an intensely rigid individual, distrustful of all intuition, will create tremendous internal conflict by suppressing all dreams and imagination. Introverted sensing types tend to resist interventions such as brainstorming. They can describe sensations in vivid and exquisite detail, but they cannot take the next step and draw meaning from those sensations.

ISTJs have extroverted thinking as their auxiliary function. They are rational, impersonal, logical, conclusive, and ready to act on their impressions. Tact and empathy are not their strong suit, just as for the extroverted thinker. Often ISTJs fail to consider the impact their decisions have upon others. The ISTJ needs to balance the secondary function with empathy and feeling.

ISFJs are tactful and considerate. They use extroverted feeling when dealing with the outside world, and they consider all the nuances of their actions. Their personal values determine their actions, and to those who share their values, they are extremely loyal, becoming fierce defenders of their organizations' welfare and of the status quo.

Examples of Types

These descriptions are accurate, but it is difficult to convey exactly what people of these types are like. One way is to relate them to characters in movies, or to well-known personalities. I have chosen some classic and contemporary examples to illustrate these types. Some are hyperboles; others are serious character portrayals. I hope you will be familiar with many of them. If you are not, it is worth renting the movies—and enjoy a combined leisure activity and serious study.

ESTJ: Extroverted Thinking with Sensing. Wally, in *My Dinner with André*, is the opposite type of André. His concern is with the here and now. He appreciates being with his wife and waking up in the morning to a cup of warm coffee. He enjoys reading a biography of Charlton Heston and the endless details in the *New York Times*. He is confounded by the phantasmagoric idlings of André. In this dialogue between the two, we vividly see the classic conflict between a sensing and an intuitive type. Wally sees the world defined by the concrete realities of money, a job, and marriage, and derives satisfaction from the small pleasures in life and its obligations. André, however, has to transcend the here and now to look for meaning in esoteric adventures that promise new possibilities.

ENTJ: Extroverted Thinking with Intuition. Lee Iacocca is the quintessential ENTJ. He is very expressive in citing the many possibilities for growth and opportunities in the auto industry. He talked the federal government into loaning Chrysler, a private company, and moreover one that performed no vital national security function, $500 million. He has a firm value system that guides his path: "Lead, follow, or get out of the way." His dominant function is extroverted thinking, and he uses this to convince or criticize.

ESFJ: Extroverted Feeling with Sensing. As portrayed by actor Lee J. Cobb, the messenger service owner in *Twelve Angry Men* is an ESFJ. He is obsessed by repressed feeling, a set of personal values centering on authoritarianism, directed at his son. He feels violated by his son's rejection and abandonment of him. The worst-case scenario follows: As a juror, he projects his anger onto the defendant, a young boy, and loses sight of the task at hand—to weigh the evidence objectively and come to a just solution.

ENFJ: Extroverted Feeling with Intuition. ENFJs wear their values on their sleeves. They are constantly projecting, sometimes in a charismatic way, their visions for a just and better world. Martin Luther King and Jesse Jackson are excellent examples of ENFJs, as religious and political leaders. The film character Norma Rae in the movie *Norma Rae* exemplified this type in her attempt to organize the mill workers to form a union.

ENTP: Extroverted Intuition with Thinking. Jeff Bridges, in the role of Tucker, in the film *Tucker—the Man*, acts out the role of a convincing ENTP. With his innovations in the car industry and his ability to integrate complex engineering designs for production, Tucker uses his dominant extroverted intuitive function and his organizing thinking function. Like many other entrepreneurial types, however, he encounters problems when it comes to facing some of the realities of the situation, in this case, the opposition from the "Big Three" car manufacturers in terms of political clout. Other ENTPs that come to mind are Mitch Kapor, founder of Lotus Corporation, and Kenneth Olsen, retired CEO of Digital Equipment Corporation. Both were brilliant innovators but fell short when it came to running the practical side of the business.

ENFP: Extroverted Intuition with Feeling. Robert DeNiro as Rupert Pupkin in the *King of Comedy* represents extroversion at its peak. His characterization of the obsessed and frustrated talk-show host points to the need of the extrovert to be front and center. Peter Pupkin is also driven by his wild intuition and internal values.

ESTP: Extroverted Sensing with Thinking. One can find no greater extrovert than Joan Rivers, actress and talk-show host. Joan must talk! Her energy is constantly flowing. Her interviews of guests consist of an opening question, with the guest's response verbally usurped by Joan's need to express her unabashed energy as she attacks the subject matter with the jocularity of the prototypical extrovert.

ESFP: Extroverted Sensing with Feeling. The character portrayal of Mozart in the film *Amadeus* is an excellent example of a high-spirited extrovert. He bounds through life, relishing the limelight and the rewards and opportunities for extravagance that come his way. His extroverted sensing rules his behavior. The moody Salieri, an introvert (INTJ), disdains both this kind of behavior and Mozart's genius. Indeed, he resents the style—the extroverted attitude—and exuberance as much as the talent, so much so that he sinks into vengeful depression.

ISTP: Introverted Thinking with Sensing. Clint Eastwood's portrayal in *Dirty Harry* is a prime example of an ISTP. Dirty Harry deals with a situation by scanning the environment (using his sensing function) and gathering facts for internal judgment. There are long pauses in the dialogue while the camera pans from his narrowed eyes to the details of another person or a bit of evidence, then back to his eyes. Dirty Harry's facial muscles are frozen in place, his eyes fixed in a stony gaze. There is a long pause, and then finally he speaks: "Go ahead. Make my day."

INTP: Introverted Thinking with Intuition. Columbo, the television detective, is another intuitive. He is not as cultured or as smooth as André, and he dresses like he buys all his clothes at Goodwill clearance sales, but his stream-of-consciousness thinking represents the intuitive mind-set. He forgets details, like pens and note paper. He constantly scratches his head, a nonverbal sign, scanning his intuitive right brain for connections and clues to a case.

INTJ: Introverted Intuition with Thinking. Gregory Peck in *Twelve O'Clock High* represents a good example of the introverted, brooding, thinking type. Watch closely his interaction with General Pritchard in the opening scenes. He rarely volunteers information until it is dragged out by the general; he then carefully analyzes the cause of the demoralization of the bomber group. His analysis is not spontaneous but instead is the result of introverted thinking, carefully planned and scrutinized before presentation. He describes the problem as a case of the commanding officer's "overidentifying with his men." Only a pure thinking type would come up with such a harsh judgment.

INFJ: Introverted Intuition with Feeling. In *Twelve O'Clock High*, Gary Merrill, as Colonel Davenport, regresses into a rage, instigated by his feeling function, when he is ordered by the general to relieve his navigator, Zimmy, from duty. His concern and empathy are with the person, not with goals and missions. His personal value orientation kicks in. As a result, he too is dismissed from command by the general, a hard-nosed thinking type.

ISFP: Introverted Feeling with Sensing. Rick, the owner of the Café Américain in the film *Casablanca*, represents the introverted stance. He rarely shares his thoughts or feelings with anyone and he even plays chess with himself. His communications with others are oblique and terse. His past is shrouded in mystery: we find out with some probing that he was a soldier of fortune in the Spanish Civil

War, but no more. Rick has no close friends—only acquaintances and enemies. The energy of the introvert is directed inward. Rick's inner world focuses on his own set of values: autonomy, cynicism, chivalry, and existential hedonism—his own set of feeling values.

INFP: Introverted Feeling with Intuition. The classic encounter between an intuitive, André, and a sensing type, Wally, occurs in *My Dinner with André.* André lives his life in an abstract world of fantasy and possibilities. He makes loose connections between isolated events and creates associations that baffle the sensing Wally, his dinner partner. André loves to live with possibilities and change. The here and now is transformed into wild dreams.

ISTJ: Introverted Sensing with Thinking. Remember the television series "Dragnet"? When Sergeant Friday interacts with his sidekick and his witnesses, we see the quintessential sensing type: "The facts, ma'am, just the facts." In a contemporary comedy based on the series, Dan Akyroyd does a splendid job of spoofing the detailed conscientiousness of the sensing type. Focus on his elaboration of the detective's dress code: "It means there is a dress code for detectives in robbery homicide section 3 dash 205 10 point 25 point 10: short hair, suit or sport coat, leather shoes preferably with laces and a shine on them!"

ISFJ: Introverted Sensing with Feeling. Colonel Codman, Patton's aide in *Patton*, exemplifies the characteristics of the ISFJ: tactful, considerate, extremely loyal, and a fierce defender of the organization or the boss. Codman is constantly reassuring Patton that his views and actions are correct. He becomes an apologist for each and every misstep. Patton states: "When that happens again, give me a swift kick in the butt." Codman, replies: "I'll give you a gentle nudge."

Exercises for Strengthening Type
Energy Orientation

For *introverts*, the task is to:

• Attend assertiveness training classes or join a discussion group in which everyone has to talk about what is on their minds.

- At parties, conferences, or dinners, introduce yourself and interact actively with others.
- Meet with subordinates, peers, and bosses, and ask them what they need from you.
- Ask yourself, "What did I leave out in the conversation?"
- Attend some psychodrama meetings or role-playing seminars, usually held by adult education programs.
- Attend effective presentation skills classes.
- See a Marx Brothers film.

For *extroverts*, the task is to:

- Learn the relaxation response, described at the end of Chapter 2.
- Read Proust and Thoreau.
- Set aside one hour of quiet time each day.
- Take a long walk in the woods alone, and contemplate nature.
- Practice active imagination.
- Learn active listening techniques.
- Keep a diary of your inner thoughts.

Perception Orientation

The task for *intuitive* types is to develop sensing:

- Learn to cook from recipes.
- Learn a sport such as sailing that demands specificity—terms, exactitude, and precision.
- Learn computers, the most sensing task of all electronics.
- Listen to jazz for the fun of it.
- Use your hands: paint, sculpt, or fix up the house.
- Plant a garden.
- Use your eyes to focus on details in nature.
- Learn to master a balance sheet.

The task for *sensing* types is to develop intuition:

- Visit a museum with a good collection of abstract paintings, and write about their personal meaning to you.
- Construct a personal five-year plan with strategic options.
- Listen to classical music. Try to grasp the complexity of a piece, and then try to explain what the music meant to you.

- Write an explanation of why a rose is not just a rose.
- Practice exercises with embedded figures.
- Watch a Fellini or Bergman movie or *My Dinner with André*.
- Set up a discussion group with known intuitives to discuss their interpretations of a short story (an S type) and a Faulkner short story (an N type). Try to reconcile the different perceptions of the same material.
- Read poetry, especially the romantic poets (Blake, Wordsworth, Coleridge, Keats, Shelley, and Byron).

Judgment Orientation

The task for *thinking* types is to develop empathy and personal values:

- See Charlie Chaplin in the movie *The Kid*.
- Write about your most cherished values.
- Ask a very close friend about his or her most cherished values.
- Develop a more personal style. Write a letter (not to be sent) to a subordinate who gives you trouble. In the letter try to walk a mile in his or her shoes. Stay away from impersonal factual and critical comments.
- Attend an AA meeting to experience the personal pain of others.
- Interview a friend about certain critical issues. Share your views with that person.
- Ask a significant other about his or her reactions to your statements.

The task for *feeling* types is to develop balanced and logical judgment:

- Hear both sides before judging.
- Lower your personal reaction to criticism.
- Take a course in critical thinking.
- Develop delegation skills.
- Develop power bases. Power is not evil.
- Learn effective performance appraisal skills.
- Seek out a thinking type to explore this problem: "In an attempt to offset the shortage of water in several large cities, plans are being completed to dam major rivers, thus creating artificial lakes as reservoirs. Naturalists complain that wildlife will not be able to adjust to artificial lakes and will be severely affected. In several cases whole villages may have to be moved to higher ground, leaving farms and traditions behind them."

Delegation and Psychological Type

Delegation is an important management skill, and certainly a key activity for all managers, with both direct and derived benefits. It extends the tasks from what a person can do to what she or he can control; releases time for more important work; develops subordinates' initiative, skills, knowledge, and competence; and allows decisions to be made at the appropriate level.

Most managers agree that decisions ought to be delegated to the lowest possible level where they can be made intelligently and where the relevant facts and required judgment are available. Often, in practice, they violate this rule by micromanaging. Yet it does not necessarily follow that the higher the level at which a decision is made, the better the quality of that decision will be. The cardinal principal in delegation lies in the type of decision that must be made. A policy decision clearly belongs in the hands of top management. Operating decisions, however, where the problems are best solved by those with special expertise, should be made by middle and lower management.

Delegation means maintaining responsibility but relinquishing authority. Some managers reverse the process and give subordinates the responsibility to act but do not give them corresponding authority. This is *not* delegation. Other common mistakes in delegating include:

- *Dumping:* Giving no or minimal guidelines to the subordinate. The boss says, "Just fix it" or "It's up to you." If the subordinate does not pin down the boss's expectations, the boss eventually returns to criticize the subordinate.
- *Hovering:* Constantly checking on the progress of the delegated project, to the point of interfering. It leaves the subordinate feeling distrusted, frustrated, and thwarted. It is the parent side of the boss reacting to the child side of the employee.
- *Ordering:* Telling the subordinate exactly what to do, with no opportunity to question or suggest. This form of management is extremely authoritarian and invites passive–aggressive behavior.
- *Do-It-Yourself syndrome:* Doing the job yourself because you want it done right. This leads to overwork, overcommitment, stress, and underdevelopment of subordinates.

In addition, the personality characteristics of both the boss and the subordinate can have a profound effect on whether delegation takes place. Psychological type can have some effect on how a boss delegates. *Sensing types (S)*, because of their proclivity for detail, may tend to micromanage or hover over the task and take initiative away from their subordinates, while *intuitive types (N)* may not explain all the details or responsibilities to the subordinate, believing that the broad picture is enough for the delegatee to work with. *Introverts (I)* may not fully communicate all the necessary information they have; their delegation will be patchy and inconsistent. *Extroverts (E)* may wander with their thoughts and not be concise in their communications. (This problem is less likely with extroverted sensing types than with extroverted intuitive types.) Impersonal and hypercritical *thinking types (T)* can arouse anxiety and uncertainty in an insecure subordinate. *Feeling types (F)* may seek harmony and avoid conflict which will come back to haunt them later on. *Judging types (J)* may push too hard for the outcome and operate out of a crisis management mode. *Perceptive types (P)* may procrastinate by mulling over the problem or task and not delegate until a crisis explodes.

Clearly delegation is a state of mind, in both the individual and the organization. Let us see how each of the sixteen personality types tend to manage.

ESTJs give subordinates mountains of detailed information without regard to its degrees of importance, so the big picture will be out of focus. They like to organize and plan all the procedures, which they focus on to the exclusion of overall strategy. Then they hover and push for closure. They can be abrupt and hypercritical of others' performance, with delegation sometimes taking the form of giving orders and demanding results. The ESTJ type had a 22 percent occurrence in my management sample of over 1,000 middle- and upper-level managers in a Fortune 100 company.

ESFJs are sensitive to rules and regulations and, paradoxically, to the needs of people as well, so when it comes to delegation they will be caught between these two poles. Therefore, they may hover over subordinates to make sure they follow guidelines and to offer support. They are extremely social and may tend to oversell their kindness. ESFJs are a minority in management—only 2 percent in my sample.

ENTJs have a sense of self-importance. They give orders, rather than truly delegate, so control and authority remain in their hands.

They dish out criticism with no regard for the feelings of others. Twelve percent of my management sample were ENTJs, whereas 4.6 percent occur in the general population.

ENFJs are very involved with the group as a leader and as a participant, sometimes becoming overinvolved with too many tasks. "Reverse delegation"—taking on or sharing subordinates' responsibilities—can be the result. ENFJs must learn to dissociate from overidentification with others. Only 1 percent of my management sample were ENFJs, as opposed to 4.6 percent in the general population.

ESTPs, more entrepreneurs than managers, do not attend to details as much as action. Follow-up is not their strong suit. This could be why only 2 percent of the executives in the management sample were ESTPs, opposed to 14 percent in the general population.

Active and entertaining ESFPs make work a happy place. They are performers of the highest quality in their social interactions. But they must be on guard about dumping work on their subordinates without providing them with adequate guidelines. They will pay more attention to the human side than the task side. That is why only 1 percent of management jobs are held by this type.

ENTPs ponder over the scope of the problem and expend much time in defining the possibilities. They have no great sense of urgency when trying to accomplish a task. Because of the tremendous number of options and alternatives they generate, subordinates may be confused about what an ENTP really wants. Clear expectations may not be given.

ENFPs are careful not to criticize subordinates or to overburden them. But because they are so concerned about the human side of the equation, the task may suffer. ENFPs must separate the people from the problem, outline the task at hand, and be assertive in giving instructions and handing over authority. There is no time urgency for the ENFP; schedules may slip and priorities be ignored.

ISTJs focus on details, giving out only what they perceive as important information. They are likely to be very impersonal and not give rewards when the subordinate does a good job. A subordinate who does not live up to the expectations of an ISTJ will pay for it. An extraordinary 21 percent of a management group in one of my studies were ISTJs, while only 4.6 percent of the general population is ISTJ. Communication is a problem for this type.

ISFJs are uncomfortable in a position of authority. They respect authority and follow rather than give directions. Therefore, they are less likely to delegate and tend to do jobs themselves. They are underrepresented in management. Of the managers in my population sample, 2.3 percent were ISFJs.

INTJs think about the big picture but do not fully communicate their vision, believing that subordinates can read their mind. Subordinates have difficulty dealing with INTJs because they do not like others to criticize their grand design. Like ENTJs they tend to give orders and not delegate; the difference between the types is in the amount and structure of their communications.

INFJs strive toward harmony in the organization and respect the feelings of others. This is commendable, but INFJs have a tendency not to give constructive criticism when it is warranted; as a result, subordinates may not grow under their tutelage. INFJs fix their subordinates' mistakes themselves and remain silent.

ISTPs immediately attack the problem, leaving little room for subordinates to interact in defining the problem or devising a solution. The ISTP is more a troubleshooter than a manager.

ISFPs are rarely found in management. They do not plan and prepare; rather, they like to perform in the fine arts. The atmosphere of the organization is a damper on their soul. Delegation would be a hard task and an alien operation for the prototypical ISFP.

INTPs examine the task and ruminate over the possibilities. But after they have scanned all the possibilities, they give the subordinate a carefully drafted list of how to approach the task. The problem for the subordinate is that the INTP has suggested too many options, leading to dead ends and poor time management.

INFPs are impatient with details; they focus on the big picture, overlooking some needed facts and pushing on with the job. Therefore, in delegating to others, some vital aspect may be missing. INFPs do not get involved unless they feel that a project fits in with their values. In this respect, priorities may not be respected.

Using Psychological Types for Individual and System Growth

Attention must be paid to more than the individuals and their needs for completeness and wholeness. It is possible to use data from en-tire organizations to design interventions for more effective team-work and improved quality of work and relationships.

The State Department in the early 1970s discovered that 60 per-cent of the deputy chiefs of missions were cited by their bosses, the ambassadors, for failing in their jobs. An extensive research pro-gram revealed that conflict over management style was a key factor in the ambassadors' negative appraisals of the deputy chiefs. Many of the ambassadors were political appointees of an entrepreneurial bent. Most of the deputy chiefs were of the cerebral, intuitive, thinking type. The goal for organizational development was to re-move this conflict by teaching management style to everyone in-volved.

Six opportunities were targeted for organizational development:

1. Understanding individual management style.
2. Understanding the culture of the State Department.
3. Developing influence skills (positive power).
4. Developing conflict management skills.
5. Developing skills to manage stress.
6. Developing delegation skills.

Data were gathered on the distribution of type from a sample of over two hundred deputy chiefs of missions. We found in this group and a similar one of participants in a management develop-ment program that six types accounted for 80 percent of the distri-bution. Based on the percentages typical of an adult population, the number of these six types was larger than expected. The most no-table ratios were for the INTJ (8.0 to 1), the INTP (4.7 to 1), the ISTJ (4.6 to 1) and the ENTJ (2.6 to 1). Some types were excep-tionally underrepresented: ESFP, ENFJ, ESFJ, ESTP, ISFJ, and ISFP. (The last never surfaced in any of the programs.)

The implications for organizations are obvious: they need to de-velop better human interaction skills. There is a tremendous overemphasis on the task with little attention devoted to develop-ing relationships. Since companies are organized on a matrix basis, the interdependency among various groups and individuals is criti-cal to getting the job done right the first time.

4

Modifying Needs

Needs are forces that organize perception, apperception, intellect, cognition, and action. They can be something we lack but seek, or something we have and wish to keep. When we act on our needs they become manifest behavior, and we fulfill a desire. If we do not act on our needs, they remain unsatisfied. Repressed needs, unconsciously held, can lead to neurotic symptoms. Inhibited needs, consciously held but not acted on, lead to frustration.

Sherman, a project manager in a large corporation, has a high need for recognition, but the corporate culture emphasizes task orientation and little communication from the top. Sherman feels isolated and frustrated when he completes a job and receives neither positive nor negative feedback. His need for recognition is being thwarted, and he harbors ill feelings toward his boss. Joyce, on the other hand, has been promoted to section manager. Her high needs for achievement and dominance have found a fine arena for expression. She delights in being able to take charge of people and tasks and to perform at a high level. Joyce has found a position that allows her to express her natural tendencies.

Certain needs (e.g., food and water) are physiologically driven. Others are psychologically driven. David McClelland, a motivational psychologist, calls the psychological needs *social needs* because they involve a transaction between the person and the environment. Perhaps a better term is *psychosocial needs*. These psychosocial needs are the result of a combination of nature and nurture. They are like muscles. We all have them, but their mass and shape vary from person to person. By conditioning our naturally given muscles, we can build them to vast proportions, or we can cause them to wither by our inactivity. This loose analogy can be applied to our needs. If we accept the idea that needs are fostered by both innate drives and environmental influences, we can reshape them by mental exercise. The exercises in this chapter can be used to modify your needs. But first, I will explain the needs and their relationship to organizational effectiveness.

The Task Requirement Model

Any consideration of needs must factor in the task requirements. The task requirements of a sales organization, for example, should ideally be carried out by highly motivated, achievement-oriented people with no desire to direct or manage others (the need for power and influence). If any of these highly effective salespeople are promoted to the role of manager, the fit might not work. Conversely, if a person with a high need for affiliation and dominance is placed in a job requiring isolated individual effort, the result will probably be frustration and poor performance. Her needs to work with and direct others are not being fulfilled.

In the best of all possible worlds, our pattern of needs and personality type would allow us to pursue careers that suit our personality; no modification would be necessary. Some people do, intuitively or rationally, seek out the environment that suits their personalities. It is not astounding that executives tend to be high in both the need for achievement and the need for power. However, it is more likely that just as your psychological type may need modification, so too may your need pattern if you want to be successful as a manager.

The Needs

The fifteen needs I have identified as fitting within a corporate environment fall into four categories: the Management Triad of Needs, Bosses/Peers/Subordinates Relations Needs, Task Factor Needs, and Interpersonal Modifiers. (Appendix B is a form that you can use to determine your own needs.)

The Management Triad of Needs

The needs for achievement, dominance, and affiliation determine a manager's approach to the task.

ACHIEVEMENT

The need for achievement—to do one's best, to be successful, to accomplish tasks that require skill and effort—manifests itself according to the expertise and skills that a manager acquires through education, training, and experience. Over 80 percent of successful managers are high in this need.

Most managers fuse this need with the need for power, in extreme cases controlling and driving a task without regard to either delegation or teamwork. Such managers tend to give orders and to delegate little responsibility. Sometimes the need for achievement combines with the need for affiliation. In this union, the manager gives equal weight to concern for task performance and concern for positive interpersonal relationships. It is a highly participatory management style, and the manager becomes part of the team. The style can be effective if the ultimate responsibility of the manager is not sacrificed; it will be ineffective if the manager abdicates his rightful role as the head decision maker. The disadvantages associated with a high need for achievement include isolation from a network of productive inputs, excessive rivalry with colleagues, lack of delegation of tasks (the Do-It-Yourself syndrome), secrecy or redundancy of task accomplishment, perpetuation of the "Not Invented Here" syndrome, and stress from an overarching need to excel at all costs.

A high need for achievement can be a problem for managers who use it to achieve as individuals. Carried to the extreme, it leads to micromanagement and loss of focus, with the manager ending up doing tasks that others should do and ignoring the big picture. Managers must learn to meet their personal achievement needs through group success.

A study of successful and unsuccessful lead engineers, who coordinate tasks over many functions without direct authority for any of them, spotlighted the shortcomings of emphasizing achievement alone. It found that the least successful lead engineers had a high need for achievement and low needs for power and affiliation. They saw themselves as individual contributors, not as coordinators of the work flow, delegators, or team builders. Meanwhile, the functional departments saw these lead engineers as usurpers trying to take over their own roles as the engineering task performers.

These high achievers had been promoted to the lead engineer position because of their brilliant work as individual contributors in their areas of engineering expertise. The problem was that they carried over into their new position old behaviors that were inappropriate to lead engineer requirements. The study described them as archetypal cases of the Peter Principle, which states that people are typically promoted up to a level at which they are incompetent to perform the tasks dictated by their job. Had they assessed the new job requirements and their own management style, they might have modified their needs in accordance with the new conditions.

The most successful lead engineers were moderate in the need for achievement and high in goodwill power (building relationships based on mutual interests, empathy, and respect for others) and affiliation. Lead engineers interface between the program office and the functional departments of manufacturing. They coordinate funding, schedules, and customer requirements, with the actual tasks performed by task engineers. The most successful lead engineers forged collaborative attitudes between the program office and the functional departments. Individual achievement was replaced by teamwork. They did not let the need to achieve as soloist interfere with the job requirements.

DOMINANCE

The need to dominate is the need to control one's environment, to direct or at least influence the behavior of others by suggesting, persuading, or commanding: Dominance is a crude form of power. It is a natural need found in humans and animals. The development of effective power is a skill and can be learned. (Dominance itself can be broken down into eight power categories, which are detailed in Chapter 5.)

As a sole motivator of subordinates, dominance is ineffective and demoralizing, as Ken found out. Ken was the plant manager for an electronics company that produced complex radar devices. He was a loner who surrounded himself with a small and loyal staff who carried out his every wish. He relied solely on his authority as plant manager to get tasks done. He did not want to hear about problems, so his staff shielded him from any that arose, and in the case under discussion concealed some bad news about the status of the quality, cost, and schedule of an important product. When the problem ultimately surfaced, Ken denounced his staff for not recognizing the problem and then blamed them for not disciplining the people who worked for them. Actually, they *had* recognized the problem, but they were afraid to bring it to his attention. In reaction to his outrages, they turned on their subordinates, and a hierarchy of terror was the result.

This episode reached its climax when Ken's bosses found out about the severe problems with the new radar device from the customer. They were simultaneously embarrassed and angry. The customer issued an ultimatum that the company would lose its sizable contract if it did not act to rectify the problems of quality, cost, and schedule. Senior management transferred Ken to another plant, where the requirements of dependence and open communications were not as important in getting the product out.

Ken had believed that his authority and willpower were enough to get people to produce. He ignored the reality that regardless of level or rank, there are important relationships among all levels that must be nurtured in order to have all of the parts fit together. Ken is an extreme example of the abuse of negative power. He operated like one of the rulers of the Roman Empire.

The need for dominance has negative effects if it is not tempered by other considerations. If a manager operates as Ken did, he or she will:

- Disempower others.
- Overcontrol the task.
- Be blind to other opinions.
- Force premature solutions.
- Exploit others.
- Manipulate others.

Management wisely chose Ricardo as the new plant manager to replace the beleaguered Ken. He is the direct opposite of Ken; he is outgoing, he smiles, and he radiates a sense of self-assurance without conveying any overtones of arrogance. He gives clear messages to his staff that he is a leader, not an autocrat.

Ricardo is from the school of management that believes everyone has something to contribute and therefore should be treated with respect. In his first month at the plant, he met with the other managers and asked them what they thought needed to be done to turn the situation around. At first he was faced with guarded skepticism, the legacy of Ken's reign of manipulation and punishment, but within two months he had gained the trust of the department managers. Fortunately, Ken had taken his own staff of loyalists to his new job, and Ricardo could appoint replacements. He then instituted a policy of openness. "Tell me the problems first," he urged, "and the good news later."

Ricardo had the gift of being able to make people relax, and ultimately he gained their confidence. He gave back to them the authority to make decisions appropriate to their level. Delegation, which had never had a chance under Ken, was encouraged and rewarded.

After one year, the plant won a national award for quality production. Ricardo had used his power in subtle and positive ways.

AFFILIATION

Affiliation is the need to draw near and cooperate or reciprocate with an ally, to participate in a friendly group, and to do things with other people rather than alone. Those with a need for affiliation have a participative style and form strong attachments to peers, subordinates, and bosses. They like to share equally and to make group decisions.

Affiliative managers value teamwork and communicate well with subordinates, colleagues, and bosses. They prefer not to work alone. Although affiliative managers help build strong morale, they may consider tasks to be less important than relationships. Therefore highly affiliative managers should be on guard against giving too much weight to relationships at the expense of tasks.

The affiliative need is subject to the test of extremes. A need too high or too low can be problematic. Low affiliation may interfere with the ability to generate friendly reciprocal interaction with others. Very high affiliation can place overemphasis on a relationship in opposition to the task. The aim of the need for affiliation is to form a synergy: a mutually productive, cooperative, and reciprocative relation with another person. Organizations with a critical mass of managers with low needs for affiliation have difficulty in developing teams outside their function. Either their achievement or their dominance needs get in the way.

Take the case of Paul. He was given the task of implementing a total quality management (TQM) program in his company. His leadership style was high in control over tasks. He had great success in meeting cost, quality, and production schedules on all his projects. Senior management thought he was the logical choice for this important program. However, Paul did not believe in management by committee. As a result, he had a hard time implementing the team concept of TQM. In the past he had done all the problem solving and decision making. After two months of nonproductive effort, he asked his boss to relieve him from the task. It was quite obvious that Paul was low on the need for affiliation. He could not bring himself to "buy into" the team concept. Paul was replaced by Roger, who had a more balanced need for power and affiliation. The TQM planning groups, under his leadership, started to make progress. Paul's boss ordered Paul to become an active member of the TQM planning group: senior management recognized he needed to be a trainee, rather than the implementor.

Bosses/Peers/Subordinates Relations Needs

Bosses/Peers/Subordinates Relations Needs are a cluster of five needs—deference, autonomy, nurturance, succorance, and abasement—that determine how we relate on an interpersonal level to our fellow workers.

DEFERENCE

Those who have a need for deference need to respect and get suggestions from others. They like to find out what others think, and they normally follow organizational customs and respect the hierarchy. Genuine deference to another generates mutual respect and is the easiest way to build a relationship. This is the positive side of deference. But as with all other needs, this one has two faces, like the Roman god Janus. Extreme deference untempered by critical thinking can develop into sycophancy. In the negative face we see overcompliance, bowing down to, accepting without judgment, and idolatry. Too low deference is a slight to the other person's concerns and rights. In this case it can be viewed as an affront to one's being. The bumper sticker that advises "Question Authority" is rejecting deference. In this form it could be a defense against imposed deference in one's childhood experiences.

In the television series "Magnum," Tom Selleck, as Magnum, and John Hillerman, as Higgins, illustrate the extremes of the deference dimension. Higgins is a subservient, loyal, and dedicated employee of the absentee English landlord, Robin Masters. Magnum, who lives on the Hawaiian estate as a hired hand, displays all forms of disdain for tradition and pomp embodied in the protoypical English attitude of Higgins. Many of the scenes in the series portray the interplay between the highly deferential Higgins and the iconoclastic, albeit naive, Magnum.

AUTONOMY

The need for autonomy is the need to be independent in making decisions, to feel free and not obliged to conform. Those who need autonomy want to decide their own agenda, work around hierarchies, and resist coercion and restriction. They are self-sustained. Autonomous people can be a great asset when they are individual contributors and do not have to work with others. They can be left alone with minimal supervision, if they are competent and goal-oriented. The negative side is that unbridled autonomy can lead to off-base decisions, irresponsibility, and feelings of restraint. If the autonomous person does not have the same goals and objectives as the organization, he or she is trouble waiting to happen.

Sally was a marketing development manager who gained recognition as a creative copy designer. She worked for Mat, a seasoned marketing director, who tended to overlook individual idiosyncrasies in favor of performance. He characterized Sally as a maverick who was outspoken and brusque at times. Mat recommended Sally for promotion to marketing development manager.

Her new boss, Candace, is strong-willed and believes in respect for authority and discipline. She tends to be on top of all the projects in her group. Sally was accustomed to more freedom of expression and creative initiative. After two months on the new job Sally found herself in a running battle with Candace over goals and objectives. This conflict was rooted in Sally's high need for autonomy and low need for deference. These needs clearly conflicted with

Candace's needs for control (dominance) and deference. Sally over-looked Candace's management style. She continued on the same course as with her previous boss. Neither Sally nor Candace re-spected the other's style. This case highlights the interaction be-tween deference and autonomy.

NURTURANCE

People who have the need for nurturance generally feel positive to-ward others and are empathetic. They show affection and respect and want to assist others, giving them positive reinforcement when it is appropriate. Nurturance is the need to give support rather than to receive it. Nurturing managers take into account the growth and development of subordinates and serve well as mentors.

Many people believe that nurturance is a female trait, but the empirical evidence says otherwise. A study of over 2,000 managers, including five hundred women, found no difference in the level of nurturance between men and women; the mean score on nurtur-ance for both groups was in the 40th percentile.

Organizations are trying to foster better work relationships in order to build effective teams, a goal that requires most managers to develop a higher need for nurturance. This need has to be tem-pered with a task orientation. If nurturance is too low or too high, there are problems in management style. The cold, overly task-ori-ented manager creates a chasm between boss and subordinate; the excessive nurturer, on the other hand, smothers and hampers inde-pendence. A fair mix of nurturance and affiliation can go a long way to building the team spirit that is often cited as a necessity for improving American industry today.

Roland was the director of preventive medicine at Mega Hospi-tal in Baltimore. His staff consisted of twenty-two health profes-sionals who had varying degrees of experience. All of them were competent in their specialties. Roland recognized early on that most of them were not trained in the nuances of organizational be-havior. Most of the departments at Mega Hospital were run under the traditional medical model in which authority and expertise were the trademarks of the department heads. Roland decided to change the perspective of his group and encouraged them to attend training seminars in order to broaden their behavioral knowledge. The topics included conflict resolution, interviewing techniques, team building, and understanding themselves. Roland genuinely cared for the psychological growth of his staff. The result was a smooth-running team that respected themselves and the patients.

SUCCORANCE

Succorance is the need for support from others. Those with this need seek out assistance and tend to want to be continually and unconditionally rewarded and supported. Succorance is another need that can cause interpersonal problems if it is too high or too low. The needy manager or subordinate puts great pressure for time and energy on others; the stand-alone stoic does not know how to take praise or to ask for help when she needs it.

With both nurturance and succorance needs, managers have to make a distinction between conditional strokes, directed at the behavior (which can be positive or negative), and unconditional strokes, directed at the person (which can also be positive or negative). A manager can get into deep trouble by using only one of the four combinations. For example, a person who gives only negative unconditional strokes can destroy his subordinates' self-esteem. Conversely, the outpouring of positive, unconditional strokes can lead to a credibility gap with subordinates. The receiving person wonders what is behind all the inappropriate sugar and honey. There are times when a manager has to criticize or has to try to modify the behavior of a subordinate, and negative conditional strokes are proper in this situation, but they should be balanced by some positive conditional strokes. With an overly succorant person, the demand for positive unconditional strokes can lead to distortions of perception. For example, when a manager directs criticism at an employee's work behavior, the overly succorant subordinate may turn his remarks into unconditional negatives, for he or she feels that he or she has been personally attacked. The criticism of the work, no matter how muted, is converted into a personal issue.

James believed that rewards have to be earned according to high standards of performance. He was known for his lack of feedback *to* subordinates. On the other hand, he constantly wanted feedback *from* his subordinates and demanded absolute concordance with his decisions. His nonverbal messages told people to agree with him or to suffer from his displeasure. James's low need for nurturance and his high need for succorance placed undo pressure on his subordinates to give, but not receive.

ABASEMENT

Those who have the need for abasement tend to accept responsibility readily. They feel guilty when things go wrong and feel liable for actions that may not even have been their responsibility. A good way to describe them is to say that they are hyperresponsible. The abasement need was the lowest ranking need among a sample of 2,000 managers in a Fortune 100 corporation. The mean percentile was 29. It appears that people who submit passively to external forces tend not to make it up the organizational ladder. Martyrdom is not highly prized in organizations. An excessive need for abasement appears to be an undesirable trait in managers.

One could also argue that an extremely low score might result in an amoral stance and lead to unethical behavior. I wonder what the level of abasement need is for the 1980s corporate raiders, S&L plunderers, and inside traders.

Let us put these two main types of needs together and see what they can mean to a manager.

Alberta was a director of product development in a publishing company, with three curriculum directors and a director of editorial administration reporting to her. The three curriculum directors managed section heads for the various disciplines of reading/language, math/science, and modern language/social studies. The director for editorial administration had managers for product assurance, editorial services, and design reporting to him. Each of the curriculum directors had redundant functions, such as product manager, design specialist, and middle-level editor.

Alberta's boss, Rebecca, a senior vice-president, had decided to implement a program in total quality management (TQM). The goal was to look at all of the functions in the four directorates to see if more interaction among them could decrease redundancies and increase efficiency and effectiveness.

Alberta's profile on the Management Triad of Needs showed high achievement and dominance and low affiliation. Her profile on the Bosses/Peers/Subordinates Relations Needs showed high autonomy but low deference, nurturance, succorance, and abasement.

She was perceived by her colleagues and subordinates to be an extremely competent director of product development but excessively independent, aloof, and cold. Her directions to her subordinates were clear and straightforward. She was quick to point out errors or deviations from her plan, and her subordinates had learned to do their homework before they had a meeting with her.

When Rebecca approached Alberta about the TQM project, Alberta offered no open opposition even though she secretly felt it was a waste of her valuable time. After a number of meetings and trial runs, the team concept never gelled. Alberta told Rebecca that they had tried it, but that it had no relevance for their type of business.

It is not hard to see why TQM failed. First, Alberta had no serious commitment to the project. Second, her need patterns did not fit the requirements for team building under TQM.

In Japan, where TQM flourishes, the modal patterns of managers are high achievement, moderate dominance, and high affiliation. In terms of the Bosses/Peers/Subordinates Relations Needs, autonomy needs to be low, deference high, nurturance high, succorance moderate, and abasement high.

The Japanese succeed because they can readily sacrifice their individual egos for the team effort. They do not demand excessive autonomy or dominance. They readily defer to others' opinions and give positive strokes to one another. The cementing factor is that they are hyperresponsible (they have a high need for abasement) and do not want to lose face with their colleagues by failing.

Alberta is just the opposite. She wants autonomy to do her own thing. She does not defer to or reward her peers and subordinates, and she has no feelings of guilt over her management style. The failure lies in lack of commitment and contradictory needs for the task.

Task Factor Needs

Task factors—needs for change, order, endurance, and intensity—influence how individuals approach tasks, how well they fit into an organizational climate, and how well they perform within various work groups.

CHANGE

The need for change is met by doing new and different tasks, meeting new people, and altering the daily routine. Those with the change need like to experiment, to try new jobs, and to move around.

Managers who have a high need for change require new and different tasks, variations in their daily routine, and role shifts within the organization. Organizations with a dynamic orientation, where tasks and priorities change frequently, are appropriate for change-hungry managers.

The need for change is a factor that influences the person-to-organization fit. If the job is routine and predictable, a person with the need for change will get frustrated by its constancy. Conversely, a low-change person in a dynamic and fluid environment will probably feel stress as the result of continual shifts in the job. There are no normative standards for change; it is what feels comfortable for the manager within the context of the job.

Hillary left college because she was anxious to get out into the "real world" of work. She obtained a job as a solderer with an electronics manufacturer. She worked at a bench with ten other solderers. Hillary soon became bored and frustrated with her job. Her colleagues could not understand why she felt this way; after all, she had a secure and well-paying job. Hillary had a high need for change, while the other workers were content with their routine because of a low need for change. Hillary needed to find a more dynamic work environment that suited her needs.

ORDER

Those who need order seek detailed, precise order in the organization of the immediate environment. They must work to a routine schedule and they want things to function smoothly. Like the need for change, the need for order is a personal preference. One must ask, "Does the job fit my needs for change, or can I impose order when necessary?" There are no prescriptions for this need.

Mary Beth and Roger worked as graphic designers in a publications company. All the offices were arranged as open work stations. Roger was very meticulous about his work station. All his files and documents were systematically arranged. Mary Beth's work station, in contrast, was a mass of clutter. Roger constantly criticized Mary Beth's work habits. When she needed some of Roger's software she rummaged through his files and took it. She rarely returned the borrowed material and Roger in exasperation would eventually have to storm over to her desk and demand it back. Then Mary Beth would rummage through her piles of papers and floppy disks, and miraculously retrieve the missing item. Roger would breathe a deep sigh and walk away. In the eyes of their boss both were outstanding performers. The difference in their work habits was due to their contrasting need for order.

ENDURANCE

Endurance is the need to make a sustained effort at a job until it is finished. There is a plodding quality to the endurance need.

Managers who have the need for endurance like to keep at a job until it is finished. They will stick with a problem regardless of slow progress, and they will put in long hours without distraction. The need for endurance is distinct from the need for intensity, in which bursts of high energy are expended for shorter periods of time. *Intensity* refers to how hard a person works, *endurance* to how long a person works.

Endurance too is a personal preference need. Some jobs are suited to the high-endurance type, while others fit the intensity-need type. The endurance need fits best with job environments that are stable in terms of their product line, that allow time for the organization of day-to-day activities, that have a predictable future, and that involve tasks that are straightforward. Occupations that lend themselves to exercising the endurance need include accountant, production worker, surgeon, realtor, tax lawyer, and insurance company employee.

Harvey was a world-class mountain climber. Each weekend he and his fellow climbers would ascend some unforgiving mountain. The ordeal lasted for the weekend. Back at his job, as an orthodontist, he displayed the same level of endurance, working ten-hour days while restructuring molars.

INTENSITY

The need for intensity involves vigorous activity for a sustained but limited period of time. Then there is a shift from a high level of alertness and effort to a period of temporary exhaustion, followed by a gearing up to a new level of high-energy expenditure on the same or a different task. The job environments that match the intensity need have the following characteristics: dynamic and changeable tasks, daily and sudden crises, constant priority shifts, the simultaneous performance of multiple jobs, and task complexity. Some of the jobs that fit the high-intensity profile are research and design engineers, emergency medical personnel, trial lawyers, creative writers, and troubleshooters (e.g., foremen in a high-tech production unit). Creative artists such as painters and writers also fit this category.

Seth was regarded as an extremely competent task engineer who always finished a job. He worked in an orderly fashion and never missed a deadline. As a result of his success on many projects he was promoted to manager in the program office. After two months on the job he went to his boss and asked to be transferred back to his old job. His boss asked, "Why?" Seth told him that the constant changes of specifications and priorities from the customer were causing him great stress. Seth's profile on task needs was low change and intensity, and high order and endurance. Monique, who replaced him, found the program office job challenging and exciting. Her task need profile was the opposite of Seth's: high need for change and intensity, coupled with low need for order and endurance.

Interpersonal Modifiers

Three needs make up the cluster of Interpersonal Modifiers: introspection, exhibition, and aggression. These needs are called modifiers because they give a unique tone to a manager's style. For example, an achievement-needy manager with a need for aggression is very different from an achievement-needy manager who is low in aggression need but high in introspection need. The former will come across as domineering, impatient, and insensitive, while the latter is cautious, thorough, and sensitive.

INTROSPECTION

Introspection is the need to analyze one's own motives and feelings. It also involves observing others to understand how they feel and to analyze their behavior and motives.

A manager with high introspective needs is likely to analyze his own motives, perceptions, and assumptions, and to try to understand other people's points of view. The need for introspection can be a positive modifier when it helps a manager to develop empathy for others. It would benefit managers to cultivate a positive use of introspection. But a cautionary note must be sounded: morbid dark thoughts can cloud introspection and cause negative repercussions. For example, a manager might interpret someone's behavior as Machiavellian when in fact nothing is going on.

Salina had a tendency to analyze and brood over her interactions with her bosses, peers, and subordinates. She would focus on selective perceptions and come up with interpretations that were bizarre. This tendency to overwork her dark introspective need made people uncomfortable in her presence. She said little, but others could sense the scrutinizing inner ear and inner eye that she cast upon them. She was not trusted.

AGGRESSION

People with the need for aggression criticize others publicly and disagree with them actively. They often show anger or displeasure, and they also often blame others. They like to "tell it like it is."

The need for aggression is expressed in open criticism, angry behavior, and frank, blunt communication. Aggression needs bring a hard, hostile tone to a manager's style. Many organizations encourage this need by assuming that aggressive competition among departments and individuals leads to high performance. But in such situations people act as adversaries instead of collaborators, with unfavorable results.

A high need for aggression should be tempered for both the inner good of the aggressive person and for her or his effective interpersonal contacts. When such aggression is turned inward and is not overtly expressed, psychosomatic consequences can result. Outward aggression hurts others; inward aggression hurts the self. Aggression has to be distinguished from positive assertion. The major difference is the unconditional attack on others exhibited by the aggressive type. A positive-assertive person is able to communicate his or her needs, perceptions, and assumptions without offending another person.

Take the case of Mac, a manager of production. He was regarded as the man to get people moving. He had a caustic style—criticizing, berating subordinates, and demanding perfection. He was successful as long as things went right. When problems arose, he would fly into explosive rages, blaming everyone for incompetence.

His extremely aggressive style fostered a self-protective attitude that caused his subordinates to hide problems from top management. Finally, the submerged problems caught up with the division, and Mac was held accountable by his superiors. They respected his technical competence but replaced him with a manager who was noted for building teams.

EXHIBITION

Exhibition is the need to be noticed, to be at center stage, and to be recognized for one's self-worth and accomplishments. Those with this need are often witty and clever. The need for exhibition may also be called the need for recognition. People with this need demand attention for both their work and themselves. They can create conflicts in hierarchical organizations in which center stage is reserved only for those at the highest levels.

It is natural to have a need for recognition. Everyone likes to be quoted, reinforced, and affirmed by others. When this need becomes pathologically high, however, it turns into an insatiable fervor.

José was a project manager in a design group. Each project had five or six designers working on a task. In one of his projects, all six designers had a high need for exhibition, and the design meetings were like the Tower of Babel: everyone wanted to talk at once. They constantly criticized each other. Finally their jabbering got so personal that José had to disband the team and assign them to other projects.

The Fusion of Needs

A fusion problem occurs when various needs are manifested at a high level and result in negative outcomes. (But note that in some fusion cases a positive effect is achieved.) In the spirit of understanding and subsequently modifying one's style, pitfalls should be identified before action can take place.

Achievement with Dominance. This combination is the most common pattern among managers. When carried to the extreme, it leads to overcontrol, too much involvement in details, and impoverished delegation skills. This type of a manager needs to be on guard about these deficiencies and to give up the hovering and order giving that can be his or her Achilles' heel. The tendency of the achievement/dominance manager is to micromanage the task. Under stress, this type of manager pounces on subordinates and demands immediate results.

Achievement with Affiliation. Achievement and affiliation fusion can lead to a very participatory style, one that was promoted in the sensitivity training seminars of the 1960s and 1970s. Influence is exercised through affiliation and being part of the crew. This fusion is marked by a democratic manner and can be very morale building. But in its extreme form it leads to mushy management in which the manager abdicates responsibility and blurs lines of authority, leading to confusion and role ambiguity. Positive assertiveness is needed to balance the quasiegalitarianism that is projected by the extreme form of these needs.

Achievement with Autonomy. The achievement with autonomy fusion may create serious problems because the manager focuses on accomplishments to the exclusion of the needs of others. Teamwork can suffer if this fusion is carried to the extreme. In some cases, the manager loses sight of the big picture because he or she maintains such a narrow focus.

Achievement with Succorance. When succorance fuses with the need to achieve, the manager seeks constant reinforcement that he is doing well. He has a needy quality to his style, and may call group meetings for affirmation of his decisions. Subordinates will be on constant call to assist their boss and may feel oppressed by these demands.

Achievement with Abasement. A fusion of the need to achieve and the need to feel abasement indicates a sense of hyperresponsibility to both self and others. People with this combination *never* have enough time to accomplish the extremely high goals they set. The manager who is constantly bombarded by self-critical automatic thoughts will be disproportionately stressed.

Achievement with Aggression. A manager with a fusion of achievement and aggression needs may become ruthlessly competitive with colleagues and subordinates in order to achieve self-minded goals. Some such managers become self-appointed experts; others engage in overblown criticism directed at everyone else's work, in an effort to highlight their accomplishments.

Dominance with Affiliation. Dominance with affiliation can lead to using friendship as a means to gain control. In a friendly, persuasive way, the manager maneuvers the peer or subordinate to accept her control. The form of behavior is not as apparent as the warlord pattern (dominance with aggression), but is nevertheless insidious in its results.

Dominance with Autonomy. The need to be dominant and at the same time autonomous creates a barrier between the manager and her colleagues. She builds a wall around her domain, and cooperation with other units is impaired. The manager often demands strict allegiance within her group while at the same time preserving her independence.

Dominance with Succorance. Dominance with succorance is a rare pattern, but when it does occur the manager oscillates between being the boss and being needy. The manager will fall into states of helplessness and, in a childlike way, demand support from subordinate(s), who may become confused by and resentful of this behavior.

Dominance with Abasement. A manager with the needs of dominance and abasement will experience internal conflict. There may be a high need to undertake more than can be accomplished, especially from superiors, combined with guilt projected downward to subordinates, with an unhealthy outcome. Great pressure may be exerted on the team to make good on promises that are unrealistic.

Dominance with Exhibition. The combination of dominance with exhibition leads a person to be dramatically forceful in public.

Again, the impact of this pattern depends on the circumstances. In certain corporate cultures, this kind of behavior is not tolerated; in others, it is seen as a positive statement. When these needs are expressed by a boss, only she or he gets center stage.

Dominance with Aggression. Dominance with aggression can lead to an autocratic and abusive management style. This kind of manager has a warlord mentality: "Never give an inch, and make them flinch." In certain crisis situations, this type of manager can ramrod decisions through that will lead to quick fixes. But in the long run, such tactics usually lead to resentment and lowered performance.

Affiliation with Deference. People with a fusion of the needs for affiliation and deference tend to be cooperative and to have an extremely friendly manner. The problem is that their striving to be friends may override their concern for the task, leaving critical thinking suspended. However, in a positive sense, this mixture can build into a reciprocating relationship.

Affiliation with Aggression. The combination of the needs for affiliation and aggression can manifest itself in an us-versus-them syndrome, with the manager seeking allies in order to beat the other group. This pattern is common in organizations where cliques are formed around hated procedures and unfair policies and against tyrannical bosses. The behavior may be overt or under cover (e.g., by gossip and backbiting).

Affiliation with Succorance. The combination of the needs for affiliation and succorance leads to a search for a relationship with a stronger, wiser, and caring person. If the other person is a mentor, a strong bond may occur that can develop into an unhealthy dependency.

Autonomy with Succorance. The interplay between high needs for autonomy and succorance presents an internal conflict for the manager; it is difficult to stand alone yet simultaneously desire help and caring. Whichever need prevails frustrates the other need. Managers having these characteristics are caught in a double bind and typically feel at odds with themselves.

Autonomy with Aggression. A rebellious and revolutionary streak comes from the marriage of high autonomy and aggression. A manager feeling constrained by the rules and regulations in the organization could openly rebel or he or she might secretly plot revenge. In a more open and less hierarchical organization, this fusion might be tolerated and even used as a means to change some cherished stone tablets.

Autonomy with Exhibition. The fusion of a high need for autonomy and exhibition can lead to eccentric posturing and disregard for others' feelings. A manager who is seen as aloof but grandiose could foster disdainful feelings in others.

Deference with Exhibition. When the high need for deference is combined with the need for exhibition, two things can take place. First, there is internal conflict: the manager is torn between taking center stage and praising others, and the result is a flip-flop between the poles. Second, the manager may integrate these needs into an interpersonal style of dramatic flattery. At one and the same time she is on stage but deferring to others.

Nurturance with Aggression. The joining of high needs for both nurturance and aggression creates a polarity leading to internal conflict. It may be possible to have aggressive caring—for example, "You may not like what I'm going to say to you, but it is for your own good"—but the more common case is vacillation and turmoil.

Exhibition with Aggression. Managers with patterns of high need for exhibition and aggression seek attention by being verbally abusive or by playing practical jokes. The aggressive behavior is intended to show how wonderfully smart they are. If this combination occurs alongside high dominance needs in a manager, the subordinates are in for a rough time. On another level, this need pattern may result in sniping and oblique aggression if the person is unable to confront others.

Succorance with Abasement. The union of the needs for succorance and for abasement leads to constant humble pleas for aid. A manager with this fusion will be regarded as draining and probably ineffective. Most managers who reach middle-level status do not have these needs; they are more often manifested by such difficult employees as "the constant complainer."

Succorance with Aggression. The fusion of the needs for succorance and for aggression can result in a sense of entitlement and the feeling that these demands are being unfilled. The outcome may be repressed anger and resentment toward others. This is clearly a victim behavior.

Abasement with Aggression. The combination of high needs for abasement and for aggression represents an internal conflict, characterized by outbursts of anger followed by withdrawal and remorse.

Crossover Problems

Crossover problems occur when one need is high and another is low. For example, a high need for succorance by itself is a problem for a manager in that he needs constant reinforcement from the external environment, and a low need for nurturance can cause difficulties because a manager is unable to give positive reinforcement to others. When high succorance and low nurturance are combined, the result is dramatic problems. A manager should be able to give support without looking for excessive help or sustenance in return. This behavioral pattern of needs turns the job upside down. The manager acts like a needy child rather than as a role model.

The following examples show combinations of high and low needs that intensify the effect of just one need by itself.

High Autonomy and Low Deference. High autonomy and low deference can be a problem if the manager has a boss who is high in authority power. The subordinate's needs run counter to the needs of the boss. A person with this crossover pattern can survive if he or she has invaluable skills or expertise, but the tension between manager and boss will never dissipate.

High Exhibition and Low Nurturance. High exhibition (recognition) and low nurturance dooms the possessor of this pattern to defeat. Who wants to recognize someone who never gives positive reinforcement?

High Dominance and Low Introspection. High dominance and low introspection can lead to insensitivity to the impact of authority and control. This type of manager uses power without regard for the feelings and needs of others.

High Autonomy and Low Affiliation. High autonomy and low affiliation results in an avoidant personality. The drive for independence collides with the need for interdependency and positive relations in the organization.

High Affiliation and Low Introspection. High affiliation and low introspection leads to shallow and superficial relationships. If a manager lacks introspection and cannot understand the needs of the other person, communality cannot develop.

High Aggression and Low Affiliation. High aggression and low affiliation results in a standoffish, superaggressive personality. If a manager with this fusion lacks other redeeming attributes, such as specialized expertise, he or she will have serious trouble.

High Autonomy and Low Nurturance. High autonomy and low nurturance produces a cold and aloof attitude.

High Exhibition and Low Deference. High exhibition and low deference is a self-defeating pattern. The manager may be critical and indifferent. The recipient(s) of this interaction are unlikely to give recognition under these circumstances. This configuration can work only in interpersonal relationships when the manager holds the power.

High Aggression and Low Deference. High aggression and low deference can yield an antisocial attitude. The rules of the road may be ignored. A disastrously compounding factor is the addition of high autonomy.

High Aggression and Low Nurturance. High need for aggression and low nurturance leads to an uncaring and overly critical disposition.

High Change and Low Endurance. High need for change and low endurance can be a problem if the organization has a stable and consistent environment (e.g., assembly-line work).

Changing Needs by Means of
Perceptual Shifting and Countering

Beneath the surface of these needs are beliefs, assumptions, and attitudes that drive each need toward behavior. Because the strength of our needs is reinforced by our assumptions, perceptions, and feelings, (APFs) any attempt to strengthen or diminish the influence of a need must begin with the technique of *perceptual shifting*. Perceptual shifting emphasizes the following research-based assumptions:

- We selectively screen sensory data, and the brain forms these data into patterns. There are an infinite number of possible patterns, but the brain uses only a few, personal schemata.
- Themes, once formed, have a tendency to persist, unless unlearned.
- Most patterns are learned from significant others in our lives.
- The more a pattern is repeated, the stronger it gets and the more difficult it will be to remove or replace it.
- Groupthink can be a powerful reinforcer of selective perceptions.
- Themes are generally formed not on a logical basis but through emotional-experiential learning.
- Some perceptions, once formed, may be immutable. Other perceptions can be modified by changing the basis for their formation, lowering their valence and intensity.
- People in power may have the most difficulty in addressing their assumptions and perceptions.

Counters are new assumptions and beliefs that go against previously held ones; they replace damaging thoughts or beliefs that cause problems. Before you can develop counters, you have to identify the assumptions and beliefs that support the needs. There are many ways to develop counters to change underlying assumptions and beliefs, for example, by using coping statements, humorous counters, rational beliefs, label shifting, and utilitarian counters.

To show how these work, I am going to use General George Patton as an example to demonstrate the perceptual shifting and countering model. The goal will be to see if we could have suggested to Patton how he could or should have modified his style. Patton is a controversial figure in history, and his beliefs and behavior were riddled with contradictions. He wanted to be a celebrated hero-warrior, but he thought that he could go it alone, without support from his merely mortal subordinates, peers, and bosses—an egregious assumption. He was dismissed from command two times because of his overzealousness in pursuing his self-defined mission. His problem was that he, like many other people, suffered from a set of self-defeating beliefs that interfered with his effectiveness. If he only wanted to win battles, then one could say, "C'est la guerre." But he wanted more: to be recognized and immortalized. Given these goals, he was not able to manage his career by the rules of the game. He left this earth an embittered man, the glory that he sought tarnished by his downfalls.

The interaction between Patton's needs and his psychological type were major factors in his wild up-and-down career. In my previous book, I made the case that his psychological type was ENTJ. Other management style factors such as his use of power and his conflict style are important. But to demonstrate the model for needs analysis I will focus on Patton's needs to illustrate the perceptual shifting and countering model. Since this analysis serves as a model for your use and reference, I have discussed Patton's needs analysis in the present tense.

A Needs Analysis form can be used to identify pitfalls in fusion and crossover needs. Appendix C contains this form, and you can use it for your own needs assessment. To use it, first complete the Assessment of Needs located in Appendix B. Then follow the instructions for the ten steps of the Needs Analysis. The following example is based on Patton's needs and psychological type.

The Needs Analysis for General George S. Patton

Step 1. Determine your needs levels (high or low).

Management Triad	Level	Task Factors	Level
Achievement	High	Change	High
Dominance	High	Order	High
Affiliation	Low	Endurance	High
Bosses/Peers/Subordinates Relations		Intensity	High
Deference	Low	*Interpersonal Modifiers*	
Autonomy	High	Introspection	Low
Nurturance	Low	Exhibition	High
Succorance	Low	Aggression	High
Abasement	Low		

Step 2. Identify pitfalls in fusion and crossover needs.
Do you perceive any fusion problems (where both needs are high)? Look at
your needs and use the following checklist.

Fusion Needs			*Are Both Needs High?*
Achievement	with	Dominance	Yes
	with	Affiliation	No
	with	Autonomy	Yes
	with	Succorance	No
	with	Abasement	No
	with	Aggression	Yes
Dominance	with	Affiliation	No
	with	Autonomy	Yes
	with	Succorance	No
	with	Abasement	No
	with	Exhibition	Yes
	with	Aggression	Yes
Affiliation	with	Deference	No
	with	Aggression	No
	with	Succorance	No
Autonomy	with	Succorance	No
	with	Aggression	Yes
	with	Exhibition	Yes
Deference	with	Exhibition	No
Nurturance	with	Aggression	No
	with	Abasement	No
Exhibition	with	Aggression	Yes
Succorance	with	Abasement	No
	with	Aggression	No
Abasement	with	Aggression	No

Step 3. Identify any crossover problems.

Do you detect any crossover problems? Look at your needs, and use the following checklist.

The Needs	*Level* *(High or Low)*	*Potential Problem?* *(Yes or No)*
Succorance	Low	No
Nurturance	Low	No
Autonomy	High	
Deference	Low	Yes
Exhibition	High	
Nurturance	Low	Yes
Dominance	High	
Introspection	Low	Yes
Autonomy	High	
Affiliation	Low	Yes
Affiliation	High	
Introspection	Low	Yes
Aggression	High	
Affiliation	Low	Yes
Autonomy	High	
Nurturance	Low	Yes
Exhibition	High	
Deference	Low	Yes
Aggression	High	
Deference	Low	Yes
Aggression	High	
Nurturance	Low	Yes
Change	High	
Endurance	High	No

Step 4. List potential fusion and crossover problems.

Fusion Problems	*Crossover Problems*
1. Achievement with Dominance	1. Autonomy with Deference
2. Achievement with Autonomy	2. Exhibition with Nurturance
3. Autonomy with Aggression	3. Dominance with Introspection
4. Dominance with Aggression	4. Autonomy with Affiliation
5. Dominance with Autonomy	5. Affiliation with Introspection
6. Dominance with Exhibition	6. Aggression with Affiliation
7. Autonomy with Aggression	7. Autonomy with Nurturance
8. Autonomy with Exhibition	8. Exhibition with Deference
9. Exhibition with Aggression	9. Aggression with Nurturance
10. Aggression with Deference	

Step 5. Star the fusion and crossover problems that you perceive may need modification. Base your assessment on critical incidents from your past or present behavior in the organization. These incidents can involve subordinates, peers, or bosses.

Step 6. Identify any MBTI and Need combinations that are present, and consider their potential outcomes. A synopsis of the needs follows:

Achievement. There is a strong relationship between the need to achieve and the functions of sensing and intuition. The dominance of the sensing or the intuitive function determines which kind of data individuals feel comfortable using to meet their achievement needs. If a particular job is a mismatch with a person's perception function, he or she will be frustrated and feel his or her achievement needs thwarted.

Dominance. The need for dominance affects the type of data a manager wants to control. A dominant intuitive type may insist on taking a global, conceptual approach when more facts and details are needed. On the other hand, a dominant sensing type may amass too much data and miss the big picture. When combined with the thinking function, dominance can override the manager's concerns for others and cause him or her to make decisions based solely on logic and impersonal principles. High dominance needs, combined with the feeling function, may cause managers to impose their personal values on others. They may override logic or insist that others support their opinions.

Affiliation. Affiliation needs soften the critical edge of a thinking type. Low affiliation will harden the thinking function and amplify the critical, impersonal attitude.

Autonomy. Introverts tend to keep things to themselves and not involve others in critical decisions. Communications with others will be minimal.

Deference. Low deference combined with thinking will intensify the impersonal attitude. In conjunction with feeling, low deference will harden the value judgments of the feeling type.

Nurturance. High nurturance combined with feeling may induce too much empathy for others and lead to conflict avoidance so as to not hurt others.

Succorance. An introvert with high succorance needs may suffer this unfulfilled need in silence and brood over the lack of empathy of the other person.

Abasement. Feeling types with a high need for abasement will feel guilty about their failings in relationships, and they will ultimately come to resent their guilty feelings. Extroverted types with high abasement needs make it known to others how much they suffer over the cruelties of the organization. Introverts who have this need may preoccupy themselves with endless internal ruminations about guilt.

Introspection. Extroverts with a low need for introspection will be driven only by external forces. The internal assessment of their own and others' motives will be lacking. This could lead to misreading the situation.

Aggression. A need for aggression is amplified in an extrovert who publicly subjects another person to criticism. This person's need may show up in barbed wit or outbursts of temper. Among thinking and feeling types, alike, aggression adds a sharp, acerbic tone to judgments. In introverts, aggression seeks an outlet through fantasy, or it erupts as modulated criticism.

Change. Extroverts act on their need for change overtly and sometimes impulsively. Introverts will ponder the significance for change and be more cautious about meeting their need for change.

Order. When the need for order is combined with the sensing function, a nitpicking detail orientation can develop. A thinking type with a high need for order can develop an obsessive approach to managing.

Endurance and **Intensity.** There does not appear to be any discernible negative links between these two needs and the psychological types.

Need	*MBTI Combinations*	*Potential Outcomes*
Achievement	Intuition	This combination has both positive and negative outcomes. They combine to lead to brilliant strategies and victories. But Patton baffles his colleagues with his single-mindedness. His perception of the world, ruled by his acute intuition, is the only view he sees as valid.

Need	*MBTI Combinations*	*Potential Outcomes*
Dominance	Intuition	He tends to force his strategies and plans on others without their input. His sixth sense rules supreme. Details are sometimes overlooked.
Dominance	Thinking	This combination is his Achilles' heel. Since thinking is his dominant function, he assaults others with his opinions. There is no room for debate.
Affiliation (low)	Thinking	His low need for affiliation increases his impersonal style. He tells it like it is, without regard for impact.
Autonomy	Introspection (low)	His high autonomy and low introspection builds a barrier to receiving feedback from others. Without the necessary introspection, he forges ahead, at times in a blind fashion.
Deference	Thinking	His low deference intensifies his single-minded thinking. He can be abrupt and insulting.
Nurturance (low)	Feeling (inferior function)	People are looked upon as pieces in a chess game—instruments in his quest to fulfill his destiny.
Succorance (low)	Introversion	Not applicable.
Abasement (low)	Feeling (low)	He has very little sense of remorse over his actions. The combination of low feeling and low abasement can lead to callous acts.
Abasement	Extroversion	Not applicable.
Abasement	Introversion	Not applicable.
Introspection (low)	Extroversion	He is not careful about what he says.
Aggression	Extroversion	This combination leads to public outbursts and explosive behavior.
Aggression	Thinking	This combination leads him to be hypercritical of others and to force his logic onto them.
Aggression	Feeling (low)	Under stress, his inferior feeling can break through in overdetermined emotion. The slapping of the private in a tent, outrage at his men for not being heroic enough, and his

Need	*MBTI Combinations*	*Potential Outcomes*
		soliloquy at the funeral for his aide, Dick Jensen, are examples.
Aggression	Introspection (low)	He is unaware of the impact of some of his verbal interchanges.
Change	Extroversion	These attributes lead him to create and maintain a dynamic atmosphere. At times it is inspiring and productive. At other times, he can be impulsive.
Order	Sensing	Not applicable.
Order	Thinking	On the positive side, he can use his intuitive thinking in an organized, creative way. The downside is a tendency toward obsessive thinking.

Step 7. List all the fusions, crossovers, and MBTI interactions.

Fusion

1. Achievement w/Dominance
2. Achievement w/Autonomy
3. Autonomy w/Aggrresion
4. Dominance w/Aggrresion
5. Dominance w/Autonomy
6. Dominance w/Exhibition
7. Autonomy w/Aggression
8. Autonomy w/Exhibition
9. Exhibition w/Aggression
10. Aggression w/Deference
11. Aggression w/Nurtance

Crossovers

1. Autonomy w/Deference
2. Exhibition w/Nurturance
3. Exhibition w/Nurturance
4. Dominance w/Introspection
5. Autonomy w/Affiliation
6. Affiliation w/Introspection
7. Aggression w/Affiliation
8. Autonomy w/Nurturance
9. Exhibition w/Deference
10. Order w/Thinking

MBTI Interactions

1. Achievement w/Nurturance
2. Dominance w/Thinking
3. Affiliation. w/Thinking
4. Deference w/Thinking
5. Introspection w/Exhibition
6. Aggression w/Exhibition
7. Aggression w/Thinking
8. Change w/Exhibition

Step 8. Count how many times the need appeared as a fusion, as a crossover, and as a MBTI interaction.

Management Triad	Level		Task Factors	Level
Achievement	3		Change	1
Dominance	6		Endurance	0
Affiliation	4		Order	1
Bosses/Peers/Subordinates Relations			Intensity	0
Autonomy	8		*Interpersonal Modifiers*	
Deference	4			
Nurturance	4		Introspection	3
Succorance	0		Exhibition	6
Abasement	0		Aggression	9

Step 9. Rank-order the needs by occurrence.

Needs	Occurrence
1. Aggression	9
2. Autonomy	8
3. Dominance	6
4. Exhibition	6
5. Deference	4
6. Affiliation	4
7. Achievement	3

Step 10. Use cognitive restructuring to modify needs by countering techniques.

I am proceeding under the assumption that it is easier and less traumatic to change the needs than psychological type. In Patton's case, seven needs got him into trouble given his ENTJ type. This cluster and their interaction with the commandant style of the ENTJ intensifies his strong-willed personality type. He becomes almost a prototype. They are, in rank order:

1. Aggression
2. Autonomy
3. Dominance
4. Exhibition
5. Deference
6. Affiliation (low)
7. Achievement.

Were Patton doing this step, he would have come up with this list of needs to modify and the reasons for change.

The Need	Reason to Modify
Aggression	It interferes with cooperation and sets up win-lose dynamics.
Autonomy	Autonomy by itself is not good or bad, but in my case I set myself off as a god and demand absolute allegiance.

Dominance   This needs to be shaped into the positive power bases: refer-
             ent, reward, and information. At this time I overuse authority,
             coercive, and expert power.

Exhibition   My need for recognition is boundless. I lack essential mod-
             esty. I see myself as competing for center stage and trying to
             be number one.

Deference   I don't want to be like Bradley or my sycophant aide, Colonel
             Codman, but a little deference could help. Both Ike and Bedel
             Smith would agree.

Affiliation I am not a team player across organizational lines. I need to de-
             velop positive reciprocal relationships based on the *big picture.*

Achievement My achievement orientation is single-minded. I have my own
             destiny to fulfill. Sometimes this interferes with the overall ob-
             jectives of the Allied Command.

As we see, with a little introspection thrown in, General Patton is on the path
to modifying some destructive patterns. Let us follow him on the pathway to
the cognitive restructuring of his needs.

Need: Aggression

Assumptions/Beliefs	*Counters*
• Life is a battle among wills; it is win-lose	• Win-lose is appropriate on the playing fields and against destructive enemies. There are times, however, when cooperation and interdependence are necessary. I must be able to distinguish between two conditions. All glory is fleeting.
• Anger is one of the sinews of the soul; he that lacks it has a maimed mind.	• Aggression and anger can maim me as well.
• By being aggressive, I prove to myself and others that I am strong and willful.	• I can be strong and willful by my magnanimous acts as well.
• The impossible can be attained by only a struggle.	• The impossible is attained by teamwork and synergy.
• Aggressiveness got me where I am today.	• My ability as a competent soldier got me where I am. Aggression has gotten me in trouble many times.
• I must fight any challenge to my will	• There are times when others' opinions are worth listening to.
• A good fight is a hearty menu.	• Good camaraderie is a hearty menu.
• I don't want people to like me. I want them to fight!	• They like Bradley, and they fight for him as well.

Need: Autonomy

Assumptions/Beliefs	*Counters*
• I stand alone in a world that is out of step with me.	• My personal goals may be in conflict with the big picture.
• To belong to a crowd is a sign of weakness.	• There are people in the world who are worth knowing.
• I am a special person and need to be autonomous to maintain my character.	• I can still be independent without building a wall around myself.
• The superior individual has no need for boundaries.	• Some boundaries are necessary for order in the world. I am no exception.
• Who so would be a man must be a nonconformist.	• Some forms of nonconformity are antisocial acts.
• Imitation is suicide.	• My avoidance of imitation is an obsession.
• Adherence to convention produces mundaneness.	• Mediocrity has nothing to do with convention. It is a result of many other factors: sloth, lack of practice, and ability.

Need: Dominance

Assumptions/Beliefs	*Counters*
• I was put on this earth to lead men in a desperate battle against evil. I can achieve victory by my command.	• This can be an obsession that is self-defeating.
• I must be in control to achieve my ends.	• Raw dominance leads to counterattacks by others.
• By being in control, I will not lose control of my destiny.	• The use of negative power leads others to resent my unbridled control.
• There is a natural hierarchy of leaders and followers.	• In animals there may be a hierarchy, but people can be trained to be positive leaders without oppression.
• The spoils of battle belong to the strong.	• The meek shall inherit the earth. I am a Bible reader, so why did I not see this as a balancing force?
• My men would not admire me if I was not dominant.	• Admiration comes from many sources, not just raw power.
• I am like a coach who has to bring out the best in my men by reigning over them.	• When I treat someone like a child, he acts like a child, sometimes an angry child.
• I was always the commanding hero warrior in my previous lives.	• My belief in reincarnation is unshakable. I don't want to modify it.

Need: Exhibition

Assumptions/Beliefs	*Counters*
• In order to be a leader, I must stand out from the crowd. Caesar wore a red robe to distinguish himself from his troops.	• Unabashed exhibitionism shows signs of immodesty. I can take pride in having good taste without flaunting it.
• Symbols are what make a man. Therefore, my regalia must be splendid. It is the regal rooster who gets the chicken.	• My poetry and writing reflect on my glory.
• I am a prima donna. People respect me for this.	• Bradley made his mark by being humble, not a prima donna.
• I need the recognition of others to affirm myself.	• I can give myself recognition from my inner strength.

Need: Deference (low)

Assumptions/Beliefs	*Counters*
• I believe in my own judgments, not those of others	• I may need to defer to the opinions of others in order to find wise solutions.
• A good piece of criticism is necessary to assert yourself.	• Discipline without punishment is an alternative.
• Deference is not a general's prerogative	• Deference has no rank. To the right degree and at the appropriate time, it is seen as respect.
• Sycophants are deferential.	• Wow! I have a double standard here.
• I will be seen as weak if I defer to others.	• Bradley is deferential and still seen as strong and willful.

Need: Affiliation (low)

Assumptions/Beliefs	*Counters*
• I don't need friends. I need loyal followers	• I work in an interdependent environment where teamwork is necessary among my peers and bosses. I need to build networks outside my own unit.
• I choose a small number of confidants whom I trust.	• This can lead to insularity and narrow-mindedness.
• Making friends takes the competition out of the game.	• When they feel they are competitors, they are less likely to help me.

Assumptions/Beliefs	*Counters*
• Familiarity breeds contempt.	• Familiarity, in proportion, can build referent power.
• My affiliation is with the gods, not with men.	• You give praise to the gods but get help and sustenance from friends.

Need: Achievement

Assumptions/Beliefs	*Counters*
• I must fulfill my destiny. God will not allow it not to happen. His will be done.	• I can still fulfill this need by coordinating my efforts with others.
• I must prove that I am a better field general than Montgomery.	• This is childish and detracts from my overall achievements which can stand alone.
• My personal goals supersede all others	• This has gotten me in trouble in the past. I must guard against extreme hubris.
• I know best how to win this war.	• In order to achieve victory I need the help and support of others.
• I love this more than my life.	• I may cherish this but I must not endanger or destroy others.

The objective of the countering exercise is to tame, not obliterate, a need. Patton is not going to be less dominant; however, he is going to develop positive power bases that achieve his goals without a negative backlash.

The key to using counters to change underlying assumptions and beliefs linked to needs is repetition. If you have formed a set of needs based on nature and experience over your lifetime, a one-shot try at countering does not work. Just consider all the constant internal and external conditioning that went into what you are today. Therefore, some structured practice each day is mandatory. In addition, it is important that you produce your own counters rather than use off-the-shelf counters. Relaxation and meditation are two effective adjuncts to counters in that they enable you to become more receptive to your counterarguments to the assumptions and beliefs underlying a need.

If we could roll back the hands of time and have Patton try this technique, we can speculate what would have occurred. Was he following a preordained fate, or was he misguided in his personal agenda? He did say, after suffering a reprimand and a dismissal for slapping the soldier, "I wish I kissed the son of a bitch."

5

Developing Positive Power

B ob's boss told him he was being promoted to chief designer on the annual report and product brochure group for the Hermes Corporation. As format designer, he had produced layouts for the reports and brochures. Bob was an exceptionally creative artist and had put together innovative combinations of text, graphics, photographs, and typefaces that had garnered him a series of awards. Hermes' clients were impressed with him, so much so that he was always in demand. The new job was a natural step up; he would coordinate the work of other designers in Hermes, plus the work of freelance photographers and graphic designers. In addition, he would work through design concepts with the clients and offer suggestions to bring their projects to conclusion. Mary, his boss, thought Bob was ready for the new responsibilities.

Bob's new group consisted of a format designer, a photographer, and a typesetter. Bob had worked with these peers in the past, but the contacts had been casual and had little effect on his job. In dealing with clients, Bob had served mainly as a resource for Hermes' presentations. Now he would be the chief manager of these activities.

Sligo Manufacturing, a bathroom fixture manufacturer, was a new client. Joe Trebo, the founder and CEO, had worked his way up through the Kohler Corporation, rising from expediter to chief of manufacturing, before starting Sligo. He prided himself on knowing his business from the ground up.

Five years earlier he had started Sligo with his savings and money borrowed from relatives and friends. Joe felt there was a niche for a bathroom fixture company that used European designs and technology. He had built his business around avant-garde architects and builders, and he provided his clients with high-quality products.

Joe came to Hermes for his product brochure because he was impressed with its artistic touch and attention to client needs. He had met Mikael Korda, the founder of Hermes, at a cocktail party and was impressed with him. Mikael turned the project over to Mary, who in turn delegated the job to Bob.

Mikael introduced Mary and Bob to Joe Trebo at the first project meeting for Sligo's brochure. He extolled the administrative virtues of Mary, who closely monitored time and expenses, and the creative ability of Bob, as well as his computer design expertise. Mikael oversaw all projects, plus he was always on call as a consultant. Joe admitted that he usually got involved with all Sligo projects, and this one would be no exception. The meeting ended after setting a date for a preliminary presentation on the direction of the Sligo brochure.

The next meeting, at Sligo, was attended by Bob, his project group, and Joe Trebo. Joe kicked off the meeting: "Bob, let me tell you something about myself. I worked my way from the bottom up. I attended engineering school at night, and I've had courses on the history of European art. I am especially fond of the Renaissance painters and sculptors. My philosophy is that work is art, and art is work, get me? Now let's talk about Sligo's product brochure. I'm tired of receiving these drab black-and-white desktop publishing reports that have no soul. I want our brochure to reflect our product's essence: artful bathrooms."

"I have no problem with that philosophy," Bob responded. "I try to represent the client's spirit. Last project I worked on, we shot photos in the rain forest of Brazil for an environmentally responsible corporation. Our theme was that even profit-making companies can appreciate the need to preserve our natural resources. It was well received too."

"Good, good," Joe interrupted. "Now I want to use Italy as the backdrop for your photos. I want Rome, Florence, and Venice as sites. I can see the Sligo fixtures as part of a montage of the statues in Rome, the canals and portos of Venice. Two art forms joined together. What do you think, Bob?"

"Yes, I can see connecting your products with tasteful objects.

On the other hand, I always believe that you need a human element in product photos. After all, your customers are people. I think that we can combine your idea with a living Venus de Milo using your pedestal sink or a living David standing before your marble bath." (Bob forgot that Venus had lost her hands some time in antiquity and that David is nude.)

"Well, I don't like to mix metaphors, classical with Renaissance," objected Joe. "You get confused on the message. Let's stick to one period. As far as the human factor goes, maybe I can bend a bit. Why don't you and your staff take back what I have said and come up with some ideas that I can respond to. Okay?"

The meeting ended far short of the allotted time, much to Bob's dismay.

The Hermes team rescheduled an early flight back home, and on the plane Bob berated Joe: "Every second-generation Italian wants to let you know that he loves art, opera, and pasta. As if we are the unbathed!"

Shelley, the photographer, tried to act as appeaser. "Gee, Bob, I thought his idea of using Italy was quite good. You know how we are in the age of the rebirth of all things Italian?"

"Listen Shelley, I don't need a lecture from a photographer about culture. I can hold my own with anyone. You just point and shoot." Shelley looked away from Bob and dropped her eyes. Bob continued, "My god, before long he will be telling us what type to use. Max, you can't let them dictate our prerogatives. You know what I mean."

"Well, Bob, he *is* the client!" Max reminded him.

But Bob cut Max off: "Look, I got the promotion for what I know, and Mikael pays me for being the creative genius. Otherwise, you would be in my place. And you know who gives you your raise!"

"Certainly, Bob. Anything you say."

The team spent the rest of the plane ride in silence.

Late that night Bob received a call from Mikael. "What the hell are you trying to do, Bob? Ruin the account? Joe just got off the phone after telling me you criticized his taste in art and that you thought he was living in the dead past! And why didn't you listen to his suggestions? I want you, Max, and Shelley in my office tomorrow morning at eight o'clock sharp!"

Bob got off the phone in a state of shock, wondering, "What is wrong with Mikael? I'm only trying to do my job. He never criticized me for my creativity in the past. What is going on? Many times I've heard him say to Mary that a client was being unreasonable or pigheaded. Why can't I be allowed the same latitude? Shelley and Max didn't object. Well, I'll straighten this out tomorrow."

What went wrong? Was Mikael overreacting to Joe's call? Was Joe stifling Bob's creative impulses. Was Shelley a thin-skinned bleeding heart? Was Max overstepping his place? Will Hermes retain the Sligo account? Will Bob remain on the Sligo account? Did this have to happen?

The Concept of Power

Bob, Mikael, and Joe were all involved in a power moment, when personal forces clash over supremacy. Probably none of them was aware that each was striving to be dominant. Paradoxically, each person believed he was doing the right thing to do the best job. Yet something went wrong. In order to understand the situation, let's analyze the role of power in this context.

What Is Power?

Power is the capacity to influence the behavior of others through the control of your own behavior. For an individual, power exists on two levels: as a motive and as a behavior. The need to feel in control, to influence, to organize groups, to become, and to grow are examples of power on the motivational level. At this level, power is latent or potential. When these motives are translated into action, power is manifested in behavior.

Power is potential in all of us. The root of it is the need to dominate. In this form, it is crude and undeveloped. From this genetic basis, we learn how to use or misuse our need for dominance. If we accept the premise that the base form of power, dominance, is grounded in genetic factors and that all other bases are learned or conditioned behaviors, then the development of the power motive is a case of behavior modification. Thus we can apply most of the principles outlined in Chapter 2, on cognitive restructuring, to developing positive power bases.

The first step in developing positive power is to accept its existence. Many of us have negative assumptions about power that prevent us from being effective managers. In the 1970s a noted Harvard psychiatrist told me that discussion about power was uncivilized and inappropriate in the classroom, yet he manifested all the signs of an authoritarian personality: subtle, bullying, negative put-downs; excessive use of his position; and double-bind messages. He clearly had a repressed and ambivalent attitude about power, yet he used it in a destructive way.

In organizations, the potential power of individual managers is embedded in the networks of social interactions that are part of the work setting. In power interactions, the one who exercises power attempts to influence another person (the recipient). In some interactions, the attempts to influence will be reciprocal, and the recipient and the exerciser of power will exchange places.

In a one-sided relationship, there will be only one recipient and one wielder of power. From the perspective of the recipient, the behavior of the one who exercises power can be perceived as negative (P−) or positive (P+). The behavior is seen as negative when the recipient perceives it as exploitation, manipulation, or win–lose competition. The person on the receiving end is always in a losing position in these situations. Recipients see power positively when they benefit from the exchange. That benefit may be economic, symbolic, or personal. When the person on the receiving end perceives power as positive, the interaction takes on a win–win character. The recipient senses support, increased motivation, and ego enhancement.

The Behavioral Bases of Power

Theoretical and empirical studies of organizational behavior have defined eight behavioral bases of power that can be used to influence another person or group. Anyone can develop the skills to use most of these power bases in order to achieve maximum individual effectiveness in forwarding organizational goals. (Appendix D, the Influence Inventory, is a form that you can use to determine your own power bases.)

REWARD POWER

When managers give their subordinates positive strokes, some form of remuneration, awards, or any symbolic gesture that is interpreted as a compliment by the recipient, they are exercising reward power. The behaviors involved are verbal or nonverbal interactions with those on the receiving end.

By definition, reward power is P+, although its magnitude depends on the recipient's perception of the meaning of the behavior. A promotion or a sizable bonus, for example, has more positive power than a complimentary letter, and personally appearing at the employee's work site to deliver a compliment has more positive power than a compliment conveyed over the phone.

COERCIVE POWER

The manager demonstrates coercive power by injuring another person physically or psychologically. Coercive behaviors include verbal and nonverbal put-downs, slights, symbolic gestures of disdain, even actual physical attacks. Coercive power is the opposite of reward power; it is P–. Instead of praise, it directs psychological or physical force against another person. The subordinate who is subjected to coercive power will continually worry about his or her job security and safety. Coercion narrows the possibility of improved behaviors from subordinates and works against effective performance. Creating anxiety is not a good motivator to encourage effective performance.

AUTHORITY POWER

The legitimate right of a manager to control others is the exercise of authority power. This power base has both positive and negative aspects. The manager who issues imprudent orders without offering appropriate instructions or feedback can leave the recipient feeling put upon or degraded. Authority power is best considered as a potentiality rather than an actuality. Behaving as "the boss" too often may be seen as *over*powering rather than *em*powering. Its overuse leads to distancing and resentment. Recipients can short-circuit authority in subtle or undetected ways. The manager may be buying short-term compliance from his subordinates at the expense of their long-term commitment to him. But in times of crisis or need, the exercise of leadership based on authority will be perceived as P+.

REFERENT POWER

Referent power is in the eye of the beholder. Managers have referent power when someone identifies with them. The identification can be based on personal characteristics that are regarded as charismatic, but the perception of charisma is totally dependent on the recipient, who envies or feels a need to be identified with these somewhat mystical powers. One does not build charismatic power: it is there, or it is not there.

A more common form of referent power—one that anyone can acquire—is reciprocal identification, which sometimes means the same as friendship. In this case, the referent power is developed through associating with another individual, sharing personal information, or providing something of value to someone else. Managers can build on common interests, values, viewpoints, and preferences to a point that other people get to know them. This process, when used with reward and information power, leads to a reciprocal relationship. Either person feels free to call on the other in time of need; in effect, each has IOUs out that can be called in. In this context, referent power is similar to social reciprocity. We try to repay favors, invitations, and other positive gestures. Building referent power is necessary when dealing with peers and colleagues in an organization where the lines of authority are not clearly drawn, which will probably be the rule in organizations of the future.

EXPERT POWER

When managers have specialized knowledge valued by another person, they have the potential to employ expert power. Expert knowledge is a valuable commodity in an organization. People who possess expertise are constantly called on to help solve technical problems in their area of knowledge. When the need arises, this power can be exercised to help another person or a group. When expert power is solicited and the expert shares her knowledge, it is perceived as P+. The unsolicited use of power, however, can be seen as an unwanted intrusion and therefore is P–.

Expert power used by itself is a very limited power base. Its continual use can create barriers between a manager and others that may be difficult to remove. The way expert power is delivered is critical in forming the good or bad perceptions of the recipient. Expert advice given in a condescending or authoritative manner will be seen as a put-down and will be perceived as P–, as will withholding expertise in time of need.

INFORMATION POWER

The information power base depends on having access to information that is not public knowledge. Managers may have access to this information because of their position or because of their connections within the organization. For example, relationships created as the result of referent power can open useful informal channels through which a manager can keep informed about the inner workings of senior management.

But information power can exist at all levels of the organization. It is entirely possible, in some closed organizations, that executives at the top have less information about what is going on within the organization than people in the middle or at the bottom.

A staff assistant to a senior executive has information power. This can be passed on or withheld based on the motivation of the assistant. Such a gatekeeper not only has access to information, but also has the ability to control the flow of information to and from the senior executive. The more that information is shared, the higher is the synergy in the group.

AFFILIATIVE POWER

Affiliative power is borrowed from someone with whom you have a formal or informal connection, such as a boss or a friend in an upper management position. Affiliative power is effective and appropriate when a person is a legitimate surrogate and acts on the authority of someone else. However, when one acts without the expressed authority of the other person, the affiliative bond is misused. Affiliative power should not be confused with referent power or with the need for affiliation. Referent power does not borrow from higher authorities but is based on mutual reciprocity; the need for affiliation is the need to associate with people or groups for your own sake and has no connection with influence or power.

GROUP POWER

Group power is the problem-solving power of a group taken as a whole. When the group process is managed well, the result is often superior to the combined inputs of single individuals. The process must be managed effectively for group power to emerge. If the process is dominated by one authority figure, groupthink, entropy, and conformity will result. The development of positive group power will be explored below in the sections on developing specific power bases.

What Went Wrong in the Hermes Case?

Using this knowledge of power and the APF model to derive the assumptions, perceptions, and feelings of the three main actors—Joe, Bob, and Mikael—we can map out the resultant power moments in the scenario. We'll begin with Joe's APFs:

Assumptions
- His own role: *"I see myself as the creative leader. I am the boss of the show."*
- Mikael's role: *"I want his involvement."*
- Bob's role: *"He will be the artistic coordinator."*
- Power: *"I am an expert in my field and in the world of art. I have the authority and rank to command others."*

Perceptions
- *"Mikael is dumping the project onto Bob."*
- *"Bob doesn't respect my views on classical culture."*
- *"Bob is a know-it-all pseudoexpert."*
- *"My authority is being undermined."*

Feelings
- *"I am being betrayed by Mikael. He led me to believe he was going to have active involvement in the project."*
- *"I thoroughly dislike Bob's arrogance."*
- *"I am going to put my foot down; I'm paying for this!"*

Here are Bob's APF's:

Assumptions
- His own role: *"I am the creative leader."*
- Mikael's role: *"I have complete authority. Mikael delegated it to me."*
- Joe's role: *"He is the client and he will respect my expertise and authority in the design."*
- Power: *"Authority and rank turn me off. My expertise will carry the day."*

Perceptions
- "*Joe is a pompous ass. He thinks he is an expert on art. He is a pseudoexpert.*"
- "*Mikael has betrayed me. He gave me ultimate authority and is now backing down.*"
- "*My own staff has turned on me. Don't they know I am the boss?*"

Feelings
- "*I feel depressed and anxious. Why did Mikael overreact to Joe?*"
- "*I am right! My expertise exceeds Mikael's and Joe's.*"
- "*I am going to give it to my staff for being insubordinate.*"

Finally, we turn to Mikael's APFs:

Assumptions
- His own role: "*I am a senior consultant to the project. I will be called on as needed.*"
- Bob's role: "*He will coordinate the project and work along with Joe.*"
- Joe's role: "*As the client, he will tell us his needs and we will translate these into the appropriate format—with Joe's approval, of course.*"
- Power: "*Bob respects my expertise and authority and will do what is necessary to get the job done.*"

Perceptions
- "*Bob did not understand my directions. His role was to coordinate, not control, the project.*"
- "*Joe is angry. I must reassert my authority with Bob and bring him back into line.*"
- "*I may have put too much faith in Bob's ability to work with clients.*"

Feelings
- "*I am angry with Bob's lack of judgment.*"
- "*I am feeling uncomfortable with Joe. He seems to be very mercurial and vindictive. What am I going to do?*"

The lists of APFs point to a number of problems in the relationships of the actors in this scenario. As we can see, all three participants think that they have ultimate authority for the project: Joe because he is the CEO, Bob because he assumes Mikael gave it to him, Mikael because he is the president of Hermes. The first problem is a clash over authority power among all three major actors. They also clash over creative roles in the project.

Joe and Bob both believe that they are the creative force in the project. Joe perceives Bob as the artistic coordinator of his ideas. Bob sees Joe as a meddlesome distraction. Joe sees Bob as an extension of Mikael, whom he would prefer to deal with. Mikael sees himself as outside the day-to-day loop. He will act as an occasional consultant.

Bob sees his subordinates as pawns to be manipulated. He abruptly shuts them off and puts them down, minimizing their creative inputs. He is exhibiting an inappropriate use of authority and coercive power. And Mikael responds in the same inappropriate way. He reacts to Joe's criticism by displacing his anger and frustration onto Bob. He does not ask for Bob's perception of the situation but leaps to some shaky conclusions and ends by saying, "I will deal with it tomorrow."

Joe undermines Bob by going behind his back and calling Mikael, whom he assumes will act in his behalf and rein Bob in. Moreover, to a degree, Joe has misrepresented Bob's attitude to Mikael. Bob becomes confused and anxious after the telephone conversation with Mikael. Here we have a clash over roles, authority, and lines of communication.

At this point the three main actors are trapped in what I call an "iron triangle." Joe holds the upper hand because he controls the purse strings. Bob is caught between Joe's and Mikael's anger. Mikael has divided loyalties between the client and his star designer. Could this situation have been prevented? Of course!

Bob and Mikael are in charge of their own destinies, but they have let circumstances dictate to them. They did not analyze the situation correctly and then determine what needs to be done.

Mikael has not set the stage for Bob's entry into his new position by laying out a set of expectations. Bob thinks that it is business as usual—just be a creative free spirit. He is not aware of the pitfalls associated with dealing with idiosyncratic clients who have egos of their own. Moreover, Mikael has defined to himself what future roles he will play with new clients, but he has not conveyed this vision to Joe or to Bob. And neither Mikael nor Bob realizes that what worked in the past—the old power bases—may be inappropriate now.

The prescription for Bob is to:

- Recognize that he has no authority power with the client.
- Downplay authority and coercive power with his subordinates.
- Build referent power with Joe.
- Build a viable psychological contract (an explicit agreement between individuals that defines their relationship in terms of expectations) with Mikael.
- Build group power with his subordinates.
- Downplay his need to show his expert power—his creative bent.

The prescription for Mikael has three components:

- Build a viable psychological contract with Bob.
- Control his anxiety over the client's reaction, an anxiety that has caused him to use negative authority power with Bob.
- Build a working relationship with Joe by exchanging expectations about roles and performance.

At this point it may be helpful to outline some of the steps for building the various power bases. Then we can return to the Hermes case and rewrite the scenario.

Changing Your Power Bases

Developing effective power bases is a learned skill. You must understand the concept and then acquire the appropriate behaviors to carry it out. Each power base has a distinct set of behavioral components. These behavioral components will be outlined in the following sections.

Reward Power

Reward power is the ability to give other people something they value. The reward may be tangible, such as money, a gift, a promotion, or career development opportunities. More frequently the reward is intangible: conditional praise directed at a person's behavior or unconditional praise directed at the person. When the praise is appropriate and genuine, it binds relationships and encourages productivity. When it is indiscriminate and hollow, it loses effectiveness.

An effective communication style is the key to developing reward power. Some people find it hard to give positive strokes under any conditions. They tend to be stoical individuals who believe that the least amount of praise will spoil the child. I emphasize the word *child* because what they are projecting onto the other person is a child–parent relationship. In most cases, the self-fulfilling negative prophecy comes true: an angry child results. A person who holds this belief is defying all the research on the power of positive reinforcement. Behavior or performance improvement grows with intermittent positive reinforcement.

The ideal time to give reinforcement is at the completion of a defined task. If the task is a project that has a long completion time, say two years, reinforcement should be given at various junctures along the way. Effective managers negotiate psychological contracts with their subordinates and take the time to check on their progress. That's when the appropriate strokes should be given.

Coercive Power

Coercive power is the opposite of reward power. Instead of providing positive reinforcement, it directs unconditional criticism at another person and can be very harmful. Coercion can take the form of personal abuse or threats to another's security and safety. Studies on negative reinforcement show that it has the power to shut down behavior, even appropriate behavior necessary for productive performance. In some cases, it may engender passive–aggressive behavior, sniping, and psychological withdrawal. If the person subjected to coercive power has some protection from being fired, punishment can actually lead to the escalation of the undesired behavior and develop into a power struggle. Coercion narrows the possibility of improved performance. It is not a power base to develop.

On the other hand, confronting problems is part of a manager's job. Just as there are people who abhor positive strokes, there are others who shy away from giving constructive criticism. They may be afraid of conflict or worried about harming others' egos. However, there are times when conflict cannot be avoided. The psychological effect of avoiding a necessary confrontation leads to shame, guilt, anger, resentment, and retaliation. Some people store up anger and explode. The suitable way to handle the situation is to change one's mind-set from either coercion or avoidance to positive problem solving. The following steps are helpful for developing discipline skills:

1. Focus on the specific behavior (e.g., chronic lateness, absenteeism, missing deadlines). The conversation must take place in an adult-to-adult fashion. Many managers slip into the parent-to-child mode and create greater difficulties than first existed— either dependency or hostility. Adult-to-adult communications avoid power struggles and involve three stages:

   • Cultivating the ability to express initial positions: saying, active listening, symmetry (the balance of communication between speaker and listener), and a summary statement of "our" problem.

   • Exploring the underlying concerns associated with the problem by saying, listening, and using symmetry of interaction. Developing a "we" attitude of cooperation and summarizing the concerns of all sides.

   • Choosing solutions: making suggestions that are win–win, defining explicit options to be implemented, summarizing a plan of action, making sure there are no pieces of unfinished business, and getting final closure on the solution plan (these adult-to-adult communication patterns are more fully developed in Chapter 6 under Communication Process Considerations).

2. Outline the rationale for the desired behavior, grounding it in organizational policy or procedures. For example, defense contractors cannot introduce flextime in production operations because of government regulations, regardless of managers' desires. A clear rationale allows people to see the logic of your point of view, and the illogic of their own.

3. Negotiate contracts based on mutual expectations, and secure agreement for the change. Plan follow-ups on these negotiated points, and give positive reinforcement when they are met.

4. Confront any broken agreements as quickly as possible, again separating discipline from punishment. Renegotiate new agreements, and then follow up.

Authority Power

Authority power is the legitimate right of managers to control others' actions within their domain. Authority power is best used sparingly if at all: it is best left as a potentiality. Giving constant orders like a drill sergeant is detrimental to the growth of the competence of others. Noel M. Tichy, in *The Transformational Leader*, cites six characteristics of leaders versus transactional managers: they identify themselves as change agents, they are courageous individuals, they believe in people, they are value-driven, they are lifelong learners, and they have the ability to deal with complexity, ambiguity, and uncertainty. One might add to this list that they know how and when to delegate. The traditional authority-based manager ignores these principles. Tichy is defining the positive side of authority power—when it is silent and other actions govern.

Referent Power

Referent power is based on goodwill and mutual respect. It develops gradually as a manager spends the time getting to know the motivations, preferences, values, and interests of others. Relationships can be built on shared interests, motivations, and goals. Those that are not shared should be nevertheless respected.

Referent power can be built using these guidelines:

- Use reward power and positive reinforcement. Giving positive strokes, when deserved or needed, is the easiest way to build a relationship. Remember that the key to motivation is the need to be competent. When you affirm the competence of other people, they value you.
- Invite reciprocal responses to show that you respect and want to hear the perceptions, opinions, and information others have to offer.
- Share your expertise and share information, especially when the recipient will recognize that you will not benefit from the results of your good-intentioned interventions.
- Minimize status concerns. Other than in its charismatic aspect, referent power is based on reciprocal identification. People tend to relate to equals, not to superiors. You do not need to abandon your authority or your responsibilities, but you should leave the

trappings of office in their proper place, and bring them out for display sparingly and at the proper moment.

- Become an expert communicator. People value straightforward and noncontradictory messages. Develop both your verbal and your nonverbal channels of communication.
- Get to know the informal structure of the organization. The formal structure does not tell the whole story. In some instances you may be able to build relationships without regard for the formal authority structure. In other cases, you may have to go through channels. By learning to correctly read the corporate culture, you can avoid embarrassing incidents.
- Get to know how people react to stress and crisis. Trying to negotiate requests when another person is under stress may doom your attempts.

Expert Power

Expert power comes from superior knowledge that is appropriate for an organization's needs. When a need arises, this power can be used to help another person or group. When expert power is solicited and generously given, it will be seen in a positive light by those who benefit from it. However, unsolicited expert power can be viewed as an unwanted intrusion. A person regarded by all as a know-it-all expert will be perceived as a difficult person.

Expert power used by itself offers a very limited power base. When used in conjunction with referent power and reward power, however, it can help to constitute a very solid power base.

Accumulating expert power depends on the manager's motivation, interests, and ability to learn. This is a task of labor. The ability to use it correctly and in conjunction with other bases determines how effective you are. Follow these rules to employ expert power effectively:

- Use expert power objectively, *never* to put down another person.
- Use expert power sparingly, and only when needed.
- Avoid becoming the superexpert. You will be regarded as a bore.
- Do not get into expert-to-expert power plays.
- It is difficult or impossible to be an expert in everything. Pick the appropriate area(s) and delve deeply.

Information Power

Information power resides at all levels in the organization. For example, workers on a production line may know more about certain manufacturing processes than the industrial engineers who write the specifications. This is because they have on-line experience with the procedures. If the information about faulty and costly methods is not shared, is hidden and guarded, then the problem remains a chronic one. When upper levels of management encourage the sharing of information, the process can be fixed and the problem disappears. Sometimes people at the middle and lower levels are reluctant to bring up problems because they fear reprisals. Managers who overuse coercive power invariably shut down the information network.

Opening up the lines of communications—information flow—is the responsibility of everyone in organizations. When there is excessive competition, this flow slows down to a trickle. Building solid bases of information power is part of a mind-set. The more you give, the more you get. When information is withheld from those at the lower levels, rumors and gossip spread.

Information should flow upward as well as sideways and downward, and it should not be filtered, or distorted. It can be disseminated formally, in written bulletins, memos, newsletters, or speeches, or informally, in conversation, and it must always be accurate. A final caution is to avoid information overload. This can be as bad as no information.

Affiliative Power

Affiliative power is borrowed from an authority source with whom a person is associated. For example, executive secretaries and staff assistants reporting to high-level officers can manifest affiliative power by acting as surrogates for the authority figure. When they act according to the wishes of the person who has the authority, they are using power legitimately because the boss has delegated it to them. But if they are acting out of self-interest, the power is clearly negative.

Negative affiliative power also occurs when critical interfaces in the organization are used to obstruct or block performance. For instance, when the wielder of power interprets accounting or personnel policies rigidly and borrows authority from his or her interpretations of rules and regulations, those on the receiving end see this as negative power. Affiliative power can be used in a positive way when someone approaches the staff assistant or executive secretary with a legitimate request to be relayed to the boss, and the assistant paves the way. Goodwill is the result.

Group Power

In the day-to-day operations of most organizations, managers regularly and inevitably lead or participate in problem-solving groups. And just as regularly group participants leave the meetings feeling frustrated. Perhaps the meeting was controlled by the most vocal and power-oriented individuals, or dominated by high-status people, or it drifted into the groupthink mode (discussed in Chapter 6).

To be effective and synergistic, group problem solving needs to draw on positive group power. To achieve this goal, both facilitators and participants need behavioral guidelines:

- Ensure a climate of openness to opinions, perceptions, conflicts, and possibilities.
- Use positive reinforcement to reward contributions.
- Ban the use of negative criticism of individuals.
- Clarify the objectives of the meeting. Is the agenda intended to find opportunities? To solve problems? To evaluate or to implement?

Divide the group process into four phases: (1) the generation of opinions, perceptions, and alternatives; (2) the development of criteria for judging alternatives; (3) the trade-off phases, where the criteria are applied to the alternatives; and (4) the identification of action steps for implementation. These phases can take place in one session or over many meetings, depending on the complexity and the stage of problem solving.

The most contributions and reciprocal influence will be made when there is some structure to the group, achieved by assigning roles to individual group members. Important roles include:

- The *gatekeeper*, who tries to involve all participants in the problem-solving process, minimizes the use of premature evaluations, and brings hidden conflicts to the surface.

- The *clarifier*, who restates the opinions, perceptions, and attributions of others.
- The *critical evaluator*, who analyzes and evaluates potential decisions at the end of any phase of the group process. There can be as many critical evaluators as members in the group.

The different styles represented by group members can be a positive force for change. Identifying the range of differences in the group brings potential biases into the open. The gatekeeper can use an understanding of these differences to elicit maximum contributions and to prevent conflicts over style rather than substance.

Each meeting should set aside time at the end for the group to evaluate the process that took place at that meeting.

The New Scenario for Bob and Joe

We pick up the conversation between Bob and Joe after Joe has explained his philosophy of business. He continues, "Now I want to use Italy as the backdrop for your photos, Bob. I want Rome, Florence, and Venice as sites. I can see the Sligo fixtures posed in front of the statues in Rome, the canals and portos of Venice. Two art forms joined together. What do you think, Bob?"

"Sounds very interesting to me. Maybe you can expand a bit about your concept—say how it fits with your business philosophy."

"Sure. I'm glad you had a positive feeling about my initial idea. It was just a rough start. I could expand on it if you want."

"That's what I want. If you tell me your perspective, Joe, I can build on it with my ideas. That way we collaborate, and we all win."

"Okay, Bob, let me tell you about my travels in Italy and Greece. I had some profound experiences in studying the art forms in both countries. I would like to work some of those feelings into the photos of the products that will be in the brochure. What I want to convey is that in our own way we are artists too."

"Now I see what you're driving at. I had the same experience when I traveled to Asia. My whole perspective on life changed. I found a passive mode of expression that helped me in my work."

"Well, Bob, I see we are kindred souls."

"Joe, let me put together some of your ideas with some of mine, and I'll come back with a number of options for the first crack at the photos for the report. Could you send me some photos of your favorite shots in Italy and Greece?"

"Hey, that's a good idea! They won't be up to your caliber, but you'll get the idea. Right?"

"Joe, I have respect for everyone's artistic expression. I know they will be helpful."

"I will be looking forward to our next meeting, Bob. Good luck."

Bob is well on the way to building positive power with Joe. In this short scene, Bob has:

- Given affirmation to Joe's ideas (reward power).
- Encouraged Joe to give more input to the project (group power).
- Shared common experiences with Joe (referent power).
- Downplayed criticism and negative input (controlled his coercive power).
- Did not assume the role of expert unless asked (expert power when appropriate).

The project is solidly underway, and Bob has avoided the pitfalls in the first scenario. Both Joe and Bob have power, although of different sorts. In the first scenario, both Bob and Joe exercised negative power, and both lost—Bob with his boss and Joe in gaining expert knowledge.

6

Conflict Resolution

Conflict is part of life. Dealing with conflict requires searching for its sources but also understanding the process of conflict resolution, or the strategies adopted to handle it. Our manner of facing conflict is predominantly learned but is influenced by our biological roots. The fight-or-flight response is our instinctive means of handling conflict; our culture, family influences, religious backgrounds, professional training, and organizational experiences shape our subsequent conflict strategies.

The Fight-or-Flight Response

When we feel threatened, our reflexive reaction is an integrated physiological response that prepares us to fight or to flee. At this primitive level, conflict resolution is driven by nature. Whether we fight or flee depends on our assessment of the threatening situation. If we perceive an overwhelming threat, we are likely to retreat. If our cognitive judgment estimates a weak threat, we may advance to meet the enemy. The fight-or-flight response is controlled by a spectrum of hormonal and endocrinological processes tempered by our perception. It remains as our most rudimentary reaction to conflict. But as we grow up we are trained to exert more control over our basic physiological reactions, and from then on our learning experiences shape our conflict strategies.

The Learned Responses

The Role of Culture

Each culture has a set of assumptions, beliefs, and values about how conflict should be addressed. As a result, the culture one lives in has a profound influence on how one controls conflict. These cultural attitudes toward conflict resolution can be extremely complex. Different strategies may be considered culturally appropriate for distinct classes of individuals. In some hierarchical societies, for example, the upper classes may be expected to challenge when faced with a threat, while the lower classes are expected to submit or to retreat. People from northern Europe are likely to approach conflict by allowing one party to finish stating his case before the other party begins stating hers. In more expressive southern European cultures, interruptions are expected and tolerated.

In America, where competition reigns supreme, our culture consciously and unconsciously promotes a win–lose style of conflict resolution. Here too socioeconomic position has an imprint on our style of handling conflict. The upper classes embrace win–lose tactics when they compete in business, but try to avoid conflict in polite society.

Thus culture has a marked influence on our conflict resolution strategies, though its predominance is modified by other factors in the environment.

The Role of the Family

Families, with their wide variety of ethnic backgrounds, religious orientations, and degrees of education for their members, are even more diverse than cultures. In addition, each family structure can be classified as healthy or dysfunctional. A family unit that is unable to talk about its problems, that suppresses conflict, or that creates a climate of intimidation is dysfunctional; its members are stunted in their ability to negotiate positive solutions. Susan Heitler, a family psychotherapist, identifies "the critical factor in a well-functioning family is not the presence of stresses, change, or trauma per se but whether the system's conflict negotiation capabilities are adequate to the task. Can the family assimilate ever-changing data about each member's needs and adapt to each new set of circumstances? Healthy families continue to function as a cooperative team through even the most stressful circumstances."

Families can also produce inconsistent styles of negotiation and unacceptable outcomes, and too few of them actively teach their children effective ways to handle conflict. The family influence on conflict negotiation patterns can carry over to other situations in life, for example, to how we interact in organizations.

The Role of Religion

Christianity, with its emphasis on Jesus' teaching, promotes forgiveness and turning the other cheek. We Christians are urged by our ministers and priests to seek harmony in relationships, obey our father and mother, and join the community of God. In addition we are urged to strive for distributive justice. This religious orientation clashes with the national U.S. drive for competition. Christian Americans are caught in a double-bind situation. We pray one way and act another.

Judaism teaches the faithful to have a profound respect for authority. The male head of the household is responsible for resolving conflict based on the word of the Torah, which is God's word and must be obeyed. The Torah is unchanging, and God sees all. The righteous will be rewarded and the wicked punished. There is no room for compromise in these principles.

Islam, which means "surrender," demands total allegiance to God and belief in humanity's servile or slave status in relation to him. The Koran contains the revealed law whereby conflicts are adjudicated. One of the Five Pillars of Islam decrees "Believe in the Qudar [the timeless knowledge of God]. . . . Nothing in the universe takes place without God's preknowledge and determination." When conflict arises within a family, the eldest male takes on the role of interpreting the situation in light of the Koran and resolves the conflict. A person yields his or her own personal goals and obeys what is ordained.

Buddhism professes the striving for perfection. Among the perfections Buddhists seek are generosity that gives without expecting reward, respect for and love of others, acceptance of things the way they are, and the insight to discover their true natures. Buddhists stress harmony and cooperation with others and nature.

It is not hard to see how these assumptions about humanity can shape a personal style for handling conflict.

The Role of the Organizational Culture

The last influence is the organizational culture to which we belong. It is one of the last experiential ingredients that shapes our conflict style. Every organization has its own unique way of negotiating conflict that may not be consistent with what we have already learned. In spite of the fact that we may want to handle conflict in a functional manner, the organizational climate may have contradictory themes that prevent us from doing so. These contradictory strains sometimes present themselves as mixed messages that may be confusing when conflict arises. Four mixed messages are predominant:

- *Individualism versus the team.* In today's climate of total quality management, the public message is "Be a team player." The organization, however, may well give out rewards based on individual efforts. The manager hears the public message but will learn to seek rewards on an individual basis. The result is covert competition within teams.
- *Internal and external competition.* The organization may promote the idea that competition breeds success, so units that should be cooperating may waste time, energy, and resources by competing.
- *Authority versus collaboration.* The decision-making process may be entirely in the hands of the top managers, precluding the valuable inputs of subordinates. Under these circumstances, lower level managers adopt passive methods of handling conflicts and problems.
- *The no-mistakes policy versus productive problem solving.* Top management does not want to hear about problems and views them as heinous. Anyone who is the bearer of bad news will suffer. The resulting conflict management style is characterized by avoidance, and sometimes by outright deception.

Conflict versus Competition

Conflict is a state of being in which people have different concerns in achieving their goals. Competition is one strategy for resolving this clash of energies. But competition takes into account only the maximization of personal gain. The purely competitive strategy seeks to maximize the individual's gain relative to the gain of the other. As we will see, there are many other strategies for managing conflict. Since "competition" is sometimes mistakenly confused with "conflict," a deeper look at the two is now necessary.

One of the cornerstones of current conflict resolution theory is that competition is a learned response. Alfie Kohn, in his book *No Contest*, explores the human nature myth, which proposes that competition is part of the natural order for both animals and humans. Kohn, by carefully exploring the scientific literature in the biological and the psychosocial areas, concludes that we are taught to compete. The eminent evolutionary scientist Stephen Jay Gould supports this view; he finds "no a priori preference in the general statement of natural selection for either competitive or cooperative behavior." Indeed, Gould argues that natural selection does not *require* competition; it *discourages* it. But in the United States and most other industrialized countries, the economic system is not based on nature, and is based on competition, a paradox with serious consequences for people who work within organizations that demand interdependent cooperation but also send a hidden message that individual achievement is the key to the most sought-after rewards.

Many managers assume that competition leads to success. They have other related assumptions as well: for example, that competition is inevitable, that competition is exciting, and that it builds character. Let's suppose that the managers of the production control and the quality control units in a plant buy into these beliefs and compete to outdo each other in the manufacturing sector. Are not these the two units that must *cooperate* to attain the objectives of lowest cost, highest quality, and on schedule? If top managers set up competition between the two groups, their action is self-defeating.

My research with numerous corporations indicates that when top management combines win–lose dynamics with coercive power, the workers develop a lose–leave or yield–lose attitude. When problems or conflicts arise, they tend to deny or hide them. The net result is that the problem is pushed to a breaking point, and everyone loses.

Psychologists have demonstrated that the induction of fear results in an avoidance response. Employees who are repeatedly chastised for bringing bad news or problems to their superiors tend to ignore or sidestep these unpleasant incidents. By constantly reinforcing employee fear, corporations build a climate of conflict avoidance. Moreover, just as they inadvertently reinforce conflict avoidance, they encourage intergroup competition. The value of competition is reinforced by the symbols and myths of our society that foster learned competition. Sports metaphors constantly bombard our senses with win–lose situations and teach us that winners are rewarded with fame, huge salaries, and other benefits, while losers suffer shame.

Executives must recognize this paradox in order to deal rationally with the duality. It is one thing to act from a desire to do something better than somebody else. It is quite another thing to act with a view to getting something done as well as possible. If groups within organizations perceive it is in their best interest to get the job done rather than to foster individual interests, a truly cooperative effort becomes possible. But first we must recognize the perniciousness of competition in the workplace. When we work from the position of mutually exclusive goal attainment, the task suffers.

Conflict Management Styles

Conflict management styles are behaviors used to resolve disputes based on the assumptions and beliefs of the participants. They have been shaped by our educational, organizational, training, cultural, and religious experiences. (To assess your conflict style, see Appendix E.)

The Win–Lose Style

The win–lose style is the ultimate competitive stance. It emphasizes maximum concern for personal goals and minimal concern for the relationship. Underlying it are these beliefs:

- A conflict is a contest of wills.
- The participants are adversaries.
- Opponents cannot be trusted.
- An entrenched position is effective.
- Threats and posturing are effective.
- The goal is victory.

Adherents of the win–lose style assume that winning is the only thing. They see differences of opinion and conflict as natural and inevitable, and they believe that some people have the skills and the will to win while others do not.

The Lose–Yield Style

Here personal goals are sacrificed for the value of the relationship. Behind this "Let's be friends" position are these assumptions and beliefs:

- Conflict must be avoided.
- The participants must remain friends and should be trusted.
- Concessions and offers will improve the relationship.
- Pressure demands submission.
- The goal is agreement.

The lose–yield participant abhors conflict, perceiving it as evil and a destroyer of good will. This kind of person assumes that sugar catches more bees than vinegar. Appeasement is the goal. Neville Chamberlain's diplomacy with Germany before World War II epitomizes this style. Since it is an avoidant style, honest attempts to marshal positive energy to resolve the conflict are abandoned. The focus is shifted from the substance of the problem to being nice at all costs. A lose–yield type who interacts with a win–lose type is putting his neck on the chopping block.

The Lose–Leave Style

Total avoidance of conflict is the hallmark of this style, which is the least effective one. Managers who employ this style distance themselves from conflict by blanking out and shutting off all channels of communications, shifting to another topic, or leaving the room (physical distancing). Their style is probably the most frustrating style of all. The lose–leave style may be used to avoid internal conflicts or to avoid hurting others, or the participants may be forced into that position by someone else's overpowering style. All of these aspects need attending to.

The reigning assumptions and beliefs of the lose–leave style are:

- Conflict is irrational.
- Conflict can be ignored.
- Avoidance behavior is acceptable.
- Observers of a conflict need not be participants in it.
- The goal is compliance without commitment.

The Compromise Style

Compromisers are willing to concede something in order to gain something or to move the bargaining process forward. They may start with a firm position on an issue, but they are willing to compromise if necessary and assume that other person(s) will do the same. Compromisers hold to the principle that you have to give up something to get something. Most labor–management disputes are handled in this way, and most adversarial political systems are based on compromise. Often the outcomes of this process fail to address the underlying problems, leaving them to be fixed another time with another compromise.

The compromising style is based on these assumptions and beliefs:

- Conflict will be resolved by hard bargaining.
- The participants must follow the stated and unstated rules.
- The participants must show goodwill by exchanging concessions.
- The participants can exaggerate their demands, knowing that they must eventually grant concessions.
- The participants must be tough.
- Rhetorical appeals to justice and the common good are effective and expected.
- The goal is compromise.

These assumptions are flawed, and may well lead to an ultimate decision that is half-baked or totally wrong. Let's say that three people go to a Chinese restaurant with the premise of sharing six dishes but that each of the three has different opinions about what to pick from the menu. They remain adamant up to the point at which a compromise is struck that allows each person to select two dishes. The result could be a gastronomic catastrophe. The compromise may affect the harmony among the dishes.

The Win–Win Style

This is the collaborative approach, or principled bargaining. The participants see themselves as problem solvers trying to arrive at a wise decision. They emphasize the interests of all the participants.

The win–win style assumes that:

- Conflict is natural but can be solved.
- The participants are problem solvers.
- All the participants should be involved.
- The interests of all the participants deserve respect.
- Firm or bottom-line positions should be avoided.
- Objective criteria and reason are essential to problem solving.
- The goal is a wise outcome, effectively reached.

The collaborative approach examines the intense interests that participants bring to a problem, knowing that understanding those interests will shed light on the problem and that satisfying them must be part of the solution. It pools the intellectual resources of all the participants to generate a variety of mutually beneficial options. Options that are not apparent at the beginning surface through active problem solving. The focus is not on coercion or persuasion but on problem solving and principles. A wise decision is the happy outcome, and all the parties feel that they have benefited from the process and the result. There is no sacrifice of either goals or relationships.

The wisdom to carry out this approach does not come naturally. The win–win style must be learned and then reinforced through practice.

The Contextual Style

The five previous parts of this discussion presuppose that the persons in a conflict have a well-established, consistent style. But there are individuals who shift from one style to another based on the situation; some are capable of using all five techniques depending upon the circumstances. For example, a manager who needs to be deferential may adopt a lose–yield position with the boss. The same person could shift to a win–lose style when encountering subordinates. When in conflict with peers, she may adopt the compromise position. If she fears negative consequences in a high-stakes situation, she may adopt the lose–leave style. In most organizations, this chameleon-like, contextual style is the most common form of conflict resolution.

A manager who uses the contextual style is seen as inconsistent, confusing, and weak. There are no benefits to the use of the contextual style.

The Paradoxical Style

In this style, two opposite patterns are used simultaneously or sequentially. For example, a person using a win–win style shifts to a win–lose pattern, either gradually or abruptly. No matter how the change takes place, it jolts the process and confuses the participants. People who constantly use the paradoxical style usually have competing assumptions about conflict that are internally inconsistent.

Techniques for Resolving Disputes

When the outcomes of conflict have serious consequences, there is a moral imperative to deal with it in the best way possible. After World War II social psychologists began to search for effective ways to resolve disputes and conflict. The psychologist Leon Festinger put forth a pragmatic plan, and since then interest has increased in refining the techniques he discussed.

Among all of the theories put forth, five of them, including Festinger's, presented in an article in *American Psychologist*, stand out. Roger Fisher and William Ury, lawyers and negotiators who run Harvard University's Project for Negotiation, set forth a win–win strategy in their book *Getting to Yes*. Susan Heitler, a psychologist, has adapted their model to psychotherapy and family counseling in her book, *From Conflict to Resolution*. She reminds us that these techniques go back to the late 1950s when social scientists started exploring conflict resolution and competition. Dudley Weeks develops a formula in *The Eight Essential Steps to Conflict Resolution*. Finally, Thomas Crum's *The Magic of Conflict* applies the principles of aikido, a martial-art form, to conflict resolution by using it as a metaphor for shifting our way of thinking and acting in conflict situations. Although each of these authors has a somewhat different focus, they all share a number of assumptions about conflict resolution, including:

- Conflict is natural and normal; it cannot be ignored.
- Conflict is not a contest.
- There are functional and dysfunctional strategies for handling conflict.
- Clarification of perceptions, positions, and interests is necessary.
- The process must be managed by a third party or a facilitator.
- Effective communication is one of the cornerstones of conflict resolution.
- Options must be set out before judging. Premature decisions must be avoided.
- Emotions must be acknowledged and managed.
- Expectations for the future need to be expressed.

Communication Process Considerations

Fisher and Ury have synthesized the techniques for setting the stage for effective conflict resolution, addressed the perceptual shifts that are needed to go from one approach to another, and outlined the assumptions and beliefs that distinguish their guidelines. Their theory is in line with cognitive restructuring.

Effective communication patterns will lead to effective negotiations. When the process is based on talking, not on verbal, nonverbal, or physical violence, and it is predominantly cooperative, not avoidant, competitive, antagonistic, or coercive, the outcome will be a settlement that all participants find acceptable because it addresses their concerns.

Heitler lists the following communication processes that need attending to:

- *Saying:* The verbalization needs to be explicit, nonthreatening, and focused on data.
- *Listening:* The listener has to be focused on what the other person is saying. That means holding back on judgment, rebuttal, or distractions.
- *Symmetry:* Equal strokes for equal folks. One party should not do all the talking while the other does all the listening.

- *Summarizing:* Each participant should paraphrase what he or she thinks the other person has conveyed.

There are other behavioral components of the communication process. For example, both parties must show willingness to listen, communicate interest in and facilitate the other person's relating of concerns, and communicate respect for the individual's worth, integrity, and abilities. In order to assist *willingness to listen,* employ the following behaviors:

- Keep a relaxed posture.
- Maintain consistent eye contact.
- Assume a suitable seating distance (not too far or too close).
- Move your shoulders toward the other person.
- Make relaxed gestures toward the other person.
- Face square toward the other person.

To foster and facilitate *interest so the other person can voice his or her concern,* use the following devices:

- Use positive nods of the head.
- Keep a facial expression that shows interest.
- Maintain a modulated voice tone consonant with the content.
- Never interrupt.
- Don't ask single or open questions.
- Paraphrase or restate what you hear as you hear it.
- Repeat key words that emphasize your concerns.

In order to communicate respect for the individual's worth, integrity, and abilities, employ the following devices:

- Avoid evaluation.
- Use the other person's name.
- Make positive statements about the other person.
- Review the options with the other person.

These communication guidelines, as affirmed in all the literature on this subject, should ensure a positive process.

Another view of the complicated communication process, known as the "Satir Modes," is presented by Virginia Satir. Through her clinical work, she has isolated five modes of language behavior that people use under stress and notes that we tend to adopt one of these modes as a habitual pattern.

Blamers use unconditional negatives directed at the other person to control the communication process. Examples of unconditional negatives include:

- "Why are the parts always late?"
- "How could you do that?"
- "Everything you say was twisted and turned. What do you take me for, an idiot?"
- "Well, smarty, as usual, you really fouled that job up. Why can't you be more careful?"

Placators, using an apologetic tone, seek approval from others and want to avoid unpleasantness. Their nonverbal cues—lowering the head; wide, begging eyes; possible fidgeting—plead for help. They will make remarks such as:

- "Oh, you are so right. I will try to get the parts on time."
- "Well, I really didn't mean what I said. You know me. Let's forget about it."
- "I'm an idiot. I'm so sorry. I didn't mean to upset you. Anything you want is all right with me."
- "I guess I'm careless. This job is overwhelming me. Please forgive me."

Advocates of *computer language* avoid reference to themselves (the "I" message) at all costs and show a minimum degree of emotion and a high degree of impersonalization. The person sounds like Mr. Spock on "Star Trek." These people's nonverbal cues are as blunted as their verbal ones. They make remarks such as these:

- "It has been shown that there are many factors involved in the late delivery of the parts. There appears to be a pattern that needs attention."
- "On certain occasions, research has shown that automatic acts happen."
- "There is no reason to panic. The position as stated is neutral."
- "The job has been carefully planned. It is on schedule."

Distractors shift from blaming to placating to computing, thoroughly confusing the listener. A distractor might say something like this: "Well, you could have come to me before everything was fouled up. After all, I am trying. You know I am loyal. Then again, you share responsibility too! But heck, let's be friends. Reasonable people know that mistakes happen. But what can I do?"

Clearly, participants in negotiation should avoid the blaming, placating, using computer language, and distracting modes, and should quickly work to reshape them if they rear their ugly heads. The best mode, which conveys direct, honest communications, is the *leveler* mode. Levelers use statements such as these:

- "Tom, the reason that the parts were not delivered was that I had higher priorities than your job. I hope you understand my position."
- "I did that because I thought it was right."
- "Sometimes I do, and sometimes I don't. I am that way."
- "I would like to clarify the issue with you. Let's set up a time."

Note the directness and the affirmation in the leveler's statements. The levelers say what they think, feel, or observe. Unlike blamers, they do not accuse. They are different from placators in that they are not giving mixed messages. Unlike distractors, they are congruent in their verbal and nonverbal messages. And in contrast to users of computer language, they are direct and personal.

Groupthink and Conflict Resolution

Another pitfall for conflict resolution is groupthink, a mode of thinking in which people engage when concurrence seeking becomes so dominant that it tends to override realistic appraisal of alternative courses of action. The concept arose from observations by psychologist Irving Janis when researching high-level governmental decision making in the 1970s. Janis noted that groupthink was more prevalent in cohesive groups where the drive to reach agreement hinders the group's capacity to evaluate the impact of their decision. Group pressure is exerted to transform minority opinions to conformity with the norms of the majority of the group. The majority norms can be shaped by the leader, who influences a critical mass in the group. Pressure toward achieving conformity is verbally and nonverbally enforced. The enhancement of the "we feeling" becomes the dominant force. Janis states: "The more amiability and esprit de corps there is among the members of a policy-making group, the greater the danger that independent critical thinking will be replaced by groupthink, which is likely to result in irrational and dehumanizing actions directed against out-groups." Janis labels the members of groupthink as victims. They are unaware that their decisions eventually will come back to haunt them.

A Case Example

The following case illustrates violation of the three principles of conflict resolution: (1) the appropriate use of conflict resolution strategies, (2) the need to address the sources of conflict in the group, and (3) the need to avoid groupthink.

Sam is the president of a contract engineering firm, H & M Company, that mainly does defense work. It has yearly sales of $200 million but little cash or other assets. The worth of the company is in the brains and marketing ability of the staff and the key engineers who procure government contracts.

Sam is a very pleasant and amiable boss. His main weakness is that he does not like conflict. Sam was an honors graduate at Cal Tech, where he majored in mechanical engineering. Sam took over H & M when the previous president retired, almost by default; he was the last remaining founder of the company and owned 20 percent of the stock. The board of directors felt obliged to let him ascend to the throne.

Sam operates the company as a family unit, demanding loyalty and conformity to his visions, projects, goals, and whims. In the past five years he has become more of a dilettante engineer, working on scattered esoteric projects that have brought little revenue into the company. He is tolerated by everyone since they are given autonomy over their own projects as long as they pay homage to Sam. Sam is happy as long as his subordinates act like loyal and trusting family members and bring in new contracts. He rarely knows what is going on with any particular contract, and he does not care. The engineers are highly motivated and talented, and the clients are satisfied with their work.

Sam has become fascinated by the potential for robotics in replacing human effort in dangerous situations. He learned that the government is interested in building a robot that can dismantle a bomb and plans to use some H & M development money to fund a project in this area. He has called a staff meeting to propose an independent effort whereby they will build a prototype, patent it, and sell it to governments around the world. On the surface, it is a brilliant idea.

His senior staff, who act as individual project directors on various contracts, view Sam as a frustrated genius who should be indulged in his whims to allow them to go on with their autonomous projects. Individually they think the robotics venture is a waste of time and money, but one that could be tolerated if kept within bounds.

The meeting goes like this:

SAM: "I guess you all got my proposal to start work on "Bomb Smart." I think it will be a project that will bring in both revenue and good publicity, two things we could use to boost our image in the R&D field. Right?"

GEORGE [the senior design engineer]: "I understand you want to sell to foreign buyers. Are there legal restrictions on this?"

HARRY [the legal consultant]: "George, you are always the pessimist. I can take of care of that. Besides, we've performed very well for the Department of Defense and other agencies. We have an unblemished reputation in Washington and they like the work we do."

MIKE [the financial adviser]: "I have some concern over the amount of investment versus the long-term profit. I. . . ."

JOE [the senior manufacturing engineer]: "I think Sam has worked it out to my satisfaction, and we will all benefit. The startup costs are peanuts."

LAURA [the senior engineering consultant]: "I understand that the Japanese are already into this area. Can we compete with them?"

TOM [the senior engineer]: "Hey, we're first-class contract engineers! We're not building Toyotas or TV sets. They can't conceptualize the way we do. Sam is a genius in mechanical design."

BRAD [the new business manager]: "I talked to Bruce in design, and he has some concerns about draining resources from some of the other big potential projects that are on the doorstep. I thought he was going to attend the meeting."

TOM: "I told him not to come. He is negative and would disrupt this meeting. Every time he opens his mouth, he does nothing but criticize. He never contributes anything positive to the discussion."

MIKE: "Well, I'd like to hear what he has to say." [Four group members side with Tom and shut Mike out, saying, "Let's get with the program."]

SAM: "I like this project, and I want to do it. I think we can help stop terrorism, and I don't see what's wrong with making a contribution on this level and making money at the same time. You all know how I feel about terrorism. It has to stop. I want H & M to be the leader in developing products that can help to deter terrorism."

JOE: "I'm with you."

SAM: "So, what's the verdict?"

They all voted yea. Sam enthusiastically embarked on the Smart Bomb project and designed, built, and sold ten units, but the cost far exceeded the revenues that were generated. The Smart Bomb project was quietly shelved when Sam started a new program on super sensors.

What went wrong? The basic problem was that the meeting was dominated by groupthink. George, Mike, Laura, and Brad still harbored some reservations about the project but decided to drop the subject. They wanted to maintain cohesiveness to allow them to get on with their autonomous work by giving a bone to the boss. All critical thinking was suspended in order to achieve this goal. This decision was an excellent example of a collusive psychological contract. The president wanted concurrence on his pet project; most of the group was willing to go along because Sam would pursue his own project, leaving them to pursue their own independent goals. The president was oblivious to the consequences of his actions and cost the company something they could ill afford, money.

The proposal was adopted without addressing the feasibility, the consequences, and the cost. Only one alternative was considered due to the groupthink mentality. The H & M group failed to examine the consequences of the groupthink decision. The leader of the group, Sam, had made up his mind before the group had convened. The other members of the group wanted to maintain cohesiveness and move on with their own private agendas. In their minds, agreeing to fund the Smart Bomb project was a small price to pay.

The other factor that fostered groupthink was Sam's management style. His behavior, based on his overall management style, was quite predictable. He was an INFP, internally ruled by his dominant feeling function. Sam had a strong set of values, inculcated by his upbringing. In an interview, Sam revealed that three values ruled his life: God, family, and country, with God and family intertwined. He came from a patriarchal family where authority was never questioned and conflict was handled by an invisible hand. Sam was a conflict avoider because he felt that his subordinates should not confront his authority. This is how he ran his family life, and he expected the same in the organization. Sam retreated psychologically and physically from confrontation, preferring to sit in his office and work on his esoteric projects.

The staff differed in style. Many were confronters who sometimes challenged his authority. When they did, Sam would silently give nonverbal messages of disapproval. They learned quickly that if they also avoided conflict, the illusory group harmony placated Sam, and they could go their own ways. The bubble would burst when they directly challenged any proposal that Sam had invested his ego in. When this happened and the usual nonverbal signs did not produce acquiescence, he would avoid direct discussion and retreat from the problem. He would privately brood over the matter, convinced of the virtue of his position, then revert to his position of authority and impose his decision: "My way or no way!"

In this way, Sam uses a paradoxical style of conflict management. He is a superagreeable conflict avoider and then switches to a win–lose pattern. He stores up his repressed thoughts of anger at the group for not being "family corporate types" and then spasmodically explodes.

The groupthink decision reflected the usual pattern of the organization. The staff hoped that by placating Sam, he would do his own thing and they would do theirs. They erroneously assumed that the outcome of their acquiescence would have minimal financial consequences. They were wrong.

The H & M company lacks leadership, vision, and a process for resolving conflict and making wise decisions. All of the actors have to make a perceptual shift away from their embedded view of territoriality. Each member of senior management acts as an individual, optimizing personal goals at the expense of the overall effort. They need to become a team. There is conflict over goals, roles, and interpersonal style. All of these elements need to be addressed.

7

Managing Stress

The 1990s can be viewed as the age of stress. The pressures within our occupations, competition from Japan and other Asian nations, the volatility of the economic markets, the downsizing of organizations, and the uncertainties of life in general all contribute to the contemporary stress syndrome.

Hans Selye, a well-known stress researcher, first reported a scientific description of the stress reaction in 1936. The formal name he gave it was general adaptation syndrome (GAS). GAS, he said, is precipitated by an alarm reaction to a noxious agent and attenuated by the following stage of resistance to the agent. In the current view, positive events—for example, winning a lottery—as well as negative ones—such as losing your job to downsizing—can bring on the GAS. Selye defined four variations of stress:

Hypostress occurs when we suffer from lack of self-realization (e.g., physical immobility, boredom, or sensory deprivation).
Hyperstress occurs when we have exceeded the limits of our adaptability; this results in an overload or exhaustion response.
Eustress occurs when we feel a positive challenge and a pleasure in what we are doing and flow with the experience.
Distress occurs when internal and external events cause dysphoria or bad feelings; this results in a threat response.

"Our goal," he concluded, "should be to strike a balance between the equally destructive forces of hypostress and hyperstress, to find as much eustress as possible, and to minimize distress."

The distinction between a challenge and a threat is one of the crucial factors in dealing with the people, events, and things that cause stress (i.e., the stressors). The issue is whether you focus on mastery of the situation (a positive emotional tone) or submission to it (a negative emotional tone). When you are in the challenge mode, you look for solutions to defeat or surmount the stressor. When you are in the threat mode, a negative emotional tone is in operation, and you think in terms of accepting defeat or fleeing from confrontation with the stressor. When the threat response is pervasive, physical illness can result. Those who deal with stressors by accepting defeat or fleeing are doomed to suffer the stress syndrome and its consequences, including gastric ulcers, disorders of the immune system, and even coronary heart disease.

To understand stress, you must understand the components of the stress reaction:

- One's appraisal of a situation involves active, ongoing recognition of the relevant stressors and the stress reaction.
- One's cognitive structuring of a situation is responsible for mobilizing the stress response.
- One's subsequent behavior depends on one's state of mind at that moment. Depending on the content of the cognitive structuring, the behavior may be flight or attack, avoidance of the stressor or rising to the challenge. Associated feelings may include anxiety, sadness, anger, or exhilaration and a sense of mastery.
- Stressors lead to a disruption of one's normal activities.
- People vary widely in their specific sensitivities; what is a stressful situation for one person may be a neutral or a challenging situation for another. Differences in personality structure—for example, psychological type, need patterns, or conflict style—account for some of the wide variations in individual sensitivities to stressors.
- The principal stressor may be internal, such as negative or self-defeating thoughts, and have no apparent specific reference to the outside world.
- Stressful interactions with other people form mutually reinforcing cycles of maladaptive behavior.

A Cognitive Approach to Stress

A transactional analysis of stress involves how we process information from our environment. I advocate a cognitive approach to understanding and dealing with stress. The key components of the cognitive model are assumptions, perceptions, and feelings—the APFs.

Assumptions. As we pass through life, we build up an assumption system of what is, what should be, and what ought to be. These assumptions are beliefs we develop from encounters that we take for granted. The range and depth of our assumptions depend on the complexity of our experiences. Assumptions are thoughts or internal scripts that we bring to situations. They usually precede perceptions and can affect them.

Perceptions. Perceptions can alter our assumptions if we broaden our viewpoint. Perception is material processed through the five senses or how these sensations are interpreted by means of intuition. Sensing types rely on what they perceive as facts and details in the situation. Intuitive types can arrive at a perception without being aware of the concrete basis for it. They make leaps from the present to future possibilities. Given that there are different ways of processing a situation, there is tremendous latitude in what we perceive. There are both general laws of perception and individual "spins" on a given case.

Feelings. Feelings are emotive and affective reactions generated in response to a specific encounter. These feelings are triggered by our perceptions shaped by the context of the encounter and our previous assumptions. If our assumptions are negative, we selectively pick out perceptions that reinforce our negative assumptions, leading to negative feelings such as frustration, anger, and hate. If our assumptions are positive and no stress is introduced into the situation, we trigger positive feelings such as joy, happiness, contentment, or exhilaration. Feelings can impact on our perceptions. For example, when we are in a distraught state, we can turn what normally would be benign perceptions into catastrophic thoughts that have no basis in reality.

Stress on the Job

Job-Related Stressors

Work can be considered at best a mixed blessing and at worst an absolute curse. Some people work because they must satisfy their basic needs for food, shelter, and safety. Others work because they consider it a moral obligation or a gender obligation (men must be breadwinners). A fortunate few work because it satisfies some intrinsic need. Albert Camus, referring to the Greek myth of Sisyphus, who was condemned by the gods to spend eternity rolling a great rock up a hill, only to have it roll down again as soon as he reached the top, concluded: "The struggle to the top alone would make a human heart swell. Sisyphus must be regarded as happy." This statement reflects Camus's belief in the intrinsic rewards of work. Robert Holt, a psychologist, points out that all research on occupational stress is "a pointer to the dark side of work." In keeping with this philosophy, there are at least six work stressors that lead to the stress reaction:

1. *The characteristics of the job.* Stress can be caused by too much or too little work; time pressures and deadlines; having to make too many decisions; fatigue induced by the physical conditions of the work environment, excessive travel, or long hours; constant changes in priorities; and micromanagement by dominant-task-oriented bosses.
2. *The problem of role clarification.* Role conflict can result from role ambiguity, role overlap, role overload, and role competition.
3. *The quality of one's relationships with bosses, peers, and subordinates.* Some organizations are overly task-oriented, to the point where the human side is overlooked or dismissed. In addition, certain individuals are stress carriers because of their pathological personalities. Difficult people exist everywhere in life; the organization is no exception.
4. *The problem of career development.* This refers to anxiety over job security, redundancy, obsolescence, or early retirement. Related to these fears is status disparity (under- or overpromotion) or the frustration associated with reaching a career ceiling.
5. *The organization itself—that is, the culture and norms of the organization.* Some organizations place severe restraints on au-

tonomy, enforce dress codes, place limitations on decision making, and foster an us-versus-them attitude to promote competition within organizational units.

6. *The conflict between organizational and outside life.* This is the problem cited most often by middle- and upper-level managers. Family problems and loyalties clash with the demands of everyday work priorities. The rigid rules of organizations restrict the amount of time that a person can devote to family, hobbies, and self-development beyond the confines of the organization.

The key to healthy adaptation is managing the stress process and its consequences.

Individual Needs

Our needs are the driving force for achieving individual competence. Most of the time the needs exert a positive impetus to goal attainment. But if the intensity of the needs become overwhelming and pervasive they can act as *internal stressors*. Certain needs lead to personal stress:

Achievement. This high-achieving type is constantly trying to reach higher levels of success without taking the time to assess past achievements. They set high standards for themselves and berate themselves when they perceive that they have not lived up to these standards.

Succorance. A person with a high need for succorance is acutely perceptive to rejection, exclusion, separation, and abandonment. Such people require regular reassurances by others that they are all right.

Autonomy. The autonomous type is on the alert for cues from the environment that suggest interference, intrusion, coercion, or restraint. Such people perceive the world as trying to fence them in. Their reaction may be hostility or depression, depending on the circumstances. They can become extremely stress-prone when they are pressured to conform.

Dominance. This type feels uncomfortable when they perceive that they do not have control of a situation. They sense that something catastrophic is going to happen, or they fear losing their competitive edge and their sense of self-esteem.

Abasement. These hyperresponsible individuals feel that they must conform to a high standard set by others. If they perceive that they have failed, they blame themselves. With this self-blame comes a feeling of worthlessness and a need to atone.

Exhibition. In excess, this need pushes the person into an overwhelming effort to meet the demand. It is sometimes a self-defeating effort because people of this type try so hard that they alienate others. Their stress levels then skyrocket.

Aggression. This is a typical type-A person who looks out on a dog-eat-dog world. Every encounter is viewed as competitive. In the organizational world, this type of aggressive behavior can be met with resistance or counteraction. The person with this internal stressor develops psychophysiological reactions, such as muscle tension, headaches, and gastrointestinal symptoms, when thwarted.

Aaron Beck has identified and elaborated on two types of stress-prone individuals, calling them the "autonomous" and the "succorant" types. Let us look at them in greater detail and apply the cognitive model of APFs to develop insight into the dynamics of these individuals.

Autonomous types react to any incursion into their life space. They become hostile if interrupted while talking, working, or even daydreaming, and resent being held up in movie, grocery store, gas station, and restaurant lines. Their assumptions are based on the desire for pure freedom, individuality, and preservation of autonomy. Their perceptual filters are on the lookout for the least sign of interference, intrusion, coercion, or restraint. The sense of well-being for such persons depends on preserving the integrity and autonomy of their domain. They need to have unrestricted freedom of choice, action, and expression. They want to direct their own destinies and attain their goals by means of individual action. If put under extreme pressure they can develop hostility, claustrophobia, anorexia nervosa, and endogenous depression.

The following list includes their basic assumptions:

• I must stand alone.
• Individuality is the highest virtue in the world.
• I must fight any intrusion into my life space.

- I will be perceived as weak if I accept help.
- I should push people away when they crowd me.

The stress reaction of the autonomous person could be to fight. To any perceived threat to their autonomy, they develop hostile responses, which may range from mild irritation to anger or even rage. Their reactions are based on the assumption that they can counterattack and bully the other person to retreat.

The opposite of the autonomous personality is the overly succorant person. Their APF cluster is based on receiving. They want acceptance, intimacy, understanding, support, guidance, and positive feedback—all of which are necessary for their self-validation. If they do not receive these "supplies of outside support," they become passive and overly dependent, and may possibly develop a reactive depression. Moreover, they may become anxious and agoraphobic. The succorant type is sensitive to perceived rejection, abandonment, and deprivation. The following list includes their main assumptions:

- Everyone needs someone all the time.
- I am nothing without the approval of others.
- Life is meaningless without unconditional love.
- If I receive negative feedback, it proves I am unworthy.
- If I praise others, I will be given praise in return.

The stress reaction of the succorant type is fear. They are hypersensitive to cues that signal danger to their self-esteem. As a result they try to flee from the situation physically or at least psychologically. They become inhibited, they choke up, or they block out the experience. The sole focus of their perceptions is on the danger. As a consequence, all their coping mechanisms freeze up. The feeling tone associated with this type is anxiety. They develop fears of being appraised, of working for a dominant boss, of encountering a more expert peer or subordinate, and of making any mistake, no matter how small.

These are prototypes, not stereotypes. Two other factors come into play: perception and cognition. Not everyone has the same reaction to a given stressor. For example, a champion golfer facing a par-5 hole on the ocean side of Pebble Beach may actually experience a positive challenge. A 15-handicapper playing to impress his boss, peers, or anyone else may experience intense distress, including anxiety, muscle stiffness, and the wish not to be there (flight). The former perceives he can do it; the latter is sure of failure.

Thomas Haggard, doing research on stress, stated: "A person is able to act realistically and effectively in a stressful situation only if he/she knows the nature and seriousness of the threat, knows what to do, and is able to do it." In other words, we can convert stressful situations into positive challenges if we deal with cognitive factors. The way we perceive and then interpret these perceptions is done mostly on an unconscious level.

Stress Carriers

Stress carriers are people who, through their repeated behavior, cause distress in others. They are not always aware of their stress-causing behavior, which may be activated on a subconscious level. Nevertheless, they throw other people off balance and induce reactive behaviors. The basis for the difficult behavior resides in the personal script each person carries. Eric Berne, founder of transactional analysis, talks about feeling states such as "I'm OK," "You're OK," "I'm not OK," "You're not OK." Difficult people fall into the quadrants of "I'm not OK" and "You're not OK." This is their perceptual set. When they are stressed the "not OK" feeling sets in, and they try to make you "not OK" too. Once this task is accomplished, their feelings of powerlessness are reduced because they have disempowered you. Your challenge is to cope with the stress carrier by righting the power balance, a task that begins with understanding the types of difficult people and how to deal with each of them. Robert M. Bramson has identified nine types of difficult people, described below.

The Difficult Types

Sherman Tanks come out charging. Their very demeanor expresses "attack." Aggressiveness is the main need of Sherman Tanks. They are arbitrary and arrogant. They attack the person, not the problem. They seek to humiliate or to arouse a counterattack. The former response only adds fuel to the fire. Sherman Tanks love to bully the weak and squeamish. One of the distinguishing features of the Sherman Tank is the constant barrage of verbal and nonverbal threats he or she subjects people to. Some Sherman Tanks are crass; others are subtle and smooth in their attacks. Either way the victim is robbed of power.

Snipers never attack directly. They wait for a convenient time, such as a meeting, where they constantly attack by using side talk and subtle (and not-so-subtle) nonverbal gestures of disdain. Another form of sniping consists of talking behind your back to colleagues or boss.

Unlike Sherman Tanks, *Exploders* are unpredictable and spasmodic. Something triggers an adult version of a child's tantrum in the Exploder, and he or she erupts like a volcano. It is as if the Exploder is under the spell of a demon. When the tantrum is over, the Exploder may blink and feel remorseful or just go on as if nothing has happened.

Complainers constantly find fault with procedures, policies, workloads, and people. Everything is a problem for them. The problems they complain about are usually not legitimate problems. Nonetheless, they are constantly whining about something. Some have a pet complaint that they constantly bring up. They are adept at putting people on the defensive; when this happens, all actors are caught in the accusation-defense-reaccusation game.

Clams are silent and unresponsive. They shut up when you need a response to a problem that you are both involved with, so the conversation becomes asymmetrical: you are doing all the talking and responding. The behavior is a learned response to a number of predisposing conditions, including avoidance of commitment to painful interpersonal situations, calculated aggression, and evasion.

Superagreeables tell you what they think you want to hear: "The component will be ready tomorrow. You can count on that." They are stress carriers because you believe them, but they invariably let you down. They tell you all the good things you want to hear because they seek approval from you while ignoring the realities of the problem. By saying the words you want to hear, they unconsciously think they please you. But by being nice today they set you up for a fall tomorrow.

Negativists' favorite phrase is "There's nothing we can do." It is an unconditional negative, backed up by references to previous experiences, selected data, and firm conviction. The Negativist derails problem solving because the phrase "Here's a solution to the problem" is not in his or her vocabulary. Negativists suffer from existential power-lessness and project this feeling onto others. Sometimes the recipient of Negativists' remarks falls into the trap of agreeing with them.

Bulldozers are know-it-all experts. They are usually highly trained in their specialty and exude a sense of superiority that often overwhelms people. In contrast to some of the other stress carriers, Bulldozers are highly productive. What makes them difficult is that their expertise spills over into all areas. Their opinions are expressed in a tone of absolute certainty. They use paralogism to make others look incompetent and stupid. They like to one-up people. They leave little room for anyone else's judgment, creativity, or resourcefulness. In Albert Ellis's terms, they suffer from the irrational belief that they must be perfect. They try to achieve perfection by being expert in everything. They want to be in control of the world. A Bulldozer high in the needs for achievement and dominance can be the worst of all stress carriers.

Balloons are phony know-it-all pseudoexperts. Often, they are curious people who collect random scraps of information and then try to make these scraps look like wisdom. They are not liars or con artists, who know they are skillfully manipulating you. Balloons, because of a faulty ego system, are fooling themselves. They seek admiration from others by acting expert. The Balloon is more of an irritant than a serious problem. If you know you are dealing with a Balloon, the best strategy is not to take the person seriously.

Stallers are indecisive and hold off making decisions in hopes that the problem will go away. Eighty percent of the time this tactic works. (Pareto's Law states that 80 percent of organizational decisions are trivial: only 20 percent count.) The underlying concern of the indecisive Staller is not to hurt anyone by making an unpleasant decision that might distress someone. They try their best to avoid the problem. They are the ultimate conflict avoiders.

Coping with Stress Carriers

The first principle to understand is that stress carriers are not going to change. Most of them have what psychologists call "personality disorders." Any clinical psychologist or psychiatrist will tell you that people with personality disorders are the hardest to treat, and that they create the greatest frustration for therapists. If you accept this truth, you can deal with stress carriers by gaining control over your own responses and reactions to them.

The second principle is to understand the behavior patterns of the stress carriers you work with, to identify them by type, and then to treat the problem. In medicine there is no magical cure for all diseases; treatment is specific to the illness. The same principle applies to stress carriers: after identifying a stressor's behavior patterns, you can develop a plan specific to that stress carrier.

The third principle is that you must develop new behaviors to handle stress carriers, and then practice these behaviors repeatedly to become proficient in them. Many people give up after the first try, ignoring the importance of the learning curve: any new behavior is acquired at a slow rate during the early trials, but if practiced it will eventually come easily and naturally.

The fourth principle is that you may be contributing to the problem because of *your* management style. What are your stress reactions? Do you explode at an Exploder? Clam up when faced with a Sherman Tank?

The following methods for coping with the various stress carriers come from Robert M. Bramson and other leading cognitive-behaviorist therapists who deal with personality and character disorders.

Sherman Tanks are hostile-aggressives, and you must not back down or flee from them. If you remain calm, you are in a good position to cope with them. You are in charge of your internal reactions and can best balance the power ploy of the Sherman Tank. Consider these coping suggestions:

- Give the Sherman Tank time to run down.
- Get his or her attention. Change your posture. Say his or her name. If possible, get him or her to sit down.
- Maintain eye contact and project a calm, receptive manner.
- Do not argue or counterattack.
- Try to get into the problem-solving mode. Proceed in an adult-to-adult manner.

Snipers need a different approach because they are subtle and cunning:

- Surface the attack by questioning the Sniper.
- Provide an alternative to open warfare.

- Seek group confirmation if the sniping takes place in a meeting.
- Deal with the underlying problems in a private meeting with the Sniper.
- In general, try to remain in the questioning mode until the issue comes clearly to the surface.

Since *Exploders* erupt without much warning, you will be rocked back on your heels and must make a quick recovery. Use these coping suggestions:

- Give the Exploder time to run down.
- If the explosion continues, ask the Exploder to stop.
- Try to get at the reason for the explosion by eliciting their concerns.
- Perhaps get some distance from the problem, and deal with the Exploder in private.

Remember that *Complainers* need to be understood as powerless people trying to make you feel blame for their plight. They see the world only in terms of "oughts" and "shoulds." These moral imperatives are part of an internally generated script. The best strategy is to shift the Complainer into an active problem-solving mode. In order to do this you should:

- Listen attentively to what the Complainer is saying.
- Acknowledge her or his perceptions by paraphrasing what you heard.
- Ask pertinent questions.
- Neither agree nor disagree.
- Try to surface objective facts, and move into the problem-solving mode.
- Try to get agreement on limited tasks.
- Don't be persuaded by *never* or *always*. Try to question the validity of these statements.
- Remain calm under all circumstances.

Silent and unresponsive *Clams* can have three underlying motivations for being a difficult person: clamming up is a way of avoiding a potential conflict, it can also be a form of calculated aggression because its intention is to hook you into feeling frustrated and angry, or it can be a method for sidestepping potential failure, a fear often characteristic of Clams. Regardless of the motivations, the Clam must be coped with:

- Ask open-ended questions.
- Wait for the Clam to open up.
- Don't try to give him or her a response.
- Cope with your inner frustrations with the Clam.
- When they open up, allow them to say whatever they want to say.
- Restate what the Clam has agreed to do, and ask for concurrence.
- If the Clam remains closed, end the meeting with an intention to continue at another time.

Superagreeables desperately need your approval at all costs. They will say anything to please you; they will promise you the moon, even if it is impossible to deliver. Your goal is to make honesty non-threatening. This is not an easy task because Superagreeables have been self-brainwashed to believe that they must please all the time. They view unpleasant news as a potential rebuke—an ego-threatening dart. You must:

- Try to understand the underlying issues that preclude Superagreeables from being straightforward.
- Build a personal relationship with them on some aspect of their lives that is important to them.
- Listen to and interpret their humor.
- Consider that there are some hidden messages in their remarks.
- Be ready to negotiate if a conflict is surfaced.

Negativists want us to buy into their state of despair. All of us have suffered from the slings and arrows of fate, and, consciously or unconsciously, we can empathize with their negativity. But if we allow ourselves to be too empathetic, we will be trapped in their game. The key to dealing with Negativists is to empower them because the root of the negativism is their sense of powerlessness:

- Evade getting drawn into their state of mind.
- Be optimistic about the possibilities of solving the problem.
- Focus on the realistic steps that can be taken to solve the problem.
- Dream up a worst-case scenario and discuss this with the Negativist.
- Use a "force field" analysis to get on with the problem, listing the forces against and the forces in favor of any alternative(s).
- Don't argue, or he or she will dig in more firmly.
- In extreme cases, go around the Negativist and do it yourself or through others.

Bulldozers have supreme confidence in what they are expert in. Carl Jung would call them "psychopomps," people who compensate for some deeper fault. Nevertheless, they overwhelm and micromanage any task. The person facing the Bulldozer is left with little sense of competence and a high degree of frustration. Coping with Bulldozers requires the following steps:

• Be on top of the problem by doing some serious research so that the Bulldozer will not be able to put you on the spot.
• Listen to and acknowledge what the Bulldozer says.
• Question in an adult-to-adult manner.
• Avoid trying to seem more expert than her or him.
• If the behavior is incessant and the Bulldozer is your boss, let the matter go.
• If the Bulldozer is a peer, seek out other colleagues' input to solve the problem.

Balloons seek admiration and respect from others (they have a high need for succorance). In order for these needs to be met they compile a great deal of extraneous and esoteric information. They put these bits and pieces together in a collage of self-determined knowledge. They may read an article on the new information network in the Sunday *New York Times Magazine*. From that moment on they become self-appointed experts on the topic. The problem is they have not fully assimilated what they read, nor have they carried out other investigations on the topic. These curious people, armed with partial information, are not aware that they are out of their depth. The coping steps for Balloons are these:

• State the facts as an alternative version.
• Do not call a Balloon's bluff.
• Give her or him a tactful way out—for example, by "postponing" in-depth discussion of the topic for another time.
• Cope with Balloons alone. Groups allow them to feed on their need for admiration.

Stallers postpone decisions and hope they will go away. To cope with Stallers:

• Try to get the Staller to give you reasons for the delays.
• Look for indications that help to expose the problem.

- When the underlying issue is on the table, try to suggest ways of proceeding with the task.
- If a Staller tries to indict you as part of the problem, accept this indictment and try to work things out, looking forward rather than backward.
- Always give positive reinforcement to the Staller's attempts to go on with the task.
- Establish a decision-making chart and timetable with which you both agree.

The Psychological Types and Stress

Psychological type reveals some predictable reactions to stress based on how the person perceives and judges reality. The functions of sensing, intuition, thinking, and feeling play a large role in how a person reacts under stress. Since the functions are stable patterns of behavior, a person under stress falls back on strengths (the dominant function) and is vulnerable to weaknesses (the inferior function).

The judging types are more prone to the stress reaction than the perceptive types due to their desire to achieve closure. The judging types have an inordinate sense of time urgency. Decisions must be made, so they are in a state of anxiety until they achieve closure. Perceptive types are more likely to think a problem over and then react to it. Some extreme perceptive types can bring on stress by their habits of procrastination.

Judging Types

Extroverted thinking (ET) types (ENTJs and ESTJs), particularly highly dominant extroverts, are stressed when their self-imposed sense of order, based on principles and reason, is attacked. The stress reaction can be externalized in every form from benign Socratic debates to explosive outbursts. Extroverted thinkers can be formidable stress carriers because they so often insist that everyone else obey *their* formula for reality.

ETs have a tendency to repress feeling and they lack empathy. Their repressed feelings may become distorted, leading to false judgments about character. These distorted judgments can then be thrust upon others in a win–lose manner. In addition, their submerged feelings can give rise to secret prejudices—for example, a readiness to misconstrue any opposition as a personal attack. All of these propensities lead to proneness to the stress reaction. The following stress-reducing tips may help them:

- Practice relaxation techniques.
- Reduce automatic thoughts.
- List assumptions about the situation. Then list counters that may challenge this preconceived view of reality.
- Try to imagine what it is like to be the other person, looking at the world through their perceptual frame of reference.

Extroverted feeling (EF) types are stressed by disruptions to their cherished values and sense of harmony, which are based on prevailing objective sentiments and general values. They may feel rejected and invaded. The stress reaction can be a mild or strong form of acting out.

Their world is ruled by an external formula for what is "correct" in the harmonious aesthetic sense. Any fact that disrupts this balance is rejected (thinking is therefore repressed). Harmony based on internalized conventional rules of correctness is their goal. When harmony is disturbed, stress results. EFs can try to ward off stress by:

- Practicing relaxation skills.
- Listing their important values.
- Determining what values are being challenged in the stressful encounter.
- Considering alternative approaches to the problem.
- Examining why the threat seems catastrophic to harmony.

Introverted thinking (IT) types (ISTPs and INTPs) are stressed by challenges to their highly developed inner concepts. They become extremely annoyed when their thoughts or routines are questioned, upset, or merely interrupted. Intensity of thought is the goal of ITs. They become stressed when they are forced to objectify their deep inner thoughts. If the reception accorded those thoughts is less than total acceptance, they become stubborn, headstrong, and unreceptive. Their stress deepens when demands for clarification of their position are intensified. Then they withdraw, possibly alienating the other party. In extreme cases, the IT can become a prototypical Clam. ITs seeking to reduce stress can:

- Practice relaxation techniques.
- Objectify the thoughts that are controlling the situation, and determine whether they are in accord with objectively verifiable facts.
- Explore their own *feelings*.
- Identify the impact of their plans on others.
- Discuss the circumstances with the relevant parties in the conflict.

Introverted feeling (IF) types (ISFPs and INFPs) are stressed when their treasured values, which are usually hidden, are transgressed. They take this transgression as a personal assault and shrink within themselves, creating a barrier between themselves and the assaulter. Irrational thoughts may be conjured up and dwelled upon. Their true motives remain secret, guarded by inner values, as opposed to the EF's external correctness. When their inner harmony is threatened, IFs can demonstrate either murderous coldness or blanket avoidance. IFs under stress see the outside world as a place of mean thinking directed at them, scheming evil plots and secret intrigues, and so they devise counterplots. All of this is trying for IFs who want only inner harmony and total privacy. The pathological symptoms are chronic fatigue and possible exhaustion. IFs should take the following steps:

- Practice relaxation techniques.
- Identify what is upsetting about the conflict.
- Identify what values are being violated.
- Determine some of their most feared consequences, and assess these consequences by analyzing the probability of their occurring.
- List positive thoughts for solving the problem.

Perceptive Types

Extroverted sensing (ES) types (ESTPs and ESFPs) are guided by actual experiences and concrete objects. Their aim is to live life to its fullest through the accumulation of new experiences (sensations). ETs love tangible reality and do not have the inclination for reflection (intuition), so they are stressed when a situation calls for deep reflection and making connections that are not immediately apparent to them. Under these conditions, they grasp any clue in the immediate situation and focus on its tangible aspects. Once they can get back to tangible reality, they can breathe again.

ESs have great difficulty in defining their underlying assumptions and become stressed when they are pressed to do so. The stress reaction deteriorates into hairsplitting pedantry and lack of focus on the future, behavior that can become compulsive and annoying to others and self-defeating to the stressed ES. ESs can try these stress-reducing tips:

- Practice relaxation techniques.
- Make a list of assumptions that guide their behavior.
- Single out the assumptions that get them into trouble.
- Look at the big picture, listing priorities for the next month and then rank-ordering them.
- Ask others involved in their work how they see these priorities.
- Build a matrix of how their work fits in with that of others.

Introverted sensing (IS) types (ISTJs and ISFJs) are stressed when their internal order is disturbed. They internalize the objective facts that fit their needs and rigidly hold to them. When this delicate balance is shaken, they become unstrung. They can conjure up all types of plots and dangerous possibilities that lurk in the external world. IS types can become extremely rigid under stress. These stress-reducing tips will help them:

- Practice relaxation techniques.
- Arrange a meeting with the significant role players in their job.
- Engage in a brainstorming session where everyone gives personal perceptions of what is important in the current project. The ISs must withhold judgment until the session is over.
- Take home the lists generated in the brainstorming session and calmly look them over, trying to see the merits in various perceptions.
- Arrange a follow-up meeting to synthesize the lists into a master list, where all perceptions are interconnected.

Extroverted intuition (EN) types (ENFPs and ENTPs) are stressed by being overwhelmed with minutiae and structure. Their propensity to look for and seek possibilities may be thwarted by a sensing-type boss who tries to force his or her perception of reality on the EN. ENs want acknowledgment for all of their fantastic insights. When reined in by reality, they can become morbid. Stable conditions suffocate them. They can try these stress-reducing tips:

- Practice relaxation techniques.
- Arrange a meeting with an ISTJ or ISFJ and seek his or her approach to the problem. Then ask the rationale for their approach and contrast it with your own approach. Identify the critical differences in the two approaches, and reconcile the differences by integrating the two approaches.

Introverted intuition (IT) types (INTJs and INFJs) are stressed by attacks on their internal visions. Lack of structure, which in the case of introverted sensation causes stress, is of no concern to ITs. They seize on a vision and grasp all nuances and possibilities that relate to its internal reality. Because of the intensity of this vision, they may seem oblivious to the concerns of others and push on in determined pursuit of their dream. When the possibility of the dream being realized is challenged or reputed by external facts and they cannot forcibly maintain their position, they experience a severe stress reaction. The following stress-reducing tips are recommended:

- Practice relaxation techniques.
- List all assumptions and expectations about a project or a problem at hand. Arrange a meeting with subordinates and distribute this list to them. Have the subordinates mark the assumptions and expectations on the list as known (K), unknown (U), and partially known (P).
- Note the amount of agreement among the lists. Ask the subordinates if this degree of agreement on perceived shared assumptions and expectations is usual.

Coping Patterns for Stress Reduction: A Case Study

Coping with stress begins with the recognition that stress is a problem. The next step is to identify its sources: internal, external, organizational, or any combination of these. Once the diagnosis is made, five coping elements come into play:

1. Remove unnecessary stressors.
2. Do not allow neutral events to become stressors.
3. Develop skills in dealing with situations you cannot avoid.
4. Develop relaxation skills.
5. Develop diversions from the demands of life.

The following case study, pulling together all of the important concepts in this book, will illustrate how one manager dealt with stress.

The Scenario

Louis is a section manager in a manufacturing company that produces electronic components. He is an ENTJ with high needs for achievement, autonomy, and exhibition. Twenty people—all engineers—report to him. The MAXIM project is one of his many responsibilities. It is not under his direct control: it is managed by a program office that directs work to his section. Harry, the lead engineer, contracts with Louis to do various tasks for the MAXIM project. Louis's group is also doing work for Jim, another lead engineer in the program office, on the Apex program, and working as well on some independent research programs funded by the research department. Louis is constantly juggling priorities for these tasks because each lead engineer sees his task as the highest priority one.

Harry is an ESTJ with high needs for achievement and dominance, not an uncommon pattern in the company. He is a hovering type (a micromanager) who constantly interferes with Louis's engineers. He sees himself as an expert and tries to second-guess the task engineers who are working on his projects. None of them has a direct line of responsibility to Harry.

Jim is an INTJ with the same high needs for achievement and dominance as Harry. His style is very inconsistent. He is known to change the task requirements without questioning or talking to Louis. He also thinks that others can read his mind, so he does not share his inner thoughts with Louis and the task engineers.

It is Monday morning, and Louis has arrived at his desk to find Harry pacing around his office while nervously sipping coffee. Before Louis can even get his coat off, Harry blurts out, "Louis, I just came back from the people in Washington who are funding the MAXIM project, and we've got to make significant changes in the design of the switching component. We have to move fast. On Friday I asked Jill and George [two task engineers] to stop everything and get cracking on these changes. I worked all weekend on how this should be done."

Louis is flabbergasted. "What? You can't do that! George and Jill are already committed to finishing some work on the Apex program. I can't just stop things to make you happy."

"You darn well will do it. I control the money, and you will do what I say—or else!"

Louis starts to feel his blood pressure rise and his anger level increase. Before he can get control of himself, he explodes at Harry and tells him to leave his office. Harry bristles back, "Louis, control your temper. You are acting like a kid—you know K.I.D.!" Louis, now even more enraged, stalks out of his office, finds Jill and George, and orders them to get back to the Apex tasks. Meanwhile, Harry stomps off.

Louis returns to his office and slams the door. It opens a moment later and Jim walks in. He asks, "Well, Louis, are my Apex components ready for testing?"

Louis blurts out, "What testing? You never told me that was part of the bargain. I thought we were going to build prototypes and fine-tune them, not test them. What the hell is going on?"

Jim, true to type (INTJ), replies: "I am dead sure you and I agreed to a final testing. You can't back down on this agreement! I promised the customer that we'd be ready. I'll give you until Wednesday to get the job done. Take some people off other jobs, and get to it. I'll be upstairs all morning in a program review, and can't be disturbed. Call me in the afternoon about how everything is going."

"Wait!" yells Louis, but Jim has already disappeared.

As if things aren't bad enough already, now Jill comes in looking distressed: "Louis, George had a car accident and can't come in today. It's nothing serious, but he's all shook up."

At that point she starts to explode and complain about how much overtime she has been spending on both projects and how she can't take it anymore. After the explosion, she breaks down in tears.

Louis is flooded with mixed emotions. Should he put on his coat and leave this mess? Go to his boss and complain? Ignore them all and just do what he thinks is best? None of these actions is win–win, and he feels he is in a no-win situation. As he slumps in his chair and starts to reflect, he remembers that this is not the first time these sorts of incidents have occurred. Jim has always assumed more than what was agreed on; Harry always tries to manage the task engineers even though he has no authority; and Jill and George *are* overworked—and so is he.

"Damn it," he thinks. "This company is like a pressure cooker. Everyone has A1 priority. All these projects with different program managers and lead engineers. Why can't we work together? I get confused over what *my* role is. Top management talks about team-work but encourages competition and self-promotion. No one up there cares about the man in the middle. No wonder I need two drinks at night to relax. When I go to my boss, he spouts that old cliché, 'Conflict should be resolved at the lowest level.' Any good manager knows that. Besides, I have other priorities and constant pressure from my boss. My wife listens to my complaints. But what can she do? Sometimes I want to go to Iowa and grow corn.

Suddenly there is a knock on Louis's door. Louis thinks, "Oh, no, not another problem!"

The Menu for Change

This case can be analyzed at several levels, each of which will help us to understand the transactional nature of stress and coping.

Louis's menu for change begins with recognizing the problem, iden-tifying the stressors, and following the stress-reducing tips for ETs:

- Practice relaxation techniques.
- Reduce automatic thoughts.
- List assumptions about the situation. Then list counters that may challenge this preconceived view of reality.
- List what he perceives to be the APFs of the other people in order to build empathy.

The next step is to identify Louis's APFs:
Assumptions about the Organization:

- "They don't care about the man in the middle."
- "Change can't take place."
- "Everyone is out for himself or herself."
- "Everyone is a difficult person—except me."
- "Everything is futile."

Assumptions about Himself:

- "The only one who listens to me is my wife."
- "I need cigarettes and martinis to relax."

- "I am out of control over the situation at work."
- "Fighting is the best way to handle conflict."
- "My authority has been undermined by Jim and Harry."

Assumptions about Others:

- "Jim is secretive. He hides things from me."
- "Harry is a know-it-all expert and disrupts my section."
- "Jill and George are complete complainers."
- "My boss does not help; he leaves me in the middle."
- "Program managers hinder rather than help."

Louis, like most other stress-prone individuals, is primed to make extreme, one-sided, absolutist, categorical, global judgments. He polarizes the situation by calling on black-and-white dichotomous reasoning. He has a number of untested assumptions that confirm his perceptions about the current incident and reinforce his helplessness.

As a distressed person, Louis is always threatened and unable to feel in charge of the situation. He does not see problems as challenges to be mastered but as demons that haunt him. The following characteristics contribute to his particular reactions:

His stress curve: Louis is a stress reactor with a low tolerance for pressure. His autonomic nervous system is alerted to either fight or flee at a moment's notice. He does not remain calm and in charge when he is presented with a challenge.

Type of stress carrier: Louis uses the fight mode to resolve his stressful condition. He is an Exploder.

Psychological type: As an ENTJ, an extroverted thinking type, his dominant function is thinking (a judging type). Judging types, as we have noted, are more prone to stress than more open-ended perceptive types.

Needs that are stressors: His high need for achievement drives him to take on many tasks without setting realistic priorities and deadlines, and his need for autonomy is in conflict with his need for recognition. Since neither is fulfilled, he is in a constant state of frustration.

Finally, we must examine the external stressors within the organizational climate. Clearly this is a dysfunctional environment where pressures are pushed off onto others. The difficult personalities of the participants exacerbate the reactions.

Louis is subjected to three sets of stressors that threaten to overwhelm his psychological and physiological systems: Harry's arbitrary actions, Jim's hidden agenda, and George and Jill's plight. Each of these people reacts according to his or her own personal needs. Jim is a silent and mercurial type who leaves people in the dark about his needs and intentions; he is a very difficult person to deal with. Harry is a micromanager. Although he has no authority over Louis's task engineers, he interferes with their work priorities. George and Jill are overworked and become Complainers when the work burden increases. Moreover, Jill has a tendency to explode. Both George and Jill have become difficult people for Louis to manage. He feels that he is in a no-win situation, a perception that prompts a sense of powerlessness, frustration, and anger. Louis then puts himself in the distress, or threat, mode.

Louis's multiple responsibilities create role ambiguity. He is confused about priorities and his lack of time management skills is compounded by the culture of his organization.

Armed with this knowledge, Louis can now apply the five coping steps to his situation:

1. *Remove unnecessary stressors.* Louis is burdened with self-imposed expectations and demands, especially in the needs area, that make him distressed. He is an irritable achiever who exaggerates both the importance and the difficulty of the task. He sets almost impossible goals for himself. He is only happy with total success and he becomes hostile when he perceives that his colleagues are impeding his progress. Louis should use perceptual shifting addressed to the pattern of needs that get him into trouble. Moreover, he has to determine the real priorities in his job and learn not to set impossible goals for himself.

    He needs to learn to work in cooperation with others (for example, he needs to adjust his high autonomy need). Although he should be working with Harry and Jim in a collaborative way, he perceives their input as imposing on his turf and disrupting his operation. To the extent that Harry and Jim have their own agendas, Louis is partially right. But his explosive behavior prevents productive compromises. Expectations are not shared and negotiated by the players.

He needs to ask himself, "Is my behavior self-defeating?" He wants recognition for his accomplishments, but because of his alienating behavior, he is virtually ignored (e.g., Jim leaves the room when Louis is in midsentence).

The coping steps for dealing with excessive need were outlined in the chapters on cognitive restructuring and changing one's needs. Louis has to follow the steps outlined in these chapters. They include making perceptual and philosophical shifts.

As an ENTJ, he is not going to change his core characteristics, but he can recognize that judging types are more prone to stress than others. Since his dominant function is thinking, feeling is his inferior side. When the inferior feeling side remains ignored and hidden in the unconscious, it can break through in the form of subjective emotions and values, causing trouble for both himself and others.

2. *Do not allow neutral events to become stressors.* Louis's APFs are blown out of proportion. He views all events as if he were the central character in the drama, failing to recognize that his colleagues are under as much pressure to perform as he is. He needs to deal with his APFs with more objectivity and perspective. Louis must distance himself from his reaction to events so that he can look at his experiences rationally rather than become absorbed by them. His APFs are largely created by him.

3. *Develop skills in dealing with situations you cannot avoid.* Louis has to accept Jim, Harry, George, and Jill as they are. To a large extent, they too are stress carriers who need to be coped with rather than reacted to. Louis becomes powerless when he lets them hit his hot button. These are external stressors that interact with his internal stressors and drive up his stress level. Louis must follow the guidelines for dealing with stress carriers.

4. *Develop relaxation skills.* Louis should practice relaxation every day. This will put him in calmer frame of mind and enable him to handle the stressors in his life.

5. *Develop diversions from the demands of his life.* This is sometimes hard for career-driven individuals like Louis, but it is essential. Diversions are a matter of personal taste. Some people enjoy exercise; others may engage in more passive activities such as reading or working on a project not related to work;

still others find diversion in spiritual or soul-supportive activities. However, it is essential that some diversion be developed in order to achieve balance and wholeness.

Handling Stress in the Future Organizational Environment

Stress in the 1990s has a different character than it did in the past. Our anxiety base and our stress level has now expanded. The large, more-or-less paternal organization that served as the typical manager's business, "home," is starting to disappear. Organizations are downsizing, decentralizing, and becoming more amorphous in structure. But if we learn to read the signs of the times, we can cope. The following trends in organizations are based on the observations of current corporate culture watchers.

Decentralized, Collaborative Organizations

In a recent *Harvard Business Review* article, Larry Hirschhorn and Thomas Gilmore observed that "companies are replacing vertical hierarchies with horizontal networks, linking together traditional functions through interfunctional teams, and forming strategic alliances within and without the company . . . without distinction of title, function, or task." They call this form of organization the "boundaryless company."

The organizational linkages are psychological rather than functional distinctions. Rather than appearing on the organization chart, they are based on role maps of interdependencies for task execution. Louis was operating in such an environment, but he and his fellows were seemingly unaware of the new requirements of their organization and went on doing business as in the past. All actors need to make philosophical and perceptual shifts in order to cope with the new stresses and to be competent in their new interdependent jobs.

For the future organization to be both efficient and effective, the new structures depend heavily on teams. Teams are not new, but in the past they were not trained. A team must look at both the process and the task rather than simply reacting blindly to the job. "Fix the process, not the problem" is the watchword for today's problem solvers. Teams fail when they ignore the management of process in problem solving, and they can be gripped by groupthink, which leads to entropy rather than synergy. Today's total quality management programs are examples of caring for the process of problem solving. They demand a perceptual shift from pure individual effort to constructive collaborative efforts.

Adaptability to Change

Organizational specialists Phillip Slater and Warren Bennis view adaptability to change as paramount: "For adaptability to changing conditions, for rapid acceptance of a new idea, for flexibility in dealing with novel problems, generating high morale and loyalty . . . the more egalitarian or decentralized type seems to work better. One of the reasons for this is that the centralized decision maker is apt to discard an idea on the grounds the he/she is too busy or the idea too impractical."

Walter Wriston, former CEO of Citicorp, agrees: "The job of the manager today [is to] find the best people you can, motivate them[,] and allow them to do the job their own way."

In keeping with that theme, Bill Walsh, former coach of the successful San Francisco Forty-Niners, states: "Management today recognizes that to have a winning organization, it has to be more knowledgeable and competent in dealing with and developing people. . . . The coach must account for his ego. He has to drop or sidestep the ego barrier so that people can communicate without fear." Many organizations play the "kill the messenger" game. This can result in covering up problems because of fear of reprisal. In the long run, these communication barriers lead to failure and disaster.

The successful manager can distinguish between the skills and techniques that can be taught individually and those that require groups. Teams are not the sole solution to organizational problems. The ability to know when to use these techniques and when to shift is crucial.

The Age of Information

Alvin Toffler calls this "the information age." He says that more workers than ever are handling symbols (information) than things. Therefore, knowledge is the primary resource for individuals and the economy overall. The economist's traditional factors of land, labor, and capital have become secondary, a change that demands a perceptual shift for future managers. Peter Drucker concurs, but cautions that knowledge must be integrated, and not just specialized.

Individual Adaptations

Drucker identifies individual adaptations that managers must make. One is that you must assume responsibility for your career and your own development. Another is to develop self-knowledge. Engage in a change of assumptions about your job. Rather than ask "How can I prepare for the next promotion?," think "What do I need to learn so that I can decide where to go next?"—either laterally or up the corporate ladder. And rather than allowing a big-company mentality—where you are taken care of from hiring to retirement—to prevail, take ultimate responsibility for knowing yourself so as to manage your *own* career. Know both what you are good at and your limitations.

Drucker states, "Perception is more important than analysis." He means that effective managers recognize patterns and can anticipate the future. He also makes a distinction between subject/technical knowledge and self-knowledge. Subject knowledge must be blended with people knowledge in order for collaboration and integration to take place.

Developing Competencies

Managers and executives have to know themselves, their organization, and the outside environment. They must figure out the interdependencies for their role. This means that groups within organizations must do away with the us-versus-them syndrome because competition within can lead to poor morale, redundancy, and inefficiency. The specific competencies that managers should develop in order to manage themselves and know others are these:

- How we perceive and judge the world—psychological types.
- How we manage conflict.
- What motivates us and others.
- How to use positive power skills.
- How we react to stress.

Power Shifts

Power, as we have seen, has both positive and negative forms. The outcome depends on how it is used. In this regard, most organizational analysts see a shift from the use of authority and/or legitimate power to the uses of more subtle influence styles: referent power, information power, expert power, and group power. We need to take all these power shifts into account: executives are *managers* responsible for an area or a project, they are not the *bosses* of others. This key perceptual shift requires the development of mutual understanding and responsibility.

The corporate environment of the 1990s and beyond will reflect the needs of a dynamically changing world, and managers must recognize and respond to emerging patterns. If they cope intelligently and with understanding, they will avoid stress.

8

The Role of
Organizational Culture

A Case Study of Barriers between Men and Women: Opening Scenario

Sue Mack was ready to leave for an out-of-town marketing meeting with her regional representatives when the phone rang.

"Sue, this is Charlie. I have some bad news for you. Cancel the trip and see me in my office at eight o'clock tomorrow."

Sue tried to pry out the bad news, but Charlie, her boss and the president of the learning software division of V & L Design, refused to go into details.

The next morning Sue drove out to the corporate offices, located in the San Francisco Bay Area. She was filled with anxiety. Charlie's secretary gave her a cordial greeting and told her to go right in. Charlie was at his desk, with John, the CEO, sitting at his right. The only option Sue had was to sit in front of both men.

Charlie opened the meeting. "Sue, I guess you're aware of why we're here. Things have not been going well in the marketing area. John and I have decided that the marketing campaign is not working, and we are going to relieve you of your present position and put you in charge of advertising production."

John silently nodded in agreement. "Sue, you'll probably be more happy and content in the new position. You know we all support you, and this is in the best interest of all."

Sue mustered her courage and replied, "I don't know what to

say. The sales figures are not in yet, and we are only halfway through our campaign. Where are these negative projections coming from? I don't understand what's happening here."

"It's not a matter of sales figures," John explained, "but more of your style and fit. We need to operate as a team, and that just is not happening. Charlie and I have received some negative input from the men on your staff, and we can't ignore it. You came from a corporate culture that was different from ours, and the transition has been less than optimal."

A dismayed Sue asked, "Just what are the problems?"

Charlie interjected, "It's hard to pinpoint them, but they *are* real and they *are* related to your management style. I really think it's in our mutual interest that you accept this transfer."

Sue sat stunned and silent. Then Charlie filled the communication void: "Sue, why don't you take a few days off to make your decision." She nodded and silently left the room.

After the meeting Charlie called Peter, director of development and a peer of Sue, to have a drink with him at a nearby hotel. Charlie discussed the incident with Peter, who enthusiastically endorsed Charlie's position and his decision. This was not an uncommon happening: Charlie frequently used Peter as a sounding board for many of his decisions.

After two days of ruminating over the situation, Sue came to the conclusion that her options were limited: accept the transfer and lose face and money or refuse it and file a lawsuit.

Organizational Culture

Sue Mack's predicament illustrates the final factor I will examine in this book: organizational culture. Although the term *organizational culture* is of recent vintage, the concept is not. It encompasses the values, climate, and norms of an organization, and adds to them the shared perceptions, language, and problem-solving strategies in that organization. It involves the internal organization and its reaction to the external environment.

The strength and stability of an organization's culture depend on interacting factors: time, patterns of reinforcement (positive or punitive), and the clarity of the assumptions within the group. A well-functioning group whose members understand their goals, roles, interpersonal styles, and procedures are happy. When there is ambiguity in the group, anxiety, frustration, and stress can develop.

Two of the important elements of culture are the working environment and the organization's general assumptions. The working environment encompasses such elements as dress codes, the physical layout of the offices or plant, the degree of formality or informality, the emotional tone, and the actual products that are turned out. It also consists of the formal structure, shown on organization charts, and the informal matrix of relationships that develops independently of this formal structure.

The key assumptions of the organization are the foundation for how it operates both internally and externally. Usually these assumptions are defined by the founders and are based on their particular value systems. As time moves on, some of the original assumptions fade away, while others gain strength, and new assumptions are added to the mix. In other words, an organization's basic assumptions tend to change over time, for organizations must change if they wish to survive.

A good example of massive change in assumptions is the current infatuation in America with total quality management (TQM). Companies that once stressed the value of rugged individualism, internal competition, and instant decision making now stress the team effort. For many companies and the individuals they employ, making this shift has been difficult and painful.

Underlying all assumptions are deeply held values that lead to the generation of assumptions. In order to understand an organization's culture, you must ferret out these values. In some cases, values and assumptions are actually in conflict.

The previous chapters demonstrated how an individual can alter his or her management style to be more effective within the organizational context. Sue Mack's case will integrate the concepts of management style, their influence on organizational culture, and how cognitive restructuring can alter the organization's perceptions and assumptions.

There are times when we find ourselves immersed in a corporate culture where we are the victims of our bosses and colleagues. Under these circumstances we would seem to have just two choices: leave or continue to suffer the abuses. But there is a third possibility: the powers that be may change their stance and work toward changing the culture. The impetus for change may come from within, or it may originate outside, for example, in the form of new federal regulations regarding minorities, women, age discrimination, and the handicapped.

In this chapter the focus will be on changing the culture. No individual can undertake this task by himself. In order for positive change to take place, all or most of the organization's members must be willing to make the commitment to change. Critical factors include understanding the management styles of the key participants, uncovering their assumptions and perceptions, and then moving on to change through cognitive restructuring. In addition, this case will illustrate how assumptions and perceptions about others can be erroneous and dysfunctional.

A Case Study of Barriers between Men and Women: Sue's History with V & L Design

Sue was director of marketing for V & L Design, a medium-sized software company specializing in educational software and other teaching materials. She had been hired six months earlier to head the marketing department. Her last job was as assistant marketing manager in a much larger software firm.

Sue was anticipating an exciting challenge in her new position, but problems developed the first week on the job. Charlie, the head of the division, outlined his desires for a new marketing effort in the briefest of terms, and then arranged for a meeting with her staff. The five members of the regional teams were all males and longtime close associates of Charlie, who had been their immediate boss before his elevation to president. Sue felt an intuitive apprehension about the meeting but withheld any comments. When she left Charlie's office, she silently kicked herself for not questioning his intentions about her role. After all, he was a highly respected software guru, and he had selected her for the job. Why, she asked herself, did she feel such uneasiness?

The meeting with her staff was dominated by Charlie, who silently controlled the agenda by means of nods and grimaces. Occasionally he would slip in a private joke with Jim or Harry. Sue felt like an outsider. Later, she found out that Charlie was in constant telephone contact with all five representatives. On one occasion he had a private meeting with them—without Sue—to discuss the status of the marketing efforts. This meeting was never discussed with Sue.

In spite of this awkward beginning, Sue plunged into her new job with vigor. She held weekly goal-setting meetings with her staff and tried to introduce a sense of vitality and mission to the group. Her previous company was extremely dynamic and aggressive in its approach to marketing. But the staff here merely nodded in faint agreement or used critical negatives to stifle the discussion of introducing new methods. She immediately sensed resentment of her style and ideas. Why did they resent her style? Was it because she was a female? All the reps were male and married. Were they too rigid and chauvinistic? Was Charlie secretly undermining her efforts? Was her momentum stopped by Charlie's hidden hand? Or was she a misfit in this rather conservative company?

No clear answers or rationalizations were forthcoming. In spite of these perplexing problems, she continued with her efforts.

The Cast of Characters

See Table 8–1, "V & L Management Styles," for an overview of each of the characters' management styles.

Sue (ENTP)

Sue came from an upper-middle-class family in the Midwest. She had received a traditional Catholic education from grammar school through high school. After high school she went to one of the Big Ten colleges, where she majored in English and education. She worked as an elementary school teacher for five years, but was bored by this job and entered the software industry in hopes of finding more exciting work.

This was a time when idea people ran the industry. New start-up companies were formed by "wunderkinder" who produced new and innovative products that swept the marketplace. Sue found her niche in the marketing department. She started as an assistant to the director. Her career began to flourish, and she was promoted to assistant marketing manager. After three years she decided to move on to a larger company. She held the same position but had more

TABLE 8-1

V & L Management Styles

MBTI	Sue ENTP	Charlie INTJ	John ENTJ	Peter ENTP
NEEDS				
Management Triad				
Achievement	High	High	High	High
Dominance	High	High	High	High
Affiliation	Low	Low	Low	Low
Bosses/Peers/Subordinate Relations				
Deference	High	Low	High	High
Autonomy	Low	Low	Low	High
Nurturance	Low	Low	Low	Low
Succorance	High	High	Low	High
Abasement	Moderate	Low	Low	Low
Task Factors				
Change	High	High	High	High
Order	Low	Low	Low	Low
Endurance	Low	Low	Low	Low
Intensity	High	High	Moderate	High
Interpersonal Modifiers				
Introspection	High	High	High	Moderate
Exhibition	Moderate	Moderate	Moderate	High
Aggression	Low	High	Low	High
POWER BASES				
1. Reward	High	Low	Low	Moderate
2. Coercive	Moderate	High	Low	High
3. Authority	Moderate	High	Low	High
4. Referent	Low	Low	High	Low
5. Expert	High	Low	High	Low
6. Information	High	Low	High	Low
7. Affiliative	Low	High	Low	High
8. Group	High	Low	Low	Low
Conflict Style	Yield-Lose	Contextual	Contextual	Contextual
Stress Type	Succorant	Autonomous	Accumulator	Succorant

responsibility and earned far more money. Three years later she was recruited by V & L to head the marketing department.

Sue is an extroverted intuitive type who constantly looks for innovative ways to resolve problems. Although she is deferential and supportive of others' ideas, she is obviously in charge. This paradoxical mix of behaviors perplexes some people, who see her vacillate from agreeing to controlling, although in a soft, nonjudgmental fashion. She exercises power in terms of demonstrating expertise and rewarding problem-solving attempts. Her serious drawback is that she caves in when conflict with her bosses becomes too heated. That she prefers to avoid confrontation compounds her problems with the male cabal at V & L Design.

Sue can be characterized as enterprising, outgoing, expansive, and at times unrestrained in her zeal for results. Like her boss, Charlie, she is task-driven and exercises her power needs through her expertise. Her zest is tempered by a respectful and fostering attitude that at times is mistaken for weakness. Paradoxically, Charlie sees her as pushy and overzealous. The real story is that she is driven by a very high achievement drive. This misperception by Charlie attests to the remarkable ability of people to read into behavior what they want to see and to overlook other facts. Charlie bases his perceptions on a set of assumptions that are driven by a female archetype that do not fit this case. Charlie sees Sue as a kind of Diana, the Roman goddess of the hunt; in his eyes she is a competitor and hard-core feminist.

In truth, compared to many feminists at the lower levels in the company, Sue is more tolerant of the male hierarchy. But since Charlie has virtually no contact with these women, he cannot distinguish between radical feminism and Sue's more moderate brand of feminism.

Extroverted intuitive types of people are normally enterprising, outgoing, expansive, and unrestrained. Their dark side manifests itself as exploitive, defiant, irresponsible, unstable, ruthless, and irritable behaviors. Sue's dark side is repressed because of her low tolerance for conflict. At times it seeps out in expansive but unrealistic plans. She becomes irritable and pouty when her enthusiasm is not shared by others. Then she thinks defiant thoughts and imagines revenge.

Charlie (INTJ)

Charlie is highly intuitive and introverted. He is very independent and self-absorbed, and at times he manifests an attitude of entitlement. He comes from a middle-class family with strict rules for conduct. He graduated from a small college in the East and went directly into teaching. Charlie was unable to attend graduate school because of his financial obligations. His lack of superior academic credentials still haunts him today, and he tends to pander to any academics he comes in contact with. Disenchanted with the low status of his teaching job and its small salary, he obtained a position in the sales department of a small start-up software company. With his obsessive work ethic, he quickly rose in the organization and soon became director of sales. The offer to join V & L Design was the opportunity that he was waiting for: a chance to play in the big leagues. After a short and productive interview, he accepted the position. Following a successful stint in sales, he became director of marketing and then finally the president of the division.

Charlie's management style includes a high need for power and task control. He habitually sets standards too high for others to reach and then does their work himself. He usurps authority that he delegated by intervening in projects where he doubts performance progress. He then gives little or no direct communication or feedback. Introverted intuitives operate as sensual and prophetic persons. They are the most independent of the psychological types. Charlie's introverted intuitive style makes him an enigma to most of his employees. What does Charlie really want? Because he puts barriers between himself and others, no one ever directly confronts or truly understands him.

In the past five years, his division has been the most profitable in the company. Because of his success in this area, he is untouchable. Charlie has a fear of self-disclosure and of others getting too close to him. In a clinical sense, he is an avoidant personality. These propensities contribute to a terribly flawed management style.

Charlie has a close working relationship with John, the CEO, and the financial officer of the company, who allows Charlie almost total reign of his division. Besides his divisional duties, he is executive vice-president of the company. These dual roles give him a large measure of authority and affiliative power, which he exercises to his advantage. The CEO is embroiled in personal problems, and so has ceded Charlie some of his responsibilities. In Charlie's eyes, this is an opportunity for increasing his power and authority, which plays into his personal needs and goals.

When under pressure, Charlie can be openly critical and bombastic, to the point of embarrassment to others. When he is possessed by his dark side, logic and contrary evidence have no meaning for him. He clings to his version of reality by compulsive nitpicking. His sense of self-entitlement is a defense against his feelings of inferiority engendered many years ago. He then retreats into his shell and chases after every irrational possibility in his unconscious. When the spell is over, he is his rational but condescending self again.

Charlie regards Peter, the director of development, who has the same authority and rank as Sue, as a prodigal son who can do no wrong. Certainly Peter is charming, but he is also mercurial and unpredictable. It is rumored that Peter has had some influence on Charlie's decision to "downsize" Sue. Peter plays the role of Cardinal Richelieu to Charlie's king of France with exquisite aplomb. He never criticizes in meetings, offering good cheer and a smiling face. Behind the scenes, however, he is ruthless and scheming. Charlie secretly envies Peter's charm and expansiveness. The envy has been transformed into a positive bond with Peter, who is his alter ego and his projected self.

John (ENTJ)

John, president and CEO of V & L Design, was brought up in an upper-middle-class family and attended an Ivy League college in New England. He is a patron of the arts and attends many social functions. He has an affinity for style and grace. *Impeccability* is the word that defines his persona. He is well mannered and gracious to all.

John is an extroverted thinker; the basic driving force of this type is to lead and give structure to whatever they do. His motivational drives, however, moderate the stereotypical pattern of this type. He has no autonomy need, is deferential, and is open to change. He uses referent and information power and underplays his overt authority. To many of his colleagues and subordinates, he is an easy but distant person to work with. His presence is felt by his subordinates but not openly imposed on them. The main weakness in his management style is his contextual style of managing conflict; he flits from one style to another depending on his moods, the severity of the conflict, and his relationship with the individual(s). He is a complex person.

On the surface, he is charming and low key. He has a smile for everyone and is perceived by most as a gentle father figure. Beneath the surface, however, he is a brooding, secretive, and single-minded person. He looks for confirmation of his decisions in closed meetings. Therefore, the surface calm is undermined by his insulated decision-making style. As a result, most subordinates are in the dark about major decisions.

Peter (ENTP)

Peter is director of development and, like Sue, reports directly to Charlie. Peter is a tall, thin, and very engaging person. Some women at V & L see him as Prince Charming; others think he is a male chauvinist. He recently divorced his first wife and married one of his staff assistants. Sue does not like Peter, although she has never expressed this feeling to Peter or to anyone else.

Like Sue, Peter is an extroverted intuitive type, but he uses his charm to manipulate people. Behind the gracious facade hides a heavy-handed authoritarian. The three managers who report to him are all women, and they complain that he is dictatorial and inconsistent in his treatment of them and their subordinates. Charlie sees none of this and brushes off the complaints as "typically female."

Peter will do anything to curry favor with Charlie. Since Charlie has a high need for affirmation, this seals the bond between them.

On paper Peter and Sue are at equivalent levels in V & L. However Peter has a behind-the-scenes, collusive relationship with Charlie. They frequently go to lunch together since V & L does not have dining facilities, which gives Peter more access to Charlie than Sue has.

The Corporate Culture at V & L Design

V & L Design is made up of a highly decentralized group of divisions that have a low degree of integration. A high degree of autonomy exists in each division, with a duplication of effort in areas where economies of scale could be achieved. No one wants to give up turf. "Why tamper with success?" is the company's catchphrase.

The upper-level decision-making process is concentrated in the hands of John, Charlie, and Peter. Other members of the organization are treated as hirelings who merely carry out orders. An undercurrent of resentment is directed toward this iron triangle of power by their subordinates. Group power is rarely used as a source for problem solving or of input to make decisions. The company atmosphere is best described as "paternalistic."

The middle managers are achievement-oriented and driven by power. Thus the fact that decision-making power is concentrated at the top, leaving them little room for initiative, creates frustration and alienation among them. Only when a problem demands special expertise does John or Charlie consult with other managers. Most of the time, the other managers are expected to carry out their functions in their isolated cocoons.

The organization never holds group meetings dealing with goals, roles, and procedures, and orders are directed downward without a clear rationale. Charlie likes to have one-on-one discussions with his staff and he thinks that he delegates authority, but most of the time he undermines the delegatee by going directly to people who are performing for the manager to whom Charlie gave the original directive.

The most serious flaw in V & L's collective culture is its style of handling conflict; conflict is attended to in private and hushed up in public. Conflict is not recognized as a source of power that can be used to promote wise decisions. Most of the upper and middle managers do not have a defined style of conflict management; they simply employ contextual or avoidance behaviors.

Conflict management is a real source of problems for this company. How can its managers address real conflicts when they are met with blanket avoidance or win–lose rebuttals? Problems exist at all levels of V & L Design, but upper management believes that its "divine guidance" is sufficient to take care of any situation.

There is a great similarity in the problem-solving styles at all levels of management. The vast majority of managers are intuitive-thinking types, just like John, Charlie, Peter, and Sue. The corporate culture is driven by this approach to problem solving. Ninety percent of the managers are thinking types, which results in impersonal, logical, and sometimes critical problem solving. The criticism is voiced mostly by members of disgruntled cabals. The power of these intuitive thinkers is diminished by the closed attitudes of the iron triangle. Direct confrontations are avoided, and behind-the-scenes sniping takes place. Leveling is not part of the culture.

Management Styles: A Comparison

There are no gender differences in management style at V & L. Rather, it is the structural problem within V & L's corporate culture of access to power and the assumptions and perceptions of key individuals that determine the outcome in Sue's case.

There are more commonalities among the four main characters than differences. Their temperament patterns as assessed by the MBTI are the same: they are intuitive thinking types. There is a striking similarity in their needs profile in terms of the Management Triad Needs. All three are high in achievement and dominance, and low in affiliation.

Their Task Factors Needs are identical: problem solving, control over the job, and approach to the task. They are essentially clones.

On the Interpersonal Modifier Needs, Sue and John are similar: high in introspection, moderate on exhibition, and low in aggression. Charlie and Peter too are alike: moderate in introspection, high in aggression, and moderate or high in exhibition.

On the Bosses/Peers/Subordinates Relations Needs, all are low on nurturance. Sue, Charlie, and Peter are all high on succorance, while John is low. All are low on autonomy except Peter, who is high. Charlie is low on deference while the rest are high. Sue is moderate on abasement and the others low. On the MBTI and the needs profiles Sue does not stand out as having a different management style from her male peers or superiors.

All four have different clusters of power bases. Charlie uses authority, affiliative, and discipline power bases, in keeping with a "captain of the ship" image. John, the CEO, uses information, expertise, and referent power. This fits his image of being a behind-the-scenes manager who tries to influence people with goodwill and competence. He rarely manages by "walking around." Sue uses information, expertise, reward, and group power. Although she maintains task control (high dominance and achievement), she tries positive ways to involve her staff in achieving objectives. Peter uses authority, discipline, and affiliative power. He is almost identical to Charlie on his use of power, except that Peter has more charm and finesse. Sue's biggest difference is her lose–leave conflict style. The others use contextual styles. This is a serious problem in that it impairs her ability to confront a conflict and resolve it in a collaborative manner.

Analysis

If we conclude that the V & L hierarchy does not involve conflict over dissimilar management styles, what is actually wrong? The core of the problem lies in the structural components of the company. Due to the assumptions of the three males who constitute the iron triangle an implicit and covert patriarchal system has developed at V & L. None of them consciously perceives that they are operating in this fashion. In fact they would protest that they bend over backward to foster female rights. After all, doesn't the company have more females than males? But their efforts to "bend over backward" were perceived as patronizing by the female recipients of their "noblesse oblige." One perceptive male reported that dominance and personal achievement were regarded as "strong management" in males and as "bitchiness" in females.

There is an absence of explicit psychological contracts between the ruling class and their subordinates. The two main forms of contracts are double-bind—which exists when one party verbally agrees to all tenets of the contract but actually expects something quite different (e.g., Charlie and Sue)—and collusive—which are created when two or more parties agree to compete or to thwart the efforts of particular individuals in the organization (e.g., Charlie and John). Charlie and John clearly demonstrate these behaviors. Behind the scenes, Peter played his collusive role with Charlie by supporting Charlie's false perceptions of Sue. The victim is Sue.

Top Management's Assumptions, Perceptions, and Feelings

V & L's top management must recognize the role of their assumptions and perceptions in creating the problem with Sue. They could learn much from cognitive restructuring. The most innovative techniques used in cognitive restructuring derive from perceptual shifting theory, which focuses on the participant's perceptions and the impact of these perceptions on relationships.

ASSUMPTIONS

All the characters in our scenario had various assumptions about what was right and what was wrong in the situation.

Sue was hired to be director of marketing. She thought that she was delegated the authority and responsibility to carry out this job, and felt that her competence would be rewarded. Teamwork, with collaborative problem solving, was the proper way to carry out her mission. She believed that her hiring as the most senior female in the organization was a good sign and that males under her authority would not be biased in their attitudes toward her.

Charlie assumed that he was not biased toward females and that he was an egalitarian manager. However, he was the sole arbiter of all major decisions. He thought he was a brilliant strategic planner. In his biased eyes, Sue was a failed promotion: the problem was her "style." He believed that women were capable "middle managers" and very good caretakers of the routine tasks in the company but not qualified by style to become part of top management. He considered a soft patriarchal approach appropriate (a subliminal assumption). He assumed that assertive power, the ability to act effectively in behalf of one's goals in interpersonal situations, is inappropriate in the culture.

John felt that Charlie was very competent and valued him as a trusting confidant. Charlie was making all the right decisions for the division, and there was no need to scrutinize his actions. He assumed that he and Charlie were the legitimate sources of power in the company and that they could steer a steady course. He assumed that maintaining a low profile was the appropriate management style in the organization. Challenging the control system was out of bounds. After hearing behind-the-scenes comments from Charlie, he assumed that Sue was a "failed promotion."

Peter assumed that he could influence Charlie and develop a higher power base in V & L than Sue. He was not comfortable with her being his equal on the organizational chart. He also assumed that through Charlie's relationship with John he had carte blanche to go on managing in his own way and that someday he would be Charlie's replacement.

Because all the principals were intuitives, their view of what was happening was colored by their unconscious interpretation of so-called facts.

Projection has a very serious distortion bias. We distort others by forcing them into our prescribed impressions formed by previous assumptions and perceptions. The person becomes a mirror that merely reflects *our* needs and *our* complexes. Sue was a victim of groupthink distortion by a circle of males who reinforced each other's preconceived convictions about women in management.

PERCEPTIONS

Sue felt that she was doing her job according to her expectations of what she perceived to be her psychological contract with Charlie. She perceived that the marketing department needed a new approach to capture a wider market and that Charlie had given her a mandate to introduce this new approach. She thought that her role as director gave her the necessary authority to carry out her role. She empathized with the other women in the company and hoped that she could serve as a positive role model and mentor for them. Sue felt somewhat uncomfortable with John's distant style of management. She sensed that the CEO gave Charlie too much latitude and too much power in running his division and influencing other divisions in the company.

Charlie selectively scanned Sue's behaviors to reinforce his preconceived conviction that she was too assertive, thus disturbing the comfortable family atmosphere of the company. He felt that Sue had intruded on his territory of strategic planning, and noted that she had trouble managing males. Charlie saw Peter as more competent than Sue and sensed that he had more rapport with Peter and could trust his judgments.

John felt that the company culture was just fine as is, and that Sue had rocked the boat. His perception was that Charlie's opinions were more valuable than Sue's. He perceived that everyone was aware of the big picture.

Peter perceived that Charlie controlled the decision-making process and "owned" John. Charlie's admiration for him allowed Peter to do his own thing without opposition from Charlie or John. Peter thought Sue was a misinformed female who was out of her element. He had a great sense of self-importance and presumed everyone around him loved and admired his flamboyant style and wit. He felt his subordinates were incompetent and needed his strong guidance on all matters.

FEELINGS

When Sue received Charlie's call her anxiety level rocketed. At the meeting it was clear to her that she was attending a sentencing rather than an open exchange of views. Sue felt betrayed by Charlie and John. After the meeting she experienced self-doubts and depression. Her lose–leave conflict style kicked into gear. A sense of resignation and hopelessness prevailed. She also had uneasy feelings about Peter's role in the matter. She felt that Charlie treated Peter as his surrogate son and overlooked all of his capricious behavior. After Sue left V & L and took a new job, she had bouts of depression and bitterness. It was during one of these bouts that she realized that she had been railroaded. After many anxious moments of vacillation she finally took positive action.

Charlie had feelings of self-righteous justification and moral superiority in that he had performed a necessary dirty job for the benefit of the organization. When the deed was done he was relieved of a burden. He dropped a quarter in the collection box and resumed business as usual. He also felt satisfaction because John and Peter had affirmed his perceptions and judgments.

John did not want to personally deal with the problem. At times he felt irritated when Charlie kept bringing it up. Out of a desire to rid himself of the extraneous problem he agreed with Charlie and sanctioned the infamous meeting. When the case was closed he felt relieved.

Peter had a feeling of exhilaration at having wielded behind-the-scenes power. To quote Henry Kissinger: "Power is the ultimate aphrodisiac." He felt self-satisfied and smug that he could do no wrong.

The Role of Power

Power has an organizational face as well as an individual one. Power structures are organizational aspects of relationships characterized by role patterns, hierarchies, and lines of authority. These structures can vary in the extent of the imbalance of authority, of the permeability of the hierarchical boundaries, of the effectiveness in accomplishing goals of the system, and of the consensual nature of the role arrangements. At V & L Design, the power structures were dictated by a small group of men.

Besides power structures, there are power processes that shape interactional behaviors in the presence of overt or covert conflict. Power processes can vary according to the nature of the attempts to deal with conflict: dominating attempts, reactive attempts, or collaborative attempts. At V & L Design, the power processes suppressed conflict. Conflict was managed behind the scenes, usually without the participation of the involved individuals. Sue was an excellent example of this form of power process. The decision to "downsize" Sue was made without explanation, and Sue was never really allowed to defend herself.

"Boundary-setting power" refers to the ability to contain, limit, or channel the influence of others in social situations. At V & L Design this kind of power was in the hands of the powerful trio. Women in the organization did not have assertive or boundary-setting power. Experts in organizational power argue that individuals need both power bases to be effective. This lack in the power-control area seriously hindered Sue and the other women managers at V & L Design.

This brings us to the issue of access to power. Access to power is determined by structural roles in the company. In a truly democratic organization, access to power is distributed to all members. When barriers are set up, access is limited to certain groups. At V & L Design access was controlled by John and Charlie. Inclusion in the system was reserved for the ruling class.

Planned Action

In order to change the structural problems in this company, the CEO and the presidents of all divisions must make a commitment to recognize the problems and take serious steps toward achieving progress. A battery of techniques will be necessary for cognitive restructuring of the organization's culture.

An off-site retreat could be arranged to set the tone of the problem-solving process, to help the participants, through intense, in-depth discussions, to gain a mutual understanding of the problems in their organization. The format for the retreat should be based on data collected from all the participants prior to it.

V & L Design had all the necessary data on perceptions, roles, and management style to launch a retreat. The following areas deserved high priority: (1) internal gender problems, (2) change (planning for it and implementing it), and (3) reaffirmation and maintenance of positive attitudes.

A retreat cannot accomplish instant change. It can, however, provide an encouraging climate and therefore an opportunity for identifying problems and moving toward finding good solutions. Nor can a retreat change the personalities of the participants, but it can provide the format for looking at differences intelligently and putting the diversity within the organization to good use. Behaviors *can* be changed. That there is a clear distinction between personality-focused interventions and behavior change should be stated at the outset of a retreat. The focus should be on mutual problem-solving efforts, not on negative emotional judgments.

The V & L retreat should have four objectives. The first is to understand the organizational climate at V & L. This can be presented as data in summary form collected in various interviews, assessments, and questionnaires. Open discussion of the results must be permitted and sanctioned. The gender issue and access to power can be addressed at this time.

The second objective is to understand the management style of the upper and middle managers. This understanding can lead to the avoidance of many interpersonal conflicts that exist at the moment. It is *not* to be used to challenge who is right and who is wrong.

A full discussion of the implications of the management style of both individuals and the modal organization is appropriate. V & L Design has many strengths in this area, and these should be reinforced. The conflicts are the result of reactive behavior because people are not trained to understand the critical variables of management style. Sue, Charlie, John, and Peter should recognize their many similarities. This could dispel the false perception that there is a personality clash.

The third objective is to introduce the concept of force-field analysis, derived from physics: a body is at rest when the sum of all the forces operating on it is at zero, and a body will move in a direction determined by the unbalancing forces. This concept can be applied to situations involving human factors. In any case, there are forces working against and for change. Research has demonstrated that organizations can stagnate as a result of the interplay of these forces. It is necessary to identify damaging forces and why they thrive so as to maintain their pathological status in the organization. For example, what are the forces working against the inclusion of women in the decision-making process at V & L Design?

Some hypotheses regarding forces against including women in upper-level decision making might be:

- Top management undervalues the capabilities of women.
- Men enjoy a comfortable situation vis-à-vis women, and fear loss of power.
- The "us-versus-them" syndrome—men and women are engaged in an eternal struggle.
- Top management is complacent due to past successes.

But there are also forces at work pushing the organization—despite the power of John, Charlie, and Peter—to include women at the highest levels of decision making. These forces include:

- Pressure from the parent company to promote women to positions of higher responsibility.
- Pressure from women in the middle ranks of the organization for access to power and decision making.
- The assumed egalitarian values of John, the CEO.
- Successful performance by the multitude of women in the company.

The fourth objective is to use selected cognitive restructuring techniques to turn the organizational climate around. A primary diagnosis of V & L Design is that it suffers from a set of preconceived assumptions and perceptions that gave rise to the scenario presented at the beginning of the chapter. Understanding organizational culture and its management style is an initial step in setting the stage for more profound changes at the structural level. Cognitive restructuring has the goal of capturing the thoughts that are embedded in the organization that cause dysfunctional behavior and then developing counterbeliefs or counterperceptions to correct the original false assumptions with the aid of new, more productive thoughts. The following steps, orchestrated so that they form a gestalt, need to be integrated into the problem-solving atmosphere:

1. Review the retreat format and its goals and objectives.
2. Review the organizational diagnosis.
3. Discuss management style.
4. Review force-field analysis.
5. Implement cognitive restructuring techniques—both perceptual and philosophical shifting.
6. Develop psychological contracts and role negotiations.
7. Develop effective conflict management techniques.
8. Prepare synthesis and action plans for the future.

In order to promote equal access to power and build a true meritocracy, the participants must address the gender problem. Band-Aid attempts, such as isolated management training, will not resolve a corporate culture problem. In order for change to take place, commitment must be attained at all levels. This can be very painful for people like Charlie, John, and Peter who are ensconced in power and have lived a sheltered, unchallenged existence for most of their careers. They have been allowed to operate on a virtually autonomous basis. They were relatively successful in an expanding economy and had no reason to question their assumptions and perceptions. But societal pressures in the last decade have made demands on organizations to rethink their philosophies concerning women and minorities, but the results have been *under*whelming.

Epilogue

Sue accepted her demotion to manager of advertising production and moved to the South. After six months she was fired by one of her former subordinates, a close friend of Charlie, who assumed her original job as director of marketing. After considerable procrastination, she hired a lawyer, instituted a suit, and finally settled out of court with V & L Design.

The chairman of the board of the parent company of V & L was replaced by a hard-nosed ENTJ engineer noted for his micromanagement. He immediately started to scrutinize the goals and performance of all the satellite companies under his domain. V & L was a primary target. Peter, the alter ego of Charlie, was fired. John, the CEO, came under great pressure from the new chairman of the board, and autonomy was wrested from his hands. Charlie's division suffered setbacks due to the faltering economy, and he no longer had the freedom to dictate as he did before.

The idea of holding a retreat was abandoned, and the company remains under siege from the parent company to this day.

Sue eventually obtained a high-level job with a publishing firm in New York and now works in a corporate environment where women are valued equally with men.

9

Cases

What We Have Learned

The cases that follow explore different approaches to under-standing and modifying management style. All of the people in these vignettes, based on real situations, use some of the techniques discussed in the previous chapters. Each case is a *personal statement by the individual* about his or her approach to understanding and changing management style. This final chapter is presented to the reader so that he or she can identify with and learn from others the various processes that can be employed to understand and change one's management style.

Case 1, Sarah: The Sherman Tank

Sarah, an ENTJ, described herself as a take-charge person in both her professional and personal lives. An extroverted thinker, she im-pacted on those around her by using her dominant thinking func-tion. At work, she had a strong urge to create structure by defining policy rather than accepting established regulations and proce-dures—the result of her NT orientation. Her undeveloped feeling function caused problems when others did not see things her way. With a strong will toward power, she ignored input from peers and subordinates. She acted like a Sherman Tank in her quest for power and upward mobility. Fortunately, in her personal life she had found a soulmate who was an opposite type; he had a strong feel-ing function in contrast to her weak one.

After many months of self-analysis and guided training in a self-awareness group, Sarah reached a number of conclusions about herself. She realized that she was too abrupt with her fellow workers and failed to factor in *their* needs. Finally recognizing that she needed to develop the inferior function of feeling, she started a program of using the active imagination to develop her empathy for others, for example, by conducting internal dialogues with others and reversing roles in this exercise. One of her other tasks was to pay a long-overdue visit to her mother to talk about their relationship: past, present, and future.

She much preferred searching for possibilities rather than dwelling on details and facts. To handle this problem she needed to back off from the excitement of inventing possibilities and alternatives and focus on fact gathering. As an intervention, she devised a checklist for fact gathering that structured her approach and strengthened her tertiary function of sensing.

She became aware that she needed to accept the reality that people have different temperaments, needs, and so on, and to learn how to use their strengths in conjunction with her own. Prior to her self-analysis, she barely tolerated these differences, seeing them as an impediment to her struggle for ascendancy.

Having a high need for personal achievement placed a burden of stress on her: "My need to lead at a young age was obviously brought on by my parents, who provided me with opportunities to take charge. However, now that I am older and the creator of my own opportunities, I feel overburdened by thoughts of not being an important enough leader. I am not satisfied with just being a unit manager and strive to become a section manager or a project leader."

"I'm devoted to my job, 'living to work' rather than 'working to enjoy life,' which is unhealthy for anyone and results in an unhappy or burned-out manager." Sarah decided to write a personal mission statement that would include realistic goals and timetables that would moderate her obsession with achieving promotions.

She noted that as a female ENTJ she was fortunate to find a male who is not overwhelmed by her strong personality and will. But she admits that there have been some trying times in their ten-year relationship: "I am now aware of what is accepted and not accepted in my personality type by my mate. I believe it is necessary to build a relationship over time, to be patient, and not allow my strong personality traits to explode all at once." Sarah is now seeking individuation through her interaction with a significant other. The goal of individuation is completeness and wholeness, achieved through working with one's self and others. She developed four rules for her search for individuation:

- To be more accepting of herself.
- To be more accepting of individual differences.
- To develop personal strategies for conflict resolution.
- To be able to work collaboratively in an organization or a social system.

Case 2, Ruth: Ms. Know-It-All

Ruth is fifty-five years old. She was the eldest daughter in an Irish Catholic family of eleven children. She started working as her mother's "gofer" at the tender age of two. She baby sat within the family from an early age, and was baby sitting for pay outside the family by age nine. Ruth thought that her parents, and especially her mother, had taken advantage of her, but also felt a degree of pride in knowing that she had lived up to their expectations.

Ruth became a registered nurse and worked as a nurse for twenty-five years. Then she returned to school and earned her bachelor's degree. She started a new career in the public service area and became a deputy director in her agency.

Ruth describes herself as a keen observer of details; indeed, her colleagues are impressed by her phenomenal capacity to remember facts and contexts from the past. She is an ISTJ, and like people of that type she likes to plan things in advance, to the point of ruminating over each step in a process. But she finds this approach stressful and wearing on her energy level.

There is an essential paradox to Ruth's makeup: people regard her as standoffish, but she scores very high in affiliation. In other words, Ruth likes to be with people but has trouble communicating this part of her personality. In spite of having a high need for affiliation, Ruth is socially inept. She does not make friends easily and rarely socializes in settings outside work. Ruth is also extremely high in the need for achievement and dominance. These drives help her overcome any anxiety promoted by her role at the forefront of public and political activities at work. She confesses that coping with anxiety requires a conscious effort on her part. She always feels exhausted after she performs—a likely outcome for a highly introverted type. Ruth has a highly introspective side, a personality facet that balances her introverted sensing nature. She can go beyond just the facts and look for reasons, rationales, and motives, but she can also become obsessive in this regard.

Ruth discovered that she gives more feedback than she receives, with both bosses and subordinates. Her need for control is manifested in this one-sided communication style. She concluded that this imbalance impaired her relationships with her colleagues and required drastic intervention. Ruth finally recognized that she is not the perfect boss or colleague that she had perceived herself to be: "The trouble starts from my being a lazy and poor communicator. I listen well enough. I show interest in what others have to say. I take in information and absorb details, tucking them away in my computer-like brain to retrieve and deliver when opportune. I use information to gain control—to dominate a situation—and I am quite adept at this." This pattern of control carried over into her family life, where her children questioned her know-it-all attitude. Before her personal insight, she was often offended by their lack of deference. Now she concedes that they have a valid point.

Ruth clearly presents a complex profile of thoughts and behaviors, with paradoxes and internal inconsistencies, and feels the push and pull of these forces. She has achieved a number of insights about herself:

- She is a highly autonomous yet affiliative person, with a high need for control over tasks at work and at home.
- Her introversion intensifies an unbalanced communication style.
- Her introspection is her salvation. It drives her to analyze herself and move toward positive change.
- Her needs for achievement and dominance have made her into a driven person.
- Stress is caused by her internal contradictions.
- Her individuation is stunted by her ego needs. She needs to develop a sense of wholeness and completeness.

Using this self-knowledge, she devised the following plan for personal intervention:

1. Gain control over internal stress using a program of meditation and muscle relaxation.
2. Attend to the self-destructive thoughts that are exacerbated by highly ruminative introspection through cognitive restructuring.
3. Enroll in a communications workshop to develop a balanced style.
4. Develop a five-year action plan to address her future career.
5. Make nondirected play part of her daily life. Ruth had spent her childhood and youth working, and did not know how to play. Two books were recommended to aid in this restructuring of her activity: *Playing and Reality*, by D. W. Winnicott, and *Flow: The Psychology of Optimal Experience*, by Mihaly Csikzentmihaly.

Case 3, John: A Wild and Crazy Guy

John is mercurial and spontaneous, a "wild and crazy" guy with interests that range from horse racing to computer applications in photography. He is easily bored with details. His personal computer has told him so by means of repeated error messages. "I never pay attention to the slash marks or the exact file name," he admits. He states that his boredom with routine, coupled with his high need for change, is a troublesome combination. John tries to make his department, a media service laboratory, a happy place. His low need for dominance and his high affiliation and achievement needs combine to make him a strongly participatory manager. John is very good at delegation. On the other hand, he has projects that he disdains, and they never seem to get done. He describes himself as a person of the moment. John is an ENFP.

He took over a floundering department and gave it new vitality. Although he is a team builder, he has strict rules for conduct in the department. He is not always a freewheeling ENFP type. Although low in dominance, he uses the authority and coercive powers to enforce his rules. These power bases, coupled with his feeling function, make John a very opinionated manager: he expects his subordinates to see things his way. Some time ago John had a problem with a difficult employee who was constantly late. John got to the point where he was on the verge of personal retaliation. John has a very high need for aggression, and something of the trickster archetype in him. He can be seriously funny or cruelly vindictive. His task is to find the middle ground between these polarities.

The constantly tardy person had hooked John on his feeling function, and he employed coercive power by suspending her for a day. The employee retaliated by thereafter coming to work precisely on time, but then fiddling around for fifteen minutes before getting to work. Again this behavior hooked John. Enrollment in a conflict resolution workshop helped him to learn how to resolve these kinds of problems in a rational manner. Now he never lets the difficult worker see him perspire. He has gained control over his feeling function.

One of John's misperceptions was that he was a nurturing person. His personal assessment score said otherwise, as did his wife: "No, John, you are not a nurturing person." John had fallen prey to a common myth about the feeling function, that feeling types are caring of others. This is not always true, for it is their value system that is the determining cause for their actions.

John wrote a list of his problems as a manager:

- I am self-critical (personal value system and F).
- I misinterpret events (the influence of N).
- I focus on self-serving data (feeling evaluation).
- High intensity causes muscle tension (extroversion).
- I get bored quickly (high need for change and low endurance).
- I find it hard to support others' ideas.
- I endow authority figures with more power than they actually possess.
- I am too deferential due to my Italian-Catholic background.
- I find it hard to work in institutions with constraints (a paradox given his use of the authority and coercive powers).
- I easily become impatient with other people (need for aggression and F).
- I have difficulty with follow-through and with details (N and need for change).
- I require diverse activities during the day (need for change).

These personality problems are balanced by his positive attributes:

- I am excited by life and all its possibilities (his dominant intuitive function).

- I strive for authenticity (combination of intuition and feeling).
- I have a good sense of humor (extroverted intuition).
- I remain optimistic (extroverted intuition).
- I am good at getting people together (affiliation and low dominance).
- I enjoy designing new ways of doing things (extroverted intuition).
- I am attracted to the arts (highly developed feeling function).
- I am a keen and penetrating observer (intuition and introspection).

John is torn between polarities that need to be integrated. He has finally recognized that he is too polarized and he has decided to use a blend of cognitive restructuring techniques to modify his management style. He has targeted the following flaws in his style for change:

- He is too self-critical (personal value system and F).
- He misinterprets events (the influence of N) and has difficulty with follow-through and details (N and need for change). He gets bored quickly (high need for change and low endurance). He becomes impatient with people (need for aggression and F).
- He focuses on self-serving data (feeling evaluation) and finds it hard to support others' ideas. On the other hand, he endows authority figures with more power than they actually possess. Paradoxically, he finds it hard to work in institutions with constraints.
- His high intensity level causes muscle tension (extroversion), and he requires diverse activities during the day (need for change).

The first step in modifying his management style was developing a cognitive approach to self-criticism. John wrote out some of the self-talk that reinforced his negative behavior:

1. "As a manager, I must take ultimate responsibility."
2. "Sometimes I fail to meet my expectations."
3. "I can't look weak as the boss."
4. "Men can't show their emotions. I bottle them up."
5. "I lose my temper, and then I berate myself."

Then he developed counters to these self-critical beliefs:

1. "If I train my staff properly, I can delegate but still maintain responsibility."

2. "Let's assess what goals and objectives are really important and act on them. I have too many high expectations of myself and others."
3. "By using self-disclosure, I can build a bond with other people. Admitting a weakness proves to others I am human."
4. "Overcontrol of my emotions leads to tension headaches."
5. "I can practice assertive communications without blowing up."

Because his extroverted intuition sometimes clouds his perception of what is taking place, John decided he would fine-tune his neglected five senses (his inferior sensing function). He started to keep a journal of his staff meetings and his encounters with subordinates. He then shared these notes on his perceptions with his staff and asked them if they agreed. After a number of discussions, he found that he was able to focus more on the here and now and not jump to unfounded conclusions. Also, he became more focused and less impatient in his decision making.

Next, he focused on self-serving data (feeling evaluation). John, like most other feeling types, has a deeply rooted value system that guides his behavior toward others. He was asked to respond to a set of questions that drove his hidden values to the surface:

Questions: Which do you prefer?   *Answers*

Respect or popularity?	Respect
Security or independence?	Independence
Wealth or independence?	Independence
Friends or wealth?	Wealth
Health or wealth?	Health
Friends or independence?	Independence
Security or creativity?	Creativity
Popularity or being the boss?	Being the boss
Family or friends?	Family
Achievement or respect?	Achievement

It is clear that John values independence and control more than being friendly or secure. Once he was aware of his hierarchy of values, he was able to exert some control over them before he alienated his subordinates. His value system explains why he finds it hard to adhere to institutional rules. On the other hand, he demands respect from others and gives it to his superiors.

Finally, because he felt that his high intensity caused muscle tension (extroversion), he decided to take time each day to practice relaxation through meditation.

Case 4, Jane: The Superexpert

Jane is forty-six years old. She admits that she has reached the stage where "I no longer yearn to be like others and I am ready to reformulate my self-identity. Now I am ready to take the conscious step of affirming what I find personally relevant and discarding behavior patterns that have proved self-defeating."

Jane had enrolled in an intensive workshop, "You as the Interventionist and Your Impact on Others." The goals of the workshop were to focus on the strengths and weaknesses of each individual and to map out areas for self-development.

Jane was an INFJ. She was surprised to discover that she was a feeling type because she had always thought of herself as a logical, analytical type. This is sometimes the case when individuals mistake the feeling function for proficiency in interpersonal relationships rather than a preference for making judgments from a personal-value orientation. Interpersonal skills and the feeling function are two different animals. We develop interpersonal skills through experience and training, but the feeling function is part of the temperament that we bring into the world.

Jane accurately describes how her own experience with the socialization process led to functional or dysfunctional interpersonal skill development: "My socialization in my family, and at this time and place in history, duped me into seeking rewards and satisfaction from outward achievements rather than from the enjoyment of harmonious relationships."

Jane was not proficient in interpersonal skills; her needs profile showed the need to achieve coupled with a very low score on affiliation, high needs for succorance and exhibition, and a low score for deference. This needs profile, in combination with her INFJ type, suggests a "difficult person" complex. One could almost label her a dependent personality with secondary overtones of passive aggressiveness. No wonder she had the feeling that she did not fit in. Jane says: "The need for achievement combined with a tendency to be hyperresponsible led me to pursue task accomplishment as my pathway to competency. I have always implicitly assumed that achievement would bring with it the rewards of recognition and acceptance [this false set of assumptions is based on early socialization; the world does not operate that way]. However, I believe now that by not expressing a need for affiliation and by not recognizing other people's needs, I have cut myself off from the rewards of warm and enduring interpersonal relations."

The effective use of power was another area of weakness in Jane's style. Her main power bases were information and authority power, making her somewhat of a superexpert. She admitted that she had great difficulties in delegating work.

As these insights settled in, Jane took the next steps toward achieving integration and individuation. First, she worked at improving her communication skills. Jane appropriately labeled her communication patterns: she was mostly a Distracter. She would placate, blame, and be a computer all at the same time—a combination that confused others. Jane had difficulty making direct statements. In order to rectify these liabilities she decided to follow a program of interpersonal process recall, which consists of four verbal response modes: the exploratory mode, the listening mode, the affective mode, and the honest labeling mode.

Exploratory responses are open-ended questions or statements. They encourage elaboration and help Jane (or anyone) stay involved in communicating while allowing her freedom to respond. Exploratory responses encourage her to become an active participant in the interaction rather than a passive recipient of advice.

Listening responses clarify and paraphrase what the other speaker has said. Used effectively, they communicate to the speaker the listener's active and deliberate desire to hear and to show genuine interest. Paraphrasing enables the listener to reflect back the content of what she has heard. A listener statement such as "What I hear you saying is. . . . Am I hearing you right?" strengthens the probability that speaker and listener understand one another. Paraphrasing provides feedback cues for both parties in the communication loop. The focus should be on hearing the other person and avoiding interpretive, authoritative responses—a real problem for INFJs.

Affective responses focus on the feeling quality, the bodily states, and the moods conveyed verbally and nonverbally in the message. The purpose of becoming more aware of affective responses is to help the speaker/listener get in touch with her feelings, underlying attitudes, gut reactions, and values—an area Jane has trouble with.

Affective responses are sometimes vaguely understood and are consequently puzzling or even frightening. Jane was asked to practice this mode on herself and to explore the affective responses of the other person by asking such questions as: "How does this make you feel?" or "I noticed you looked away from me and your voice trailed off. Can you explain why?" In the past, Jane made only internal judgments about the feeling states of those she interacted with and never checked out the accuracy of her judgments by questioning the other person.

Honest labeling responses are direct without being brutal or rejecting. Their purpose is to encourage a dialogue that contains content and feeling, which may be difficult to disclose. Such responses communicate a willingness to deal with what was heard and encourage people like Jane to deal directly with this in order to confront her perceptions, attitudes, and values, and those of the other person.

Jane decided to review these techniques with her husband. They would then role-play and critique their interaction after each session. The goal was to develop direct communication.

Jane also resolved to enroll in an executive Outward Bound program. She recognized that she was a passive observer rather than an active participant in the events of her life. She felt that by completing this program, she would gain greater self-confidence and the poise to become an active participant.

Jane decided to build on interdependence rather than relying on her autonomy and individual achievement needs; this was a major paradigm shift for her. This new perceptual shift would build on her previous desires to develop effective communications and self-confidence. She realized that her extreme autonomy and self-reliance was a defense against being intimate and collaborative with others.

Case 5, Bruce: A Square Peg in a Round Hole

Bruce is a senior partner in a moderate-sized law firm. He has duties in the commercial, acquisition, and divestitures areas, with some litigation in family business conflicts. He is an ENFJ and wonders: "Is an ENFJ lawyer a square peg in a round hole? The feeling function operates from an individual value orientation rather than from an articulated, principled, and objective logical system. Our perception of the legal system is that it should involve the application of consistent, intelligible legal principles to the client's case. One would think that an ENTJ or an ESTJ would be much better suited to perform these basic tasks of lawyering."

Bruce is not dissatisfied; he just operates differently from his colleagues, an insight that proved to start a cathartic process for Bruce. He decided to examine the areas where he could make unique contributions; rather than change professions, he decided to look for the challenges that might enhance his performance. He felt that examining his strengths and weaknesses within the culture would be a positive step toward achieving self-integration.

He identified some trouble spots, such as high needs for autonomy and succorance. Bruce noted that a law firm operates on the principle of teamwork for beginning lawyers and autonomy for senior partners, with true autonomy achieved only by department heads. However, Bruce was very affiliative, which balanced his autonomous needs. He recognized that he could build a team with his affiliation needs. The mere recognition of these potential pitfalls was a step in the right direction.

His use of power was appropriate to the task: he relied on expert and information powers. Another favorable factor was his high introspection need, clearly reflected in his ability to dissect his own personality and then analyze his best fit within the firm's requirements.

Bruce was acutely aware that the substructure of a law firm could benefit from his strengths. As a partner in the firm, he had access to personnel resources, such as paralegals, that could carry out the laborious tasks that his NF type with its high need for change disdained, and he was astute in cultivating a cooperative relationship without being manipulative. He, unlike many other feeling types, was good at delegation and team building. On the other hand, he was alert to the pitfalls of excessive or unstructured delegation. In essence, he was going to become the manager of resources in his law firm.

He pinpointed a number of areas of potential conflict in the policy area of the firm. One was the type of pro bono work it did. Bruce wanted to extend the pro bono work to disempowered people and work on civil as well as charity cases. This desire reflected his NF style. It was met, naturally, with some resistance. In spite of the initial response, he was able to expand the range of the firm's pro bono work to include citywide art projects, public housing projects, and minority rights. He did this by avoiding a frontal assault on prior policy while emphasizing society's need for business lawyers as well as trial lawyers to do pro bono work for the disadvantaged.

He also wanted to institute change in hiring procedures, but in this area he failed. Bruce felt that the sole emphasis on law school grades was inadequate. The thinking types objected, and he eventually realized that it was fruitless to pursue this goal.

Bruce reflected on his experience as an NF in an ST and NT environment: "Understanding my constellation of styles helps me understand why my approach has often been completely different from that of the majority of my colleagues. This understanding has reduced my frustration level. In addition, it has made me more careful to ensure that quality control procedures are always in place when delegating work. Finally, in dealing with my partners on issues of administration, I take care to offer a more elaborate presentation than I would choose for myself. I set out the background and context, summarize the reasons for and against a proposition, and generally present the matter in a more formal and reasoned manner than I would otherwise do." Bruce has it together. He has recognized that differences can be managed.

Bruce already recognizes that his psychological type is not found in most law firms. His intuitive feeling functions give him the ability to foresee the results of his and his partners' decisions on others. There are times, however, when he must rotate that dominant feeling function and operate out of impersonal thinking. He also realizes that as an intuitive type he needs to explain his plans and strategies in detail. Since Bruce is highly introspective, he is able to anticipate problems in advance and plan his strategy. Bruce tries to achieve completeness and wholeness by reflecting on who he is and what needs temporary adjustment integration.

Case 6, Mark: The Enforcer

Mark has been an effective manager because he helps his subordinates reach their goals and objectives. He notes: "My management style has always been hands-on. I like to be involved in the whole process through active participation, developing motivation, and setting examples. I usually show subordinates how things need to be done, what I expect from them, and what they can expect of me. I feel good as a manager when I have control over the outcome and reach the goals." This statement of Mark's management philosophy reflects his extroverted thinking style, his need patterns, and his use of the power bases. He is an ESTJ.

Mark has high needs for achievement and dominance, which have led to many successes. For example, senior management always counts on him to handle stressful and difficult jobs. Indeed, he has earned the nickname "The Enforcer" because he has accepted many jobs for the firm that nobody else wanted to deal with and always achieves a successful outcome.

Mark believes that the ultimate responsibility for the task is his. He views his subordinates as tools to accomplish jobs and does not fraternize with them; he has a low affiliation need. He owns up to not sharing authority or responsibility with others, and, as a result, teamwork is not a strong point for him. He does not want to get attached to or friendly with subordinates because he thinks they will take advantage of the friendship.

Mark realizes there should be a balance within the combination of dominance, achievement, and affiliation. He needs to improve his participation and cooperation, and also to solicit the opinions and expertise of the group rather than imposing his will. He has discovered that he is not as friendly and communicative as he had thought. He usually goes straight to the point without any warmup, a characteristic of the extroverted thinking type.

Mark's high need for autonomy and his low need for deference can get him into conflicts with other managers and vice-presidents in the company. He realizes that the combination of high autonomy, dominance, and achievement needs is an explosive one: "I have been involved in many projects where I personally assumed responsibilities, risks, decision making, stress, and pressure because I did not delegate authority or responsibility to others. Also, I do not care for teamwork or interaction with others." All of these behaviors are reflected in his low deference, nurturance, succorance, and abasement needs.

Mark has made several mistakes dealing with subordinates. He openly criticized their performance. In addition, he vented his anger at top management when they did not implement an approved marketing campaign; he accused them of not having vision

and wasting resources. He weathered the storm but has since realized that an extroverted thinking type with high aggressiveness is a
potential loose cannon. As for task factors, Mark sticks to the job
and does it in procedurally correct fashion. On the other hand, he
demands the same attitude from others, another sign of his need to
be in absolute control.

Mark's power bases are totally in concordance with his behavior
as a manager. He states: "I try to know all the information about
rules, procedures, facts, channels of communication, and public relations with other departments." He said that in the past he
thought that use of reward power only spoiled the subordinate, and
the use of authority and coercive power ensured proper adherence
to roles and responsibility. In addition, networking (referent power)
was not one of his strong suits. It is not surprising that he did not
use group power in order to solve problems.

Mark is now searching for balance: "I need to get a balance between my dominant thinking function (thinking) and my inferior
side (feeling). I need to assess the impact of actions on others before I carry them out in both my work and my personal life. In
other words, I need to learn how to cry. I was only remotely aware
of how I came across to people. I believed that my extreme task
orientation and successes were more than sufficient to being a
whole person."

Mark goes on: "My main weakness is a low interpersonal relationship with my subordinates and with other managers. There are
steps to improve my boss–subordinate relationships. First, I should
let my subordinates and other managers share responsibility with
me for decisions that affect them. I must challenge my assumptions
about how people are motivated [a perceptual shift]. I do not need
all the weight on my shoulders. Second, I should be more friendly
and forward with subordinates [to address his low nurturance and
deference needs, and his high use of coercive power]. I need to
learn how to say 'No' without offending people. In the past I
cloaked myself in a cold and impersonal facade. Third, I need to
use techniques for developing group power and teamwork.

"I never felt a great need to build networks or to use referent
power. I now realize that these are essentials for an effective manager. My goal is to build more productive positive power bases for
the future.

"My aggressive attitude to subordinates and other people needs to be changed. I need to organize my ideas and thoughts before saying anything [learn to control his extroverted thinking]. I can be honest and direct without being a tyrant. I need to control my Sherman Tank tendencies. My need for control is extremely high and not in my best interest.

"All my negative traits reinforce my ESTJ style. I'm almost a caricature of the type! My high need for introspection has allowed me to make these brutal but necessary assessments and plans for change. The most important achievement is know yourself before trying to know others. I can change myself and as a result influence others."

Case 7, Charlie: The Task Machine

In trying to develop a long-term strategy to improve his management style and compensate for its liabilities, Charlie determined to accentuate the positive and mitigate the negatives.

Like any other strategy designed to upgrade or improve, it seems reasonable to assume that the first step should be to identify and place appropriate emphasis on existing strengths. Charlie identified the following characteristics of his INTJ type:

Creativity. One of the most positive sides of the INTJ type is in the area of response to challenges that require imagination and creativity. INTJs thrive on tasks that push their creative capabilities to the edge. Charlie realizes this and will stay in the same job area: market research. Charlie has been successful in meeting most of the challenges of his career, and he thoroughly enjoys his work. As a result of his soul searching, he now understands why. In this regard the feedback and self-analysis has proved to be a validation of his job choice.

Strategic thinking. As an INTJ, Charlie has strength in the areas of generalizing, classifying, summarizing, and intuiting when problem solving. He has been able to use the strong external thinking function (his auxiliary function) in concert with his internal intuitive function (his dominant function). These are complemented by a high need for achievement and change that allows him to visualize and articulate many different scenarios and alternative solutions.

Charlie realizes that he must use these more in the context of team-work and group interactions.

Need for achievement. Charlie has a very high need for achievement. At times this can be a liability since he is also high in the needs for dominance and aggression and low in the need for deference. However, Charlie still sees the achievement need as his main driving force. In the future, he will be mindful of the consequences of unchecked pursuit of self-serving achievement.

It is apparent to Charlie as a result of solicited feedback (he remarked that this was a tough task for him) from fellow workers and friends that the interactive combination of high achievement, dominance, exhibition, aggression, and change linked with low needs for affiliation, deference, and nurturance can cause interpersonal problems for those who live or work with him. Although he is successful on the task level, he can be abrasive on the people level. He now recognizes that to ensure his future advancement, he has to work on changing these needs. His self-prescription was to look at his fusion, crossover, and MBTI interactions and to use the cognitive restructuring methods outlined in Chapter 2.

Charlie took a unique and valuable approach to psychological type: he looked at the characteristics of his opposite type, the ESFP. He assumed that if he could identify and isolate the positive aspects and strengths of the ESFP, he could incorporate them in his own behavior. He called this the "opposite type reverse attribute" approach. I think this is a clever and very useful procedure.

In isolating the polarities between the INTJ and ESFP, he found that the ESFP tends to be witty, charming, open to the surroundings, and generally fun to be with. The opposite INTJ tends to be reserved, standoffish, intense, and less-than-exciting company. His personal experience confirmed this assessment and led him to conclude that he needs to make an effort to become more socially at ease. In addition to concentrating more externally and focusing on the other person, he thought that a course in effective listening would help.

Where ESFPs tend to be empathetic, naturally friendly, and tactful, INTJs will be less caring, more aloof, and more direct and blunt. Charlie's feedback verified these perceptions. He stated that his high sense of urgency always got the better of him; he never had time to chat or spend significant time with subordinates or peers. He stated that they felt that he did not like or care about them. This perception on their part was strengthened by his tendency to get right to the point and ignore their input. To deal with this problem, he decided to practice relaxation techniques and to become less time-urgent.

Charlie was inclined to measure his daily performance by how much he got done. He maintained a comprehensive project/time management system that included a to-do list. He admits that he was overly compulsive in this regard. He tended to "work the list" rather than prioritize and "list the work" based on importance. He became a slave to his project/management schema and neglected building strong interpersonal relationships. His use of referent and group power was very low. He concluded that he must become the master and not the slave to any system.

An ESFP will focus on people and things, gather information, and focus on the present; an INTJ will focus on ideas and concepts, intuit the "facts," and focus on the future. The ESFP is aware of people and is a good communicator. The INTJ's focus on internal concepts ignores external communications. The INTJ carries on a lot of internal dialogue but rarely reveals it to others.

Charlie has suffered great frustration because of these propensities. People reacted to him like a "task machine" who could do his job well but who related to coworkers like Mister Spock on "Star Trek." He was aware of the negative consequences of his coworkers' attitudes, but lacked the understanding that he now possesses. The problem was that he had overdeveloped his ability to conceptualize an idea, focus on it, and forecast the future consequences—behavior that stood him in high regard with a boss who reinforced these tendencies. His frustration was his inability to control these "skills." He stated that at times he seemed to be on "autopilot"; he was not captain of his own ship.

Charlie is using cognitive restructuring techniques to reassess his self-talk and to write new scripts for himself.

Case 8, Jerry: I Do It My Way

Jerry works as a manufacturing program manager and has to interact with a variety of psychological types: a goal- and procedure-minded ENTJ vice-president with an ENTP as his right-hand man, and an INFJ male technical writer. He has always enjoyed this type of a "smorgasbord" environment but was never able to understand why until he completed a management style workshop. He now understands that as an INTP, he searches for an understanding of his environment. Having a variety of characters to analyze and bounce ideas off of keeps him from being bored with the everyday redundancy found in many smaller, task-focused companies.

Jerry describes an incident that reveals a serious flaw of his INTJ style. He was helping a new quality assurance (QA) engineer to write a standard report. Jerry was in a hurry, and when the QA engineer asked for clarification, Jerry snatched the report away and said he would do it himself. This enraged the new engineer, who confronted Jerry: "If you would just take the time to show me how to do the damn thing once, then you won't be stuck doing it for the rest of your career! I may not be as quick as you, but I'm sure it took you time to learn it, and it doesn't look as if it takes a brain surgeon to figure it out." Jerry reflected on this speech and recognized that his introverted thinking type usually impeded his ability to give exacting instructions to others. His way of dealing with the outside world was through external intuition, which disregards details and facts. Now Jerry is working to convert this problem in his management style.

Jerry revealed that even as a young manufacturing engineer he had the characteristics typical of an INTP:

- He was always caught up in solving problems, often concentrating so hard that he became oblivious to what was going on around him.
- He preferred to work alone.
- He often got frustrated with others when they did not understand his analysis or could not see what was obvious to him.
- He always preferred to do things himself, feeling that others would or could not do as good a job.
- He did not give up his ideas easily and stayed away from group presentations.
- He spoke down to certain people whom he perceived were not as intelligent as he is.

This pattern was hardened by his high needs for achievement and dominance. Jerry then prepared a complete analysis of his management style:

Management Triad

Achievement	High
Dominance	High
Affiliation	Moderate

Bosses/Peers/Subordinates Relations

Deference	Low
Autonomy	High
Nurturance	Low
Succorance	Low
Abasement	High

Task Factors

Change	High
Order	Low
Endurance	Moderate
Intensity	High

Interpersonal Modifiers

Introspection	High
Exhibition	High
Aggression	High

Power Bases

Reward	Low
Coercive	Low
Authority	High
Referent	Low
Expert	High
Information	Low
Affiliative	Low
Group	Low

Win–Lose Conflict Style

Jerry looked at the management style profile and came to the following conclusions:

- His need for achievement and dominance impeded his ability to delegate.

- In spite of being high in dominance, his power bases are largely undeveloped except for expert and authority power.
- His high need for autonomy and low need for deference make him difficult to work with. It is his way or no way.
- His low need for nurturance and his infrequent use of reward power alienate his peers and subordinates. He assumes doing a good job is a reward in itself. In retrospect, he realizes the fallacy of this assumption.
- His high need for autonomy and low need for succorance helped build an impenetrable armor around him.
- His high need for abasement is reflected in his taking all the responsibility for tasks. This has led him to become overly stressed and irritable.
- His task factors fit the dynamic environment that he works in.
- His high need for introspection is positive. He has used this to take stock of himself and think about change. He has focused on his high need for aggression: he builds up negative thoughts about others within himself and then lashes out at others.
- Being an introvert and having a high need for exhibition (recognition) leaves him frustrated at times, given his standoffish attitude and do-it-yourself mentality.

Jerry's plan is to create a psychological contract with all the people in his network of interdependencies. He will explore mutual expectations, assumptions, and perceptions. He plans to keep an open mind when they differ and try to work out or resolve differences. He feels that using the APF model will greatly enhance his ability to understand and work with others.

He will start to develop his delegation skills with a clear outline of expectations, procedures, and follow-up.

As an INTP he finds himself jumping from one situation to another and juggling a large number of tasks. He plans to force himself to stay with each job longer, write down his ideas in such a way that can be coherently and logically understood by someone else, try to focus on fewer and more important areas, and surround himself with others who can interact with him and build on his ideas.

He plans to use his high need for introspection in conjunction with his newborn knowledge to understand others in an empathic way. From this base, he wants to build referent power. By systematically assessing his assumptions, perceptions, and feelings about people and the job, he will move from a reactive to a proactive mode.

Case 9, George: The Organizational Man

George represents a suitable case for the use of some of the techniques of cognitive restructuring. George had an excessive fear of his boss and felt he lacked direction in life. Unlike Bruce, George had no sense of self-assurance on the job. In order to understand his irrational fear of his boss he took an Irrational Beliefs Survey. This instrument is based on Albert Ellis's work on irrational belief. Ellis isolated ten irrational beliefs that plague people and cause anxiety and depression. The instrument is included in Appendix F. It is very useful in identifying assumptions and beliefs that are internal stressors. I have used this process successfully in stress management workshops.

George decided to focus on his irrational beliefs and try to restructure them in addition to using the usual building blocks of management style.

As an ESFP, George is a master at observing external details. This propensity is heightened by his high need for order. At his side at all times is his time management booklet. He is a slave to its dictates. His colleagues all smile at how he adheres to his routines even when more serious priorities arise. He suffers anxiety attacks whenever the sacred schedule is disrupted. Since his inferior function is intuition, he does not grasp the big picture and has been criticized by his boss, an INTJ, for this flow. George has mastered the intricate workings of the accounting information system and is always ready to help people when they encounter a problem in this area, but often they resent his long-winded explanations about the system. Because of George's expertise, his boss has tolerated most of George's shortcomings.

George scores very high on expert and information power. His high need for achievement and affiliation amplify his natural gregariousness. He is extremely deferential to his boss and always agrees with his opinions, insights, and demands. He will agree to do whatever he is asked to do even if he cannot fit the new task into his priorities. His needs for succorance and abasement increase his stress level. His willingness to undertake more than he can handle causes him to work long hours in order to follow through. When he fails to meet this self-imposed standard, he falls into a state of self-flagellation. His irrational belief in the power of authority figures to direct his destiny is compounded by his low need for autonomy. George fits the Beck pattern of the succorant personality.

One of George's positive needs was his propensity for introspection. However, at times when he was unsure where he stood with his boss, he would become obsessed with small details that did not have relevance to the situation. George would try to figure out what the small twitch in his boss's eye meant: "Does this mean disapproval of me? What am I doing wrong? Am I going to be fired? Will he move me off the project? Does he really like me?"

These morbid thoughts were reflected in his responses to the Irrational Beliefs Survey. George endorsed six beliefs. His particular cluster points to a high need for approval, dependency on higher figures, a need for perfection, obsession with future catastrophes, defining his self-worth exclusively in terms of external achievements, and seeking perfect order.

The following are George's responses to the key to the Irrational Beliefs Survey:

Belief

1. Everyone must love me. — Yes
2. One's self-worth is tied to one's achievements. — Yes
3. Some people are wicked and must be punished for their villainous behavior. — No
4. Unless conditions are just right, it is catastrophic and I can't function. — Yes
5. Unhappiness is caused by external events; we have no control over anything. — No
6. I need to worry about the possibility of some future catastrophe happening. — Yes
7. It is easier to avoid certain difficult or unpleasant events than to face them. — No
8. I need to be dependent upon someone else. — Yes
9. We're all products of our past history; we can't change anything. — No
10. There is a right and perfect way to do everything, and it is catastrophic if we don't find that way. — Yes

The script for the six irrational beliefs George discovered on the Irrational Beliefs Survey was formed early in George's life. His father was a dominant factor in his childhood. He demanded perfection, strict adherence to his standards, obedience, and achievement. George became a compliant child who never got out of the shadow of his father.

His need pattern reflects his irrational beliefs and turns them into demonlike forces that work on him to comply. His excessive fear of his boss is most likely tied to these irrational beliefs. In addition, his boss' psychological type is the exact opposite. George's inferior function is intuition while his boss' dominant function is intuition.

The extroverted sensing types are masters at observing external details. They focus on things and people and remember exactly what people said and did. Recognition of details and events are primary, while recognition of their significance is secondary. In George's case these strengths, under stress, become extreme liabilities. The obsessive ruminations over details are dysfunctional.

George developed the following counters to his present self-talk in order to gain control over his irrational beliefs.

Irrational Belief: Everyone must love me.

Counters

a. An impossible task. There are people who have a need to be critical. I cannot prevent that.
b. I can work to develop a select group of friends and build on these relationships. This will be more feasible than my other belief.
c. Anyone who demands absolute and unconditional approval for their happiness is doomed to frustration.

Irrational Belief: One's self-worth is tied to one's achievements.

Counters

a. There is more to me than my achievements. They are important but I must put them in perspective.
b. Babe Ruth hit 714 home runs but struck out 1330 times.
c. I have been successful in many areas. I must separate my genuine needs from my small failures.

Irrational Belief: Unless conditions are just right, it is catastrophic and I can't function.

Counters

a. I can't control everything in my environment. Organizations are dynamic and fluid entities.
b. I can view this as a challenge, not as a threat.
c. If there is no wind, row.

Irrational Belief: I need to worry about the possibility of some future catastrophe happening.

Counters

a. Constant worrying about losing my job has wasted valuable time that could be put to more-productive use which would ensure my job.
b. The fear that my reports will be rejected by my boss has failed to materialize. This thinking is parallel to worrying whether the sun will rise.
c. Even if I lose my current job, I have talent and skills that will get me another one.

Irrational Belief: I need to be dependent upon someone else.

Counters

a. That may have been true when I was an infant. I am now forty-six.
b. People react negatively to overdependent people.
c. If I didn't respect myself, it wouldn't matter if everyone else in the world respected me.

Irrational Belief: There is a right and perfect way to do everything, and it is catastrophic if we don't find that way.

Counters

a. Worrying doesn't change anything; it just makes me feel bad.
b. There is always an easy solution to every human problem: neat, plausible, and wrong.
c. A perfectionist takes infinite pains, and often gives them to other people.

Once George developed counters for his irrational beliefs and restructured them, he identified his strengths and weaknesses in regards to his boss. George is good at details. His boss is good at possibilities. George must avoid overwhelming his boss with just the facts and develop a sense of the big picture. The exercises outlined for sensing types in Chapter 3, "Modifying Psychological Type," are pertinent to George.

George also realized he needs to get in touch with his true self. He is an externally driven person, with low autonomy, high deference, high succorance, and high abasement. George was asked to fill out a life mission statement. He was more than a bit surprised at this request. He said that he never thought of this approach to organizing his life. He became an accountant because his father told him this was a practical and financially secure job. His natural propensity for details was a buttress to his early success in the accounting field. But at the present moment he is dissatisfied, confused, and anxious.

In the mission statement, he was asked to write about himself. Given the fact that he was an introspective person, albeit a misguided one, that should be an easy task. Writing about oneself, in most cases, is an effortless task. This has been proven to me by the countless psychological autobiographies that I encounter in my work.

The mission statement is a search within one's self for meaning. George would benefit by reading Jung's *Man in Search of a Soul*. Hillman, a noted Jungian and archetypal psychologist, wrote a profound book called *Insearch*. His main thesis was that we must get in touch with our inner core (soul) in order to become whole. "Our work seems to begin with the shadows which fall between people. . . . However, human problems are not something people have, but something people are. The problem in psychology is the individual himself, just as I am my own problem." This statement by Hillman applies to all of us.

The "insearch" began with George detecting his mission in life. Victor Frankl states: "Everyone has his own specific vocation or mission in life. . . . Therein he cannot be replaced, nor can his life be repeated. Thus, everyone's task is as unique as is his specific opportunity to implement it."

George's "Mission in Life"

FOR THE NEXT YEAR

In the next year I want to stabilize my career and my home life. At the present time I am floundering in a sea of uncertainty. My relationship with my boss has deteriorated to the point where I can no longer bring myself to work with him. I suffer from a deep sense of loss. As a result of this, my life at home has been a shambles. I work twelve hours on week days and at least six hours on Saturday. I feel that I must please my boss to the extent that I ignore my other obligations in life. My wife has been tolerant during this crisis, but I wonder how long she will continue to be tolerant of my neglect of her?

I would like to rid myself of these obsessions with performance and achievement. The feelings of guilt and shame are unbearable at times. As I write this I realize that a part of me has been lost or submerged. It is time that I get in touch with this inner self. I thought this task was going to be difficult; however, it is not. It is painful in that I realize that I have lost touch with some basic values. I am now bitterly aware that I have been under the influence of the past. My father has directed my life to the point that I see him in every authority figure. I realize that I must begin to cope with this specter of the past and move on. I must set reasonable priorities on the job.

It is time that I sat down with my boss and reached a reasonable "psychological contract" with him. At times he is enigmatic and unfathomable. This is his nature. I realize that he cannot change. It is my reaction to him that is important. I can, in an adult fashion, try to get a clear understanding of his expectations.

I want to build a more solid relationship with my wife. This has been one of the neglected areas. My wife is a very gregarious person. I need to encourage her to open up our social life with friends.

In addition I want to revive my interest in the piano. This was a solace in my adolescence as a result of my mother's urging. I have virtually abandoned this fulfilling experience in the last five years. Being an SP (sensual performer) in temperament I have cut myself off from a vital drive in my life.

I want to read more in areas other than my profession. I think that I need to expand my horizons in literature and philosophy.

I need to be in touch with my body. In the past five years I have gained twenty unneeded pounds. I would like to take a course in the martial arts. I understand that aikido has valuable lessons for stress-prone people. This also fits in with my psychological type (ESFP).

IN THE NEXT FIVE YEARS

Wealth has no bearing on my quest in life. It is a necessary convenience but not an end in itself. Therefore I am satisfied with my career choice and compensation. Although I recognize that my father pushed me into accounting, this profession is the right one for me. I like to handle details and concrete facts and organize them in an orderly way. My need structure supports this contention. My dissatisfaction lies not in the job but with myself. I keenly recognize that I have developed dysfunctional behaviors in dealing with the job. I have let the job and my boss become an obsession.

The strengths of my management style have turned into internal enemies. My need to achieve, to please, and to receive approval have made me into a pale version of the organizational man. My major goal would be to continue the personal "insearch" work that I outlined in my mission statement. I realize that this is a life's work, not just a short-term fix. During this period of self-reflection I have defined five subgoals for the next five years:

1. To expand my knowledge in the accounting field to include strategic planning. Being an overdeveloped sensing type, I want to exercise the buried intuitive part of me. This can be accomplished by courses and on-the-job training. Since this is my boss's strength, I think he would be more open to my expanding horizons. This is supported by his criticisms that I don't understand the big picture. I understand that there are creative problem solving seminars at workshops and local universities. I intend to develop these connections.
2. To become a gourmet cook. As strange as it seems this was a pastime of mine during my college years. I think this would serve a dual purpose: it would increase my own satisfaction on a sensual level and it would reduce a burden on my wife.
3. To expand my social skills.
4. To buy a summer/winter retreat.
5. To develop my spirituality.

Appendices

Determining Your Psychological Type

Extrovert or Introvert

		E	I
1.	I am gregarious.	—	
	I am reserved.		—
2.	I am relaxed.	—	
	I am intense.		—
3.	I am enthusiastic.	—	
	I am aloof.		—
4.	I speak out in groups.	—	
	I absorb information in groups.		—
5.	My energy grows at parties.	—	
	My energy wanes at parties.		—
6.	I have a large group of friends.	—	
	I have a selected few friends.		—
7.	I think out loud.	—	
	I think inside my head.		—
8.	I look for activity.	—	
	I seek quiet time.		—
9.	I like to talk.	—	
	I like to listen.		—
10.	I share my personal experiences.	—	
	I am unapproachable.		—
11.	I like new experiences.	—	
	I like stability in my inner life.		—
12.	I want to be with people.	—	
	I take a detached approach.		—
13.	I am influenced by external opinions.	—	
	I am inner directed.		—
14.	I show emotions.	—	
	I exercise restraint.		—
15.	I respond quickly.	—	
	I respond warily.		—

Total number of checks in each column.   —   —

The column with the larger number of checks indicates your attitude of either extroversion or introversion.

Sensing or Intuition

		S	N
1.	I am realistic.	——	
	I am inspirational.		——
2.	I like routine.	——	
	I like variety.		——
3.	I think about facts.	——	
	I think about possibilities.		——
4.	I like precision.	——	
	I like brainstorming.		——
5.	I am concerned with the present.	——	
	I am concerned with the future.		——
6.	I use my five senses.	——	
	I rely on my sixth sense.		——
7.	My feet are on the ground.	——	
	My head is in the clouds.		——
8.	My mind is literal.	——	
	My mind is figurative.		——
9.	I make direct statements.	——	
	I make allegorical statements.		——
10.	I pay attention to basics.	——	
	I pay attention to overtones.		——
11.	I used learned skills.	——	
	I acquire new skills.		——
12.	My focus is on reality.	——	
	My focus is on inspiration.		——
13.	I am steadfast.	——	
	I am mercurial.		——
14.	I work on solving problems.	——	
	I discover problems.		——
15.	I like details.	——	
	I like the big picture.		——

Total number of checks in each column.   —— ——

Thinking or Feeling

	T	F
1. I am logical and analytical.	——	
I have a personal value orientation.		——
2. I am critical.	——	
I am personable.		——
3. I am firm on policy.	——	
I bend the rules.		——
4. I have an impersonal orientation to problems.	——	
I have a strong personal involvement in problems.		——
5. I am direct.	——	
I am tactful.		——
6. I show justice.	——	
I show mercy.		——
7. I am hardheaded.	——	
I am softheaded.		——
8. I am fair-minded.	——	
I am sympathetic.		——
9. I focus on ideas.	——	
I focus on ideals.		——
10. I am firm.	——	
I am gentle.		——
11. I am unaffected by atmosphere.	——	
I am tuned into atmosphere.		——
12. I concentrate on the task.	——	
I concentrate on the relationship.		——
13. I prefer the honest truth.	——	
I avoid unpleasantness.		——
14. I am upset by illogic.	——	
I accept illogic.		——
15. I am tuned into designs.	——	
I am tuned into people.		——

Total number of checks in each column.   —— ——

Judging or Perception

		J	P
1.	I am deliberate.	———	
	I am spontaneous.		———
2.	I prefer structure.	———	
	I prefer to be unstructured.		———
3.	I am decisive.	———	
	I am cautious.		———
4.	I am opinionated.	———	
	I am open-minded.		———
5.	I persevere.	———	
	I procrastinate.		———
6.	I am organized and systematic.	———	
	I am flexible.		———
7.	I am self-regimented.	———	
	I am open-ended.		———
8.	I am punctual.	———	
	I am leisurely.		———
9.	I am systematic.	———	
	I am impulsive.		———
10.	I aim to be right.	———	
	I accept being wrong.		———
11.	I am geared to morality.	———	
	I am geared to the existential.		———
12.	I am critical.	———	
	I consent.		———
13.	I live up to standards.	———	
	I am open to new experiences.		———
14.	I have enduring friendships.	———	
	I have easy acquaintanceships.		———
15.	I live to plan.	———	
	I like unplanned activities.		———

Total number of checks in each column.   ——— ———

Based upon the dominant number of checks in each of these four functions, you should be able to determine your type.

My type is _____.

Assessment of Needs

Read the following statements and rate them as needs that you express *sometimes* (S) or *always* (A). Try to be objective. If you are in doubt, ask someone who knows you. Try not to be influenced by what you think you should be or by what others want you to be.

Management Triad of Needs

Need for Achievement

	S	A
1. I like to do my best in whatever I undertake.	___	___
2. I like to be able to say that I have done a difficult job well.	___	___
3. I like to be able to do things better than other people.	___	___
4. I like to accomplish tasks that others recognize as requiring skill and effort.	___	___
5. I enjoy work as much as play.	___	___

Total number of always responses: ___

Need for Dominance

	S	A
1. I argue with zest for my point of view against others.	___	___
2. I feel I can dominate a social or business situation.	___	___
3. I like to be one of the leaders in the organizations and groups to which I belong.	___	___
4. I usually influence others more than they influence me.	___	___
5. I enjoy the sense of power when I am able to control the actions of others.	___	___

Total number of *always* responses: ___

Need for Affiliation

	S	A
1. I like to be loyal to my friends and colleagues.	___	___
2. I like to do things for my colleagues and workers.	___	___
3. I share things with my friends and colleagues.	___	___
4. I enjoy cooperating with others more than working by myself.	___	___
5. I like to hang out with a group of congenial people and talk about things.	___	___

Total number of *always* responses: ___

221

Boss's/Peers/Subordinates Relations Needs

Need for Deference

	S	A
1. I conform to custom and avoid the unconventional.	___	___
2. I accept suggestions rather than insist on working things out in my own way.	___	___
3. I seek the advice of older people and follow it.	___	___
4. I like to follow instructions and do what is expected of me.	___	___
5. I like to accept the leadership of my superiors.	___	___

Total number of *always* responses: ___

Need for Autonomy

	S	A
1. I am unable to do my best work when I am in a subservient position.	___	___
2. I like to come and go as I please.	___	___
3. I resist people who try to assert their authority over me.	___	___
4. I am apt to criticize, openly or covertly, people who are in positions of authority.	___	___
5. I like to be independent of others in deciding what I want to do.	___	___

Total number of *always* responses: ___

Need for Nurturance

	S	A
1. I take pains not to hurt the feelings of my subordinates.	___	___
2. I like to help people when they are in trouble.	___	___
3. I give my time and energy to those who ask for it.	___	___
4. I like to show a great deal of affection toward my colleagues and subordinates.	___	___
5. People are apt to tell me their innermost secrets and troubles.	___	___

Total number of *always* responses: ___

Need for Succorance

	S	A
1. I like my colleagues or workers to encourage me when I meet with failure.	___	___
2. I think of myself as neglected when things go wrong.	___	___
3. I like sympathy when I am sick or depressed.	___	___
4. I am rather easily discouraged when things go wrong.	___	___
5. I experience a vague feeling of insecurity when I must act on my own.	___	___

Total number of *always* responses: ___

Need for Abasement

	S	A
1. When things go wrong, I feel personally responsible.	___	___
2. I undertake more than I can handle.	___	___
3. My friends think I am too humble.	___	___
4. I think that charity should begin with your enemies.	___	___
5. I feel depressed by my inability to handle various situations.	___	___

Total number of *always* responses: ___

Task Factor Needs

Need for Change

	S	A
1. I like to travel and experience new things.	___	___
2. I like to experience novelty and change in my daily routine.	___	___
3. I like to meet new people	___	___
4. I like to experiment and try new things.	___	___
5. I like to try new and different jobs, rather than do the same old thing.	___	___

Total number of *always* responses: ___

Need for Order

	S	A
1. Any written work that I do I like to have precise, neat, and well-organized.	___	___
2. I like to plan and organize the details of any work that I have to undertake.	___	___
3. I like things to run smoothly without any hitches.	___	___
4. My workstation is neat and well organized.	___	___
5. If I have to take a trip, everything has to be planned and and programmed in advance.	___	___

Total number of *always* responses: ___

Need for Endurance

	S	A
1. I like to work hard and long on any job I do.	___	___
2. I like to stay late working in order to get a job done.	___	___
3. I like to stick at a job or problem even when it may seem as if I am getting nowhere.	___	___
4. I like to complete a single job or task before taking on others.	___	___
5. I dislike being interrupted while at my work.	___	___

Total number of *always* responses: ___

Need for Intensity

	S	A
1. I can expend a great deal of effort in a short time.	___	___
2. I am intense with the tasks that interest me.	___	___
3. I work hard when I work, and play hard when I play. Then I feel drained.	___	___
4. Long stretches of tedious work bore me and make me feel frustrated.	___	___
5. I feel fresh, vigorous, and ready for anything, most of the time.	___	___

Total number of *always* responses: ___

Interpersonal Modifiers

Need for Introspection

	S	A
1. I like to observe how another individual feels in a given situation.	___	___
2. I like to put myself in someone else's place and to imagine how I would feel in the same situation.	___	___
3. I like to think about the personalities of people and try to figure out what makes them tick.	___	___
4. I like to understand how my colleagues feel about various problems they have to face.	___	___
5. I like to judge people by *why* they did something— not by *what* they actually did.	___	___

Total number of *always* responses: ___

Need for Aggression

	S	A
1. I treat a domineering person as rudely as he or she treats me.	___	___
2. I feel like getting revenge when someone has insulted me.	___	___
3. I like to tell people what I think of them.	___	___
4. Sometimes I use threats to accomplish my purpose.	___	___
5. I am apt to express my irritation rather than restrain it.	___	___

Total number of *always* responses: ___

Need for Exhibition

	S	A
1. I like to tell amusing stories and jokes.	___	___
2. I like people to notice me when in public.	___	___
3. I am apt to show off in some way if I get a chance.	___	___
4. I love to talk, and it's hard for me to keep quiet.	___	___

5. I like to use words of which other people often do
   not know the meaning.   _____ _____

Total number of *always* responses: _____

Scoring the Assessment of Needs

- A need can be considered as high if 4–5 *always* responses are recorded.
- A need can be considered as medium if 2–3 *always* responses are recorded.
- A need can be considered as low if 0–1 *always* responses are recorded.

Step 1. Determine your needs levels (high or low).

Management Triad	Level	Task Factors	Level
Achievement	_____	Change	_____
Dominance	_____	Order	_____
Affiliation	_____	Endurance	_____
Bosses/Peers/Subordinates Relations		Intensity	_____
Deference	_____	*Interpersonal Modifiers*	
Autonomy	_____	Introspection	_____
Nurturance	_____	Exhibition	_____
Succorance	_____	Aggression	_____
Abasement	_____		

Step 2. Identify pitfalls in fusion and crossover needs.
Do you perceive any fusion problems (where both needs are high)? Look at your needs and use the following checklist.

Fusion Needs			*Are Both Needs High? (Yes or No)*
Achievement	with	Dominance	_____
	with	Affiliation	_____
	with	Autonomy	_____
	with	Succorance	_____
	with	Abasement	_____
	with	Aggression	_____
Dominance	with	Affiliation	_____
	with	Autonomy	_____
	with	Succorance	_____
	with	Abasement	_____
	with	Exhibition	_____
	with	Aggression	_____
Affiliation	with	Deference	_____
	with	Aggression	_____
	with	Succorance	_____

Autonomy	with	Succorance	_____
	with	Aggression	_____
	with	Exhibition	_____
Deference	with	Exhibition	_____
Nurturance	with	Aggression	_____
	with	Abasement	_____
Exhibition	with	Aggression	_____
Succorance	with	Abasement	_____
	with	Aggression	_____
Abasement	with	Aggression	_____

Step 3. Identify any crossover problems.

Do you detect any crossover problems? Look at your needs, and use the following checklist.

The Needs	*Level* *(High or Low)*	*Potential Problem?* *(Yes or No)*
Succorance	_____	_____
Nurturance	_____	_____
Autonomy	_____	_____
Deference	_____	_____
Exhibition	_____	_____
Nurturance	_____	_____
Dominance	_____	_____
Introspection	_____	_____
Autonomy	_____	_____
Affiliation	_____	_____
Affiliation	_____	_____
Introspection	_____	_____
Aggression	_____	_____
Affiliation	_____	_____
Autonomy	_____	_____
Nurturance	_____	_____

Exhibition	_____	_____
Deference	_____	_____
Aggression	_____	_____
Deference	_____	_____
Aggression	_____	_____
Nurturance	_____	_____
Change	_____	_____
Endurance	_____	_____

Step 4. List potential fusion and crossover problems.

Fusion Problems	*Crossover Problems*
1. _____	1. _____
2. _____	2. _____
3. _____	3. _____
4. _____	4. _____
5. _____	5. _____
6. _____	6. _____
7. _____	7. _____
8. _____	8. _____
9. _____	9. _____
10. _____	10. _____

Step 5. Star the fusion and crossover problems that you perceive may need modification. Base your assessment on critical incidents from your past or present behavior in the organization. These incidents can involve subordinates, peers, or bosses.

Step 6. Identify any MBTI and Need combinations that are present, and consider their potential outcomes. A synopsis of the needs follows.

Achievement. There is a strong relationship between the need to achieve and the functions of sensing and intuition. The dominance of the sensing or the intuitive function determines which kind of data individuals feel comfortable using to meet their achievement needs. If a particular job is a mismatch with a person's perception function, he or she will be frustrated and feel his or her achievement needs thwarted.

Dominance. The need for dominance affects the type of data a manager wants to control. A dominant intuitive type may insist on taking a global, conceptual approach when more facts and details are needed. On the other hand, a dominant sensing type may amass too much data and miss the big picture. When combined with the thinking function, dominance can override the manager's concerns for others and cause him or her to make decisions based solely on logic and impersonal principles. High dominance needs, combined with the feeling function, may cause managers to impose their personal values on others. They may override logic or insist that others support their opinions.

Affiliation. Affiliation needs soften the critical edge of a thinking type. Low affiliation will harden the thinking function and amplify the critical, impersonal attitude.

Autonomy. Introverts tend to keep things to themselves and not involve others in critical decisions. Communications with others will be minimal.

Deference. Low deference combined with thinking will intensify the impersonal attitude. In conjunction with feeling, low deference will harden the value judgments of the feeling type.

Nurturance. High nurturance combined with feeling may induce too much empathy for others and lead to conflict avoidance so as to not hurt others.

Succorance. An introvert with high succorance needs may suffer this unfulfilled need in silence and brood over the lack of empathy of the other person.

Abasement. Feeling types with a high need for abasement will feel guilty about their failings in relationships, and they will ultimately come to resent their guilty feelings. Extroverted types with high abasement needs make it known to others how much they suffer over the cruelties of the organization. Introverts who have this need may preoccupy themselves with endless internal ruminations about guilt.

Introspection. Extroverts with a low need for introspection will be driven only by external forces. The internal assessment of their own and others' motives will be lacking. This could lead to misreading the situation.

Aggression. A need for aggression is amplified in an extrovert who publicly subjects another person to criticism. This person's need may show up in barbed wit or outbursts of temper. Among thinking and feeling types, alike, aggression adds a sharp, acerbic tone to judgments. In introverts, aggression seeks an outlet through fantasy, or it erupts as modulated criticism.

Change. Extroverts act on their need for change overtly and sometimes impulsively. Introverts will ponder the significance for change and be more cautious about meeting their need for change.

Order. When the need for order is combined with the sensing function, a nitpicking detail orientation can develop. A thinking type with a high need for order can develop an obsessive approach to managing.

Endurance and **intensity.** There does not appear to be any discernible negative link between these two needs and the psychological types.

Need	*MBTI Combinations*	*Yes or No*	*Potential Outcomes*
Achievement	with Sensing	_____	_____
	with Intuition	_____	_____
Dominance	with Sensing	_____	_____
	with Intuition	_____	_____
	with Thinking	_____	_____
	with Feeling	_____	_____
Affiliation (low)	with Thinking	_____	_____
Autonomy	with Introversion	_____	_____
Deference	with Thinking	_____	_____
	with Feeling	_____	_____
Nurturance	with Feeling	_____	_____
Succorance	with Introversion	_____	_____
Abasement	with Feeling	_____	_____
	with Extroversion	_____	_____
	with Introversion	_____	_____
Introspection	with Extroversion	_____	_____
Aggression	with Extroversion	_____	_____
	with Thinking	_____	_____
	with Feeling	_____	_____
	with Introversion	_____	_____
Change	with Extroversion	_____	_____
Order	with Sensing	_____	_____
	with Thinking	_____	_____
Endurance	with No links	_____	_____
Intensity	with No links	_____	_____

Step 7. List all the fusions, crossovers, and MBTI interactions.

Fusion	*Crossovers*	*MBTI Interactions*
_____	_____	_____
_____	_____	_____
_____	_____	_____
_____	_____	_____
_____	_____	_____
_____	_____	_____
_____	_____	_____
_____	_____	_____
_____	_____	_____

Step 8. Count how many times the need appeared as a fusion, as a crossover, and as an MBTI interaction.

Management Triad	*Level*	*Task Factors*	*Level*
Achievement	_____	Change	_____
Dominance	_____	Order	_____
Affiliation	_____	Endurance	_____
Bosses/Peers/Subordinates Relations		Intensity	_____
Autonomy	_____	*Interpersonal Modifiers*	
Deference	_____	Introspection	_____
Nurturance	_____	Exhibition	_____
Succorance	_____	Aggression	_____
Abasement	_____		

Step 9. Rank-order the needs by occurrence.

	Needs	*Occurrence*
1.		_____
2.		_____
3.		_____
4.		_____
5.		_____
6.		_____
7.		_____
8.		_____
9.		_____
10.		_____

Step 10. Use cognitive restructuring to modify needs.

APPENDIX D
Influence Inventory (Power Bases)

As a leader you are faced with many situations where you must seek the cooperation of subordinates or colleagues to get the job done. In these instances you must influence them to do what you perceive is necessary. In the influence of others we have certain assumptions about how to accomplish this task.

The Influence Inventory has a number of paired statements that reflect various assumptions about the use of power. Please circle the A or B statement that is more characteristic of your management style. In some instances both choices may suit you. In this case choose the one more characteristic of you.

1. A. They do it because I have status in the organization.
   B. They do it because I usually reward them.

2. A. I use my expertise to influence them.
   B. I give as much information as I can to help them.

3. A. I praise their abilities to accomplish the task.
   B. I set high standards and expect performance.

4. A. I use my rights as boss to decide the issue.
   B. I persuade them by emphasizing my camaraderie with them.

5. A. I use my knowledge about policy and procedures to help them.
   B. I believe in running a tight ship. Procedures must be followed.

6. A. They do it as part of a reciprocal relationship.
   B. My specialized competence is the key.

7. A. I usually provide positive incentives to do the job.
   B. I use information and data to help them.

8. A. Procedures must be enforced.
   B. My judgment is usually superior to theirs.

9. A. They listen and cooperate because of mutual respect.
   B. They do it because I usually reward them.

10. A. I provide them with the big picture and explain my reasons.
    B. They work with me because of our rapport.

11. A. My competence in this area is well respected.
    B. They feel formally obligated to follow my lead.

12. A. I set high standards and expect results.
    B. I promise them future rewards.

13. A. I keep them fully informed about what is going on.
    B. I use my expertise to influence them.

14. A. I lead by example and good faith.
    B. I use all my information to persuade them.

15. A. I am firm with them and expect results.
    B. My rank is all I need.

232

16. A. I give as much information as I can to help them.
    B. They know I will reward them.

17. A. My official authority usually carries the weight.
    B. I believe discipline shapes character.

18. A. I set high standards and expect performance.
    B. I give as much information as I can to help them.

19. A. I am responsible. Therefore, I have the authority.
    B. My expert qualifications are the driving force.

20. A. I use my expertise to influence them.
    B. I am firm with them and expect results.

21. A. They know I will reward them.
    B. They respect my authority.

22. A. They listen and cooperate because of mutual respect.
    B. I impress them with consequences of failure.

23. A. I usually provide positive incentives to do the job.
    B. They do it as part of a reciprocal relationship.

24. A. My judgment is usually superior to theirs.
    B. They recognize that teamwork and cooperation will bring rewards.

25. A. They respect my authority.
    B. I give as much information as I can to help them.

26. A. They do it because we are part of a team.
    B. They respect my authority.

27. A. I am firm and enforce strict compliance.
    B. They work with me because of our rapport.

28. A. I provide them with the big picture and explain my reasons.
    B. Lines of authority must not be violated.

29. A. They respect my ability to make the right decision.
    B. I have built a strong relationship with them.

30. A. I promise them future rewards.
    B. I use my expertise to influence them.

Influence Inventory Answer Sheet

Circle the letters that you selected on each item in the inventory.

ITEM	Authority	Reward	Power Bases Discipline	Expert	Information	Referent
1.	A	B				
2.				A	B	
3.		A	B			
4.	A					B
5.			B		A	
6.				B		A
7.		A			B	
8.			A	B		
9.		B				A
10.					A	B
11.	B			A		
12.		B	A			
13.				B	A	
14.					B	A
15.	B		A			
16.		B			A	
17.	A		B			
18.			A		B	
19.	A			B		
20.			B	A		
21.	B	A				
22.			B			A
23.		A				B
24.		B		A		
25.	A				B	
26.	B					A
27.			A			B
28.	B				A	
29.				A		B
30.		A		B		
TOTAL						

Scores: 7–10 = high, 4-6 = medium, 0–3 = low

Conflict Resolution Style Assessment

The assessment instrument contains questions about our assumptions and our tactics in dealing with conflict. The items are grouped into 10 sections containing five questions. Rank-order the five questions in each section:

5. Highly agree
4. Agree
3. Neutral
2. Slightly disagree
1. Totally disagree

Transfer the rankings for each item onto the summary-of-rankings sheet. Then obtain the total for each of the five conflict styles.

Assumptions About Conflict

Section I

Rank

1. Competition breeds success. Without healthy competition, groups stagnate. _____

2. Conflict runs a predictable course. Why sweat the issue? _____

3. It is impossible to satisfy everyone's needs. We can resolve conflict by give and take. _____

4. People have an underlying dark side that emerges during conflict. This is why most conflicts remain unresolved. _____

5. Conflict can be difficult to bear, but it can lead to increased creativity. _____

Section II

Rank

6. The task comes first; people must accommodate. _____

7. Most of the time, conflict will be resolved at top levels. I see any energy expended on the conflict as wasted. _____

8. There are too many differences among people to please all. You have to reach a settlement. _____

9. Negotiations should be undertaken with the serious intent of minimizing disruptions. _____

10. The assumption that someone has to win and someone has to lose leads to destructive competition. _____

Section III

Rank

11. Conflict is inevitable. Others want to win, and we must face a battle.

12. Most conflicts should be resolved by third-party intervention. _____

13. I believe groups should identify those issues on which agreement is impossible and those issues that they can use to reach a compromise.

_____

14. Emotions have no place in a conflict. Feelings should be controlled when a dispute arises.

_____

15. Conflict is natural and contains positive and negative energy. It is our job to harness these forces.

_____

Section IV

Rank

16. Compromise leads to more problems than it solves. Strong leadership is the only remedy to long-standing conflicts.

_____

17. Sometimes you have to walk away from the conflict and let things calm down.

_____

18. I don't mind conflict as long as we maintain our heads and give and take a little.

_____

19. Self-interest and narrow-minded attitudes drive people apart. We should all try to minimize differences.

_____

20. Conflict can be healthy. Mutual goals would be our criteria for judgment.

_____

Section V

Rank

21. The decision rests on my superior knowledge and experience. Facts and logic will prevail.

_____

22. Conflict is frustrating for all involved. There is nothing you can do when its ugly head is raised.

_____

23. I like someone who is a strong negotiator and has the ability to strike meaningful compromises when needed.

_____

24. Self-interest and narrow-minded attitudes drive people apart. We should all try to minimize differences.

_____

25. Different concerns can lead to new possibilities and new mutual options.

_____

Section VI

26. People should face facts: there is only one solution. It is my job to convince them of the right position. _____

27. I like to keep any encounters impersonal and let others fight it out. _____

28. The best way to resolve conflict is by expressing agreement with the other parties and offer suggestions on issues we both can live with. _____

29. I empathize with their position and give the other party support where I can. _____

30. I try to get the group to explore the concerns behind the various points of view. From this point we can move on to alternatives to the problem. _____

Section VII

31. The decision rests on my superior knowledge and experience. People will follow my lead. _____

32. Conflict is destructive, and we should try to avoid confrontations that increase tensions. _____

33. We should rule out the extremes and settle on middle-ground agreements. _____

34. I think conflict is frightening. Differences should be discussed without people blowing up and attacking each other. _____

35. I try to surface how others are really feeling and thinking. All issues must be brought out in the open and discussed. _____

Section VIII

36. I stand by my convictions and press hard to get them across. _____

37. I don't like people who cause anxiety and tension. When this happens, I try to avoid the situation. _____

38. I emphasize the team concept and implore the other side to get on the bandwagon. _____

39. I usually go along with the rest of the group to avoid being a barrier to problem solving and to maintain harmony. _____

40. I try to get people to explore their concerns with the rest of the group. I then ask the rest of the group to address these concerns. _____

Section IX

Rank

41. I am a hard fighter, and I like to win. This tactic usually benefits my group.

_____

42. I like people who are civil and understated when a conflict arises.

_____

43. The leader should convince dissenters that if the majority sees it differently, the dissenters should go along at this time.

_____

44. The best characteristics for a facilitator are moderation and harmonious accord.

_____

45. A leader should consider and explore all of the concerns expressed by both groups.

_____

Section X

Rank

46. I like a leader who represents our position, one who does not compromise and holds fast.

_____

47. I refuse to take sides; let the others argue and settle their own disputes.

_____

48. I appeal to the logic of the situation and try to persuade the group that we can come up with a compromise in spite of our differences.

_____

49. Facilitators and team leaders must use strict rules to prevent strong feelings from erupting.

_____

50. As a leader I try to put on the table all our concerns, see where we agree and disagree, then strive for mutual options.

_____

Summary of Rankings

Section	Win-Lose Item	Rank	Lose-Leave Item	Rank	Compromise Item	Rank	Lose-Yield Item	Rank	Collaborative Item	Rank
I	1		2		3		4		5	
II	6		7		8		9		10	
III	11		12		13		14		15	
IV	16		17		18		19		20	
V	21		22		23		24		25	
VI	26		27		28		29		30	
VII	31		32		33		34		35	
VIII	36		37		38		39		40	
IX	41		42		43		44		45	
X	46		47		48		49		50	

Total _____ _____ _____ _____ _____

Range of Scores   *Strength of Scores*
Maximum   Score = 50   36 to 50 = High
Mid-range   Score = 30   25 to 35 = Medium
Minimum   Score = 10   10 to 24 = Low

Irrational Beliefs Survey

Place a mark in the appropriate column: "Agree" or "Disagree"

	Agree	Disagree
1. I want other people to approve of me.	____	____
2. I strongly dislike failing at anything I undertake.	____	____
3. There are bad people in the world who get away without punishment.	____	____
4. I very much like hearing favorable opinions of me.	____	____
5. There's nothing anybody can do about life's circumstances; it's the system.	____	____
6. If everything isn't right, I can't work.	____	____
7. I depend upon someone else for strength in handling life's problems.	____	____
8. I try to avoid doing unpleasant tasks whenever I can.	____	____
9. I always seek others' opinions before I do something.	____	____
10. It's okay to put off doing the things you dread.	____	____
11. I expect to be the best at anything I undertake; if not, I want to try.	____	____
12. I often get upset when situations aren't as I think they should be.	____	____
13. There is a perfect way to solve most problems.	____	____
14. I tend to put off making tough decisions.	____	____
15. We are what we are, and we can't change.	____	____
16. Most people suffer unhappiness through no fault of their own.	____	____
17. I worry about risky things that could happen to me.	____	____
18. The only way to understand present events is to understand past events.	____	____
19. I consider all possible sides of all alternatives to find the perfect solution.	____	____
20. I get upset when someone else is better at things that matter to me than I am.	____	____
21. I hate to see people get away with stupid, wicked behavior.	____	____
22. I worry about future events, even those that are outside my control.	____	____
23. It bothers me when people criticize me.	____	____
24. If I can't change the way things are, I get upset.	____	____
25. Fear of some awful future makes me anxious.	____	____
26. I like people to take care of me.	____	____
27. The way we behave now is determined early in our lives.	____	____
28. The fear of being punished keeps people from being bad.	____	____
29. Things are distressing in and of themselves; we can't do anything about them.	____	____
30. I remain anxious until I find the perfect solution.	____	____

The Key to the Irrational Beliefs Survey

Check the items that you agreed with.

ITEMS			# items checked	BELIEF
1	4	23		Everyone must love me.
2	11	20		One's self-worth is tied to one's achievements.
3	21	28		Some people are wicked and must be punished for their villainous behavior.
6	12	24		Unless conditions are just right, it is catastrophic and I can't function.
5	16	29		Unhappiness is caused by external events; we have no control over anything.
17	22	25		I need to worry about the possibility of some future catastrophe happening.
8	10	14		It is easier to avoid certain difficult or unpleasant events in life than to face them.
7	9	26		I need to be dependent upon someone else.
15	18	27		We're all products of our past history; we can't change anything.
13	19	30		There is a right and perfect way to do everything, and it is catastrophic if we don't find that way.

Agree on 2 Items - tendency to hold the belief

Agree on 3 Items - strong likelihood of holding the belief

Bibliography

Athos, A. G., and J. J. Gabarro. *Interpersonal Behavior*. Englewood Cliffs, N. J.: Prentice-Hall, 1978.

Bandura, A. *Social Learning Theory*. Englewood Cliffs, N. J.: Prentice-Hall, 1977.

Beck, A. T. "Cognitive Approaches to Stress." In *Principles and Practice of Stress Management*, edited by R. L. Woolfolk and P. M. Lehrer. New York: Guilford Press, 1984.

Benfari, R. C. *Understanding Your Management Style*. New York: Lexington Books, 1991.

Benfari, R. C., H. E. Wilkinson, and Charles Orth. "The Effective Use of Power." *Business Horizons*, May–June 1986,

Benson, H. *Beyond the Relaxation Response*. New York: Berkeley Books, 1985.

———. *The Relaxation Response*. New York: Morrow, 1975.

Berne, E. *Games People Play: The Psychology of Human Relations*. New York: Grove Press, 1964.

Bramson, R. *Coping with Difficult People*. New York: Anchor Books, 1981.

Brett, J. M., S. B. Goldberg, and W. L. Ury. "Designing Systems for Resolving Disputes in Organizations." *American Psychologist*. 45(1990).

Camus, A. *The Myth of Sisyphus*. Translated by Justin O'Brien. New York: Alfred A. Knopf, Inc., 1955

Crum, T. *The Magic of Conflict*. New York: Simon & Schuster, 1987.

Csikszentmihalyi, M. *Flow: The Psychology of Optimal Experience*. New York: HarperCollins, 1990.

Elgin, S. H. *The Last Word on the Gentle Art of Verbal Self-Defense*. New York: Prentice Press, 1987.

Ellis, A. *Reason and Emotion in Psychotherapy*. New York: Lyle Stuart, 1962.

Festinger, L. *A Theory of Cognitive Dissonance*. New York: Row, Peterson, 1957.

Ficino, M. *The Book of Life*. Dallas, Tex.: Spring, 1988.

Fisher, R., and W. Ury. *Getting to Yes*. Boston: Houghton Mifflin, 1981.

Frankl, V. *Man's Search for Meaning: In Introduction to Logotherapy*. New York: Simon & Schuster, 1980.

Gould, S. J. "Biological Potential vs. Biological Determinism." In *The Sociobiology Debate*, edited by Arthur Caplan. New York: Harper & Row, 1978.

241

———. "The Nonscience of Human Nature." In *Ever since Darwin: Reflections in Natural History.* New York: Norton, 1977.

Gregory, R. L. *The Oxford Companion to the Mind.* New York: Oxford University Press, 1987.

Hogan, R., G. J. Curphy, and J. Hogan. "What We Know about Leadership: Effectiveness and Personality." *American Psychologist,* 49(1994):

Holt, R. "Occupational Stress." In *Handbook of Stress,* Edited by Leo Goldberger and Shlomo Breznitz. New York: The Free Press, 1982.

Ivancevitch, J. M., M. T. Matteson, S. M. Freedman, and J. S. Phillips. "Worksite Stress Management Interventions." *American Psychologist,* 45(1990):

Janis, I. *Victims of Groupthink: A Psychological Study of Foreign Policy Decisions and Fiascos.* Boston: Houghton Mifflin, 1972.

Jung, C. *Psychological Types.* Princeton, N. J.: Princeton University Press, Bollingen Series, 1971.

Kagan, J., and N. Snidman. "Temperamental Factors in Human Development." *American Psychologist* 46(1991):

Kluckhohn, F. R. "Dominant and Variant Cultural Value Orientations." In *Human Relations,* edited by H. Cabut and J. A. Kahl. Cambridge, Mass.: Harvard University Press, 1953.

Kluckhohn, F. R., and F. Strodtbeck. *Variations in Value Orientations.* New York: Knopf, 1982.

Kohlberg, L. "Moral Stages and Moralization: The Cognitive-Development Approach." In *Moral Development and Behavior: Theory, Research, and Social Issues,* edited by T. Lickona. New York: Holt, Rinehart and Winston, 1976.

Kohn, A. *No Contest.* Boston: Houghton Mifflin, 1986.

Levinson, H. "Why the Behemoths Fell: Psychological Roots of Corporate Failure." *American Psychologist* 49(1994):

Lykken, D. T., M. McGue, A. Tellegen, and T. J. Bouchard, Jr. "Emergenesis: Genetic Traits that May Not Run in Families." *American Psychologist* 47(1992):

McClelland, D. *Power: The Inner Experience.* New York: Irvington, 1975.

McMullin, R. E. *Handbook of Cognitive Therapy Techniques.* New York: W. W. Norton, 1986.

Myers, I. *Gifts Differing.* Palo Alto, Calif.: Consulting Psychological Press, 1980.

Rapaport, R. "To Build a Winning Team: An Interview with Head Coach Bill Walsh." *Harvard Business Review,* January–February 1993.

Satir, V. *Peoplemaking.* Palo Alto, Calif.: Science and Behavior Books, 1972.

Schein, E. H. "Organizational Culture." *American Psychologist* 45 (1990).

Seligman, M. *What You Can Change and What You Can't.* New York: Knopf, 1994.

Selye, H. "The Stress Concept Today." In *The Handbook on Stress and Anxiety,* edited by I. L. Kutash, L. B. Schlesinger and Associates. San Francisco: Jossey-Bass, 1980.

———. *The Stress of Life.* New York: McGraw-Hill, 1976.

Skinner, B. F. *Beyond Freedom and Dignity.* New York: Knopf, 1971.

Slater, P., and W. G. Bennis. "Democracy Is Inevitable." *Harvard Business Review,* September–October 1990.

Tichy, N. M., and M. A. Devanna. *The Transformational Leader.* New York: John Wiley & Sons, 1990.

Toffler, A. *Power Shift.* New York: Bantam Books, 1990.

Von Franz, M., and James Hillman. "Jung's Typology." Spring Publications, 1971.

Weeks, D. *The Eight Essential Steps to Conflict Resolution.* New York: G. P. Putnam's Sons, 1992.

Wriston, W. B. "The State of American Management." *Harvard Business Review,* January–February 1990.

Index